The Harlot and The One-Eyed Monster

Siddharth

FROG BOOKS

ISBN 978-93-52016-11-2
Copyright © Siddharth, 2016

First published in India 2016 by Frog Books
An imprint of Leadstart Publishing Pvt Ltd
1 Level, Trade Centre
Bandra Kurla Complex
Bandra (East) Mumbai 400 051 India
Telephone: +91-22-40700804
Fax: +91-22-40700800
Email: info@leadstartcorp.com
www.leadstartcorp.com / www.frogbooks.net

Sales Office:
Unit No.25/26, Building No.A/1,
Near Wadala RTO,
Wadala (East), Mumbai – 400037 India
Phone: +91 22 24046887

US Office:
Axis Corp, 7845 E Oakbrook Circle
Madison, WI 53717 USA

All rights reserved. No part of this publication may be reproduced, stored in or introduced into a retrieval system, or transmitted, in any form, or by any means (electronic, mechanical, photocopying, recording or otherwise) without the prior written permission of the publisher. Any person who does any unauthorised act in relation to this publication may be liable to criminal prosecution and civil claims for damages.

Disclaimer: The Views expressed in this book are those of the Author and do not pertain to be held by the Publisher.

Editor: Akanksha Vaishnav
Cover: Suhail M
Layouts: Logiciels Info Solutions Pvt. Ltd.

Typeset in Palatino Linotype
Printed at Repro

FOR YOU

Kumari Kandam

Image courtesy: HISTORY.COM

About the Author

To my readers,

I feel hard to put down some words here and that feels pretty strange, especially after writing this book. What I mean is that I was able to write a whole story but still find it difficult to introduce myself. Probably it's the anonymity factor. We mutually don't know each other and that is the only common point. And therefore, I feel it's a good start to tell something about me, this book and what I mean to say in it.

I am a resident of Mumbai and I done my Diploma in Mechanical Engineering. After that, I have worked in the engineering profession for almost 8 years. I took a sabbatical to write this book from my full time job. I am happy the way it has turned out with the help of my friends and editors.

I had an inclination towards writing from a very young age; but I was too shy to voice it or present it for publication. I had this idea to write or just scribble some thoughts when I was working for an engineering firm in UAE. Staying away from Mumbai, where I was born and bought up was difficult. I missed my friends and the usual hangout points where we used to jam on weekends. International phone calls were expensive, so I was obviously disciplined to make a few calls in a month. In my leisure time, when I used to stroll inside a beautiful garden near my residence, my mind would be filled with a lot of thoughts – about life, future and the world in general. Soon I started scribbling things down – some random thoughts; like we sit down to chat with our friends and usually end up having a good time. There, in UAE, in that garden, my note pad was my good friend.

Soon after a year when I reached the last pages of my book, I had become pretty comfortable in writing. What initially started as few lines had now became pages of written material. I felt that these thoughts could be put into a book or something but that was just a feeble thought; I did not have enough motivation to leave a good salary and pursue an unknown field or to write along with a job. Work was demanding and I have very little time to sit and focus on a book.

Another year passed and I was part of an interesting engineering project in my firm, which was drawing to a successful end. After that success for my company, the management decided to lay off the majority of the project team as they did not have any further projects in the pipeline. Many were given their final pay cheques, including a good colleague with whom I shared a very good rapport. He was just married at that time and he needed this job desperately the job but unfortunately he too was let go. That was a moment of realisation for me of the unpredictable nature of life. Anything can happen and that does not have to be essentially because you have done something wrong or miscalculated a step. My mind went into an overdrive and finally the thought about the things which I had wrote echoed ceaselessly make it hard for me to forget what I have known and understood about life.

Long story short, I left the job and joined another firm thinking maybe a new place may help but that lasted only a year. The thought of losing a good income was equally frustrating. But I wanted to write, that's all I knew. So I made my decision very clear and left UAE and decided to write this book.

This book is result of all my struggles and experiences both personal and observational. The journey had been lonely but now I have the opportunity to tell you the story and I thank you for listening to me.

Hope you will enjoy the story.

Siddharth

Acknowledgements

1) Mr. Arun Aravind, thank you for the patience and support throughout this journey; for your valuable arguments, brainstorming sessions and inputs.

2) Mrs. Trushal Pradhan, thank you for the relentless encouragement and tolerance.

Illustrations: Front & Back Cover: 'In her Shadows' – Art by Ms. Pratiksha Kale

Thanks to my editors, Pallavi Borkar & Apoorva Tadepalli for your patience to chip away the rough edges and make my scribbling into a readable manuscript. Thank you for your direct comments and valuable suggestion to improve my work. I cannot overlook the inputs from both of you and helping me bring this work out.

I extend my gratitude and appreciation to the entire Leadstart Team who made this book possible and I acknowledge the effort that each and everyone have put in. Thank you for support and association to make this a mutual success.

Last but not the least; I thank each and every person who had directly or indirectly been a part in the growth and development of this book.

Thank you very much.

Siddharth

Kāmamaya evāyam purusa iti |
Sa yathākāmo bhavati tatkratur bhavati |
Yatkratur bhavati tat karma kurute |
Yat karma kurute tad abhisampadyate ||

You are what your deep, driving desire is
As your desire is, so is your will
As your will is, so is your deed
As your deed is, so is your destiny

Brihadaranyakopanishat 4.4.5

Contents

Acknowledgements	7
The arrival	13
The One Eyed-Monster	50
Reflections	84
Thoughts	115
Karma	122
The Harlot	153
Vanaprastham	184
The Mystique	207
Asya	241
Epilogue	254

Once, in a huge forest, there stood a magnificent tree which was over a hundred years old. Filled with expanse, the tree exuded a sense of serenity to the forest. On this tree resided two majestic birds with beautiful plumages and splendid hearts. One among the two birds perched on the highest branch on the tree. Unmoved and calm, it radiated peace and contentment in itself, the bird used to be lost in its own splendour. The world did not seem to hinder the bird from its state and a light shone from him as a brilliant halo.

The other bird perched below on a lower place, on the tree. It had panache for adventure and mirth. It spent its whole day hopping branches, singing songs, playing with other birds and eating fruits. In midst of its activities whenever the bird used to taste a sweet fruit, his happy heart sung a song so beautiful that the animals from far regions of the forest came to hear it. The entire forest used to be absorbed and enchanted in the saccharine tune that came out the honest bosom of the bird. It sang of hope, good will and merriment. The happiness that was in his heart showed in his tune. He made more friends and there were always new things to do, new places around the tree to explore.

But while being surrounded by all commotion, once in a while the bird would peck a bitter fruit. The delight in his eyes and heart would disappear. Dejection and gloom surrounded him. He would feel lonely and sad. In his sadness he would be reminded of the magnificent bird perched above him on the highest branch. Its heart would long for the peace which the bird above enjoyed. In a hope to reach the peaceful bird's company the sad bird hopped on to a branch higher. But on the way, he soon found a sweet fruit to eat. It forgot about the bird above and spent its time singing and making merry.

Soon it tasted a bitter fruit and again it was reminded of the serene bird above. It hopped another branch towards the bird up. But there always was another fruit to be tasted, another bird to play with and another song to sing.

Over the years, after having tasted many fruits and sung many songs, the bird finally reached top of the tree where the peaceful and splendid bird perched every day. He was struck with awe and wonder by its beauty. But as it approached the bird, the form and the aura of the magnificent bird started disappearing, merging into him and his own body and heart was illumined by the same radiance. It felt immense peace and all its thirst for another fruit and song was over. In awe of his brilliant transformation, he realized that the peaceful bird above, that he always used to see from below, was none other than his own higher self.

He and the other bird were one and the same. Always.

From the Upanishads

The Arrival

The fog hung on the river as the dark night settled its journey to the early hours of the dawn. The moon was still in the sky travelling its askew path and it cast a silvery halo into the mist that had collected above the watercourse giving it the character of enlightening the whole construct like a soft cloud. The river veined out into a many distributaries much farther meeting the sea. In midst of the haze of vapour, stood a feminine figure submerged in water up to her chest. She felt the cold water flowing slowly against her soft breasts within her linen blouse. Her skin had shrunken, due to the cold but her forehead which stood steady in the heavy fog perspired. She could feel the steady current and the slow erosion of mud beneath her feet. Her long hair, too, followed course to the water flow and spread like a web of moist dry grass that pricked gently on her waist were it ended. She slowly opened her closed eyes and looked down into the water. The moon showed on the river and in the reflection of the moon she saw the thin slime of oil on the plain water that flowed. The trail of slick-flow seemed to smoothly curve around her breast line away from her linen cloth to make an outline of her body. She smiled softly at the thought of her breast so taut and how the cold water flirted with it. The woman inside her was happy one moment and in the other soon found it clouded with the soft pangs from her heart. She was being caressed by nature, unintentionally, yet she found it stirred her mind more than her body. She longed to feel the touch but it only meant the gradual increment to her melancholy. The smooth water chafed her soul into agony bringing back the things she wanted to escape for a while. The agglutination of mud at her feet, the hair pricking her back, the soft movement of water, all brought her memories of her happy past.

The area where the skin ended to give way to the areole, against which the callous water flowed, began to itch lightly and her whole body quivered a bit. She touched herself over her clothes to ease the tingle and breathed heavily. She could not take it anymore and decided to move into deeper water to avoid the growing discomfort. She felt her clothing heavy from the silt that seemed to have deposited into it. She moved, struggling, with the cloth that stuck to her thighs and nether extremities, with the underlying current, into deeper area of the river taking care that she didn't trip over. Her hairs seemed to let go of her back, relieving her of the prickly discomfort. For a moment she felt that she had stumbled upon an epiphany. As long as she moved her hairs did not stick to her back. She needed to keep on moving, she thought to herself, so the relentless thoughts in her mind would not try to pierce her soul. The grief would stream out if she moved; only stopping would mean that it would stick to her again. Her hair seemed to be reading her thought because as she moved into the depth, her hair puffed up floating around her face and some of them which lay inside the water tangled her arms and shoulders like tentacles. Tears broke forth as the discomfort gnawed persistently at her, reminding her of her misery. It simply wouldn't let her go. She wanted this to end. She did not want to cry. She pulled herself inside and opened her eyes into the water. Her scalp felt the cold water and, for a moment, and she felt a little comfort in it. All went quiet for a while. But soon her body seemed to churn out the heat and her head warmed up slowly. So did her eyes. They still wept but the clever river soaked her inexorable torment into nothingness.

She rose slowly; her squandered thighs stood straight in the water and her head alone showed above the water. She untangled her arms from the hairs and lifted them slowly in front of her eyes. The maroon smudge on her arm did not seem to wash away. The skin had sucked it in. She slightly touched her hand where the colour lay imprinted.

She remembered the first time she had it smeared on her forehead trailing back in to the furrow on her head. Her husband had spread it after the exchange of vows of companionship over the sacred fire as the priest invoked the gods to bless the couple with joy and happiness. She was married and had spent her night in the arms of her beloved. The room was filled with the fragrance of jasmine garlands which were picked in the evening to adorn their bed. She had stepped into the house of a man she loved and was fortunate to join in marriage. She could not thank her stars enough for the love and the sweet potion they had anointed her with. From the soft moments when love found her, her thoughts had converted into a dream. For the first time she had someone to wait for, to look for and to care for as her own, and to receive the same. Till then she had never thought she would actually want something out of her own life.

She would have given herself readily, but that night she had rested on his chest and fell asleep to the soft rhythm of his heart beats and he had not initiated any physical touch to arouse her. He had wrapped his arms around her and they looked into each other's eyes. The warmth of the summer night had made pearly beads of sweats on her forehead. The mutual feeling in their hearts was more intimate than any physical consummation and the next morning, she woke to find her arm with a maroon hue. The *sindoor* had slowly mixed with the sweat and dried itself out on her arm where she rested her head. She looked beside her to see him sleeping. She felt blessed. The memory, once happy, now brought her tears and sadness.

Earlier that night, she had been unable to sleep. She had lain pondering on many things on the straw mattress she had sewn the week before. The dark seemed to intensify her feelings and drove away any drowsiness. Her mind was alert and active. Her body fired up and the heat from her body was more than she could handle. The year was approaching to the winter solstice, but it did not seem to ease Asya's discomfort. Indecisive, she came out of her house. She walked the path, slowly, towards the village. The night sprayed her lungs with cold air. There was a strange feeling tonight; unlike the coziness of her warm home, the cold outside felt familiar. Her feet tingled with a slight sourness as it felt a renewed sense of cold by every passing step. She heard the river flow in the dark and her feet turned in that direction.

Soon she reached the river bank where during the day all the women from the village would come to bathe and wash their clothes. She slowly stepped into the cold water and felt it moving on her feet. Without much thought she moved inside the water mass as the water felt a little soothing on her body. But that alone was not the only reason tonight!

She again stared at the crimson hue on her arm from the vermilion, where her forehead lay rested and the water seemed inefficient to wash that away. Truly, the colour was what every woman deserved. If only the person she loved had stayed. If only his duty had not torn them apart.

The kingdom, once warring pieces of land, which was unified more than a hundred years ago, was again threatened by the invasion of a foreign rule. A century ago, a great battle of epic proportions was waged under the leadership of a wise person who had realised that it was their differences that actually made them who they were and, that alone could unite these people into a peaceful society. Dacoits and warlords and wealthy mercenaries were approached with honour for a truce, with a plan for a unified province under a single ruler. Few saw the benefits in the long run; the majority felt it to be a loss of their power and freedom. They did not want to bow down to a ruler when they had power within their own hands. A war was waged between the opposing forces which ultimately led to the founding of a unified empire. After the war, the feudal populaces were stripped of their assets and given back to the masses before banishing them from the kingdom as punishment. Those who pleaded guilty to their deeds were given a second chance and a fresh start with the new rule.

The empire flourished abundantly. People began to believe in the government and their needs and grievances were looked on with the prompt attention and care. Trade flourished, the economy was better than ever and the society upheld its name with honour in the world. People found peace in their daily lives and believed in leading a moral life; taking care of people as their own brethren. They believed it would ultimately result in a harmonious co-existence between different people. Though divided by *varna*, people led satisfactory lives content with their new found prosperity.

Over the next century, the principles on which the rule was based started becoming stagnant. Prosperity had become a common thing and people longed for the accumulation of power. The way of life changed into a quest for power and superiority over one another. New interpretations about the actions of their ancestors were derived by the new and younger ruling generations. Rules were interpreted as an aid to the growing power race among people. New regulations and guidelines were laid down in the favour of the powerful, ignoring the larger benefit of the society.

Corruption became rife within the government hierarchy, inflation soared and unemployment increased, and more and more of youth found it compelling to voice their sentiments against the autocratic rule. The discontent among the subjects rose to intolerable proportion with rising poverty and the lack of opportunity to find a suitable trade to support themselves and their families. People tired of this degradation left for more fertile grounds of trade and sustenance. Administrative sectors of the kingdom grew to be the breeding grounds for greed and power, dividing the kingdom into a small but rich and powerful group of 'haves' and the vast portion of the general population into 'have nots'. Eventually, the internal unity greatly reduced.

But none rose to deal with it. Every person was a cog of the big machinery, who albeit their willingness had to turn along with the structure that formed society.

In such a scenario, it is always favourable news for neighbouring foreign powers to know about a kingdom in shackles by its internal discontent. In prosperous times these rulers never dared to think about capturing the land in their wildest dreams. Many even had maintained good trade relations with them. But their watchful eye now caught a crack. All they had to do was to widen it.

Although it sounded to be good news, not all neighbouring kingdoms had the capacity to take over the vast nation single-handedly which was once broken pieces divided by feudal lords and rich people. A secret alliance was sought and on the grounds of mutual understanding they arrived to new agreements. Spies were sent to study and understand the exact situation within the crumbling nation and after a very intent deliberation among the foreign powers, one among the lot took the decision to capture the falling nation and make it a part of their own. The other kingdoms were to support their warring ally in arms, medicine and supplies. After their success the spoils were to be split as agreed. It was a plan worth fighting for; the bounty was tempting due its resources and so finally all the spurs in the mechanism was set forth. The war began.

The idea was to instil fear in such a way that it demoralised the opposition without much effort. This would provide ample time to plan and organise the next attack. The enemy sent out its troops in disguise as gypsies, farmers, traders along with arms and placed themselves at strategic locations waiting for the opportune moment to attack. When sufficient amount of men arrived they set the plan to work. It was a blood bath and no action was taken in a placid temper. Whole villages were burnt. Men, women, children and animals were slaughtered without any difference and their corpses hung to serve a message. The plan went like clockwork. After gaining considerable momentum, the invading forces showed the first signs of clemency. On the condition of refuge and safety, in return for their loyalty to the adversary, peoples' lives were spared and they were made to work for the enemy. Those captured were held as slaves and put to use as menial labour.

It took a while for the nation to realise that they had been hit. Much to the dismay of the proceedings, in the event of war, officials blamed each other for their negligence. In the meantime, many cities and villages had fallen prey to the encroaching rule. Independent uprising started occurring when help seemed farfetched, but in spite of all the brave and courageous movements, it lacked strategic planning and organised leadership. All the efforts seemed in vain against a well organised enemy. Many brave souls fell to the death and people fled for safety and remained in hiding.

Eventually when the administrative sector woke to their senses, a good portion of their resourceful land was already under their enemy. Slowly the armed forces were mobilised, initially, without proper planning to give enemy the idea of resistance and in the meanwhile buy some time for a strategy. Soldiers from all over the country were called in to muster resistance at the war frontier.

Asya was the wife of a soldier.

The soldier was a brave young man who believed in the principle of greater good. The village had seen the couple move in to their settlement about a year and a half ago. The newlyweds had held hands and chosen this humble settlement while entering matrimony. The village had seen them in love and share the bond so happily. The war had torn these lovers from each other. It was heartbreaking for Asya to see him go away and equally upsetting for the village folks to see the girl's misery. They never forgot the sad grief-stricken face of hers as he bade her goodbye. On the very same night she had sat down to prepare a lantern that she later hung at the entrance of the house. Every evening the village saw her light the lantern and they knew, it marked the absence of her husband. They prayed for his safe return in their hearts before moving on to their work. They recognised her sadness and felt it as their own and wished that he would return soon and the war would be over for good.

Asya felt the sadness addictive. She was all alone in her house. The whole world was moving, growing. But she felt a great void around her; a distance between the real world and the world she had known when she found love. Now she felt empty inside; earlier the feelings that gave her comfort and a new purpose in life vanished, giving way to fear of an unknown future. She was anxious about the return of her husband and each moment it kept growing, drowning the surroundings. And this insecure feeling seemed to drain the living energy from her. Everything she saw and touched and felt had lost its significance. She wanted to speak about her grief to someone, but in her heart she always felt that nobody would be able to understand her. Her day would engage herself with people around her and that would at least drown the constant feeling of the void to the bottom of her mind. She would do the things required but hardly felt that she had done anything. The daily chores were carried out but it never consumed her attention. Nights were weary and days went on by without much thought. Rudimentary life with a ruminating mind is not an ideal way to live – but she had no choice. Perhaps, it is when we close our eyes that we are in touch with our inner world and the whispers it creates either soothe us or take away our peace. All night she lay wishing for the day to start so at least she could go out and be involved in the mundane activities. Pretend that nothing is wrong with her. And each day she would walk around amongst people she knew, with a smile on her face but her thoughts would be on a relentless prayer begging to bring back the person she missed, to an empty god who seemed to have abandoned her after giving her the taste of the most precious thing that she ever had – love.

God played the game of deception well. A believer would call on him and pray to him every day. He would praise and in return be content with the feeling that infused him the confidence that when all things in this world would be against him, God would save him; would adhere to his prayer; would come to his rescue; would lead him on the right path. Man is a creature who constantly hunts for an outcome and so he wishes; he prays; he strives. But the paradoxical humour of the divine is that he can choose to be anything other than helpful when there is agony in our hearts. In the most earnest time of dismay and despair, when the path to move forward is unknown, even the most honest and virtuous man would ask God for a sign, a path, a help. He would be willing to endure it, if only he knew the path. If alone, he knew what he had to do next. And at this time, imagine if Providence decided to play mute.

For Asya the nimbus crowned entity that gave the entire mankind hope and strength had started losing its aura. She asked and prayed and begged just to know if her love would return save. But even in the most pure corner of soul, where God whispers his answers, her sincerest prayers made no ripples. God turned cold, lifeless. And as always, dead things are of no use.

All her life she had felt the cold hands of desertion. When she was born her parents abandoned her. She was found by some wandering gypsies in a forest who in turn sold her to a childless down-trodden couple. Gypsies were nomads and for them a girl child meant additional attention, extra care and most importantly extra expenditure. They only had children from the women who belonged of their own clan. Rejects and discards were not welcome. So they found it easy to sell children in exchange for money.

So it was a blessing for both the gypsies and the couple who brought her. They welcomed her and brought her up as their own child. She was named Asya. Asya meant abode, a place; and for the childless couple Asya was the abode – a place to return to and a purpose to live for. Their home was where she was.

Her father was a carpenter and her mother was a seamstress in a village. From a small age Asya was calm and level headed. She had the keenness to learn and understand. She was curious but never questioned that what seemed to be beyond her. She learned the chores of her house and always helped her mother. Carrying water from the river, watching her mother prepare food, peeling of the vegetables, learning how to sew and knit – all the things that she could do, she did dutifully.

She was content in her heart for all that she received. Her happiness lay in the fulfilment of small things that encompassed her world. She did not harbour any expectations and lived a humble life observing her parents. She believed that happiness lay in between the acts of giving and receiving. That what one gave, one would receive in return. So good would beget good and bad would beget bad. Her father taught this simple lesson.

As she grew older she was allotted the chores of cleaning and maintaining the courtyard outside the village *gurukul*. She was not allowed in the *gurukul* because of her caste and everyday in between her chores, she would hear to the hymn recitals from inside of the walls – students chanting the *shlokas*. The chorus exuded a peaceful feeling that evoked a longing for the divine in Asya's heart. It inspired her to pray; she knew not what to pray, but it inspired her nonetheless, and she felt it as an enchanting spell wooing the soft corners of her mind. The highs and lows, the variations in the pitch, the echo of the sound from within the walls tinted a picture in her mind. Holy people worthy of respect resided within the walls. God was holy and he had showered his grace on them and had blessed mankind with such knowledge that only she could hear but not understand. If it could invoke devotion by merely hearing, then the knowledge contained in the hymns were much powerful. This intensified the longing in her to know; she wanted to know. But she never knew what exactly she looked for.

Though she did not understand a word of what she heard, her heart moved to the harmony of the tune. She felt that she knew what it meant but did not understand what it said. Her idea of God grew along with her imagination. She felt the Pure and thanked God for allowing her to be here, to listen to this beautiful reverberation that transcended everything providing her peace and joy. But at the same time she felt sad due to her longing. She wondered how the thing that gave her peace could also be the reason for her sadness. She would have pursued the path if only she knew where to go; since she did not know anything prayed what she felt in her heart. And those were her earnest prayers.

She had seen the students and their teachers from outside; their poise and their confidence. Their gait was that of the people who knew what was beyond any ordinary person and they were the embodiment of the divine in human form to her. She had seen them perform their daily rituals, the offering of water to sun and all the actions symbolising the various expressions in their prayers.. She yearned to know what they spoke of, that the heavenly masters listened to them. She wanted to know if there was a better way of praying, instead of her cajoling and meekly conversation, so that the gods would also heed her words.

Once, when she was outside the *gurukul*, amidst her daily routine of sweeping and cleaning the surroundings, she heard the recital which took her attention away from her work. She stopped and sat on a stone beside the wall to hear more clearly.

The choral voices in unison reached their highest juncture and the entire landscape became boundless, melting away from Asya's vision. She was immersed in the pool of her imagination and never realised the feelings could well up inside her, that it would eventually find its way out of her eyes as tears. She felt the awareness of a divine presence within herself and surrendering completely to the novel sensations, unaware, she let her guard down weeping. If only she understood why she yearned so deeply for the divine! If only she could find out what held beneath the veil of those sacred words.

But when the flower of devotion blooms, things are meant to change. The stone she had sat while listening to the sacred hymns was the physical boundary of a brahmin's house beyond which a person from low caste is prohibited from entering. The stone at the entrance was one that a householder would place his offerings; and, timely as it could be played by fate, one of the female from the *gurukul* found a lowly *shudra* sitting on the sacred stone weeping, when she was about to clean it by water for the offerings as a part of the ceremony for which they have just invoked the god's grace. Now all the efforts were in vain. She ran inside screaming and narrated the futility of their ceremony.

A few people present inside rushed to the site. Furious at what they saw, they swore at her and it took a bit of moment for Asya to realise the commotion and adjust her senses to the present after the trance. She looked overwhelmingly happy from her extraordinary experience which just added to the rage of the onlookers. She was humiliated, cursed and beaten. And all she could hear was that they have touched a *shudra* and now they all have to cleanse themselves.

Her parents were publicly humiliated for her act. She was innocent and her father knew that. But he could do nothing. He was born a *shudra* and it was their fate that they were treated like that. He bowed down and begged for their pardon and mercy and when they felt he had pleaded enough they left with curses and a warning that Asya was never to return to the *gurukul*. Her services were no longer required.

Asya, however, was not shaken. She simply didn't understand, nor was she given a chance to say anything. She did not understand the reactions of her parents towards her either. Her mother caressed her wounds at night. All she wanted was to heal the wounds of her child but she seemed incapable of it. How was she supposed to make her child believe that they were rejects and none wanted them to be a part of their company? That they were useful but not valuable? That was how God intended their lives to be; their fates to be. But, Asya just wanted to tell them what she had felt – the mesmerising experience that she had.

Few days later, Asya, narrated the astounding and strange experience of that day to her mother. She wanted to tell her what she felt something that was remarkably uplifting and nothing was wrong with her; she was not guilty of any wrong doings. Her mother could not understand. She thought her child had gone into shock. All they did was sympathise with her and told that such a thing was not possible; not that they had heard of. They dismissed her remarks and told her to be more careful.

Asya thought, maybe this was the way parents were supposed to be. They would not allow you to grieve but would grieve themselves making you the reason for their grief, although they did not understand what you really felt. She felt one of her doors close where she had expressed herself for a long time without hesitation and doubt. Now she lost the assurance of being honest with them. All things would be looked at with doubt. Or were they really incapable of understanding what others felt; was their grief more logical and important! She built a reticent wall around her and never did her thoughts leave her without her knowing.

Years passed by and Asya did not go to the *gurukul*. Her expression of her experience was discarded as some phantasm from the beatings. Her parents paid extra attention to her activities. She helped her mother with the household and her father with his work. She learnt to cook, knit mattresses and quilts from her mother. But the question stayed with her. What was that she had experienced?

The daughter of the carpenter soon grew into a fine woman. And finally it was time for them to find a suitable groom for her. One day, when she was at the river to fill her pots, a handsome young man saw her. He had beautiful eyes, she noticed. Her heart quivered as she felt an unfamiliar, intense attraction rise in her towards him. She wanted to look again but was afraid to lift her gaze.

As soon as she filled her pots, she rose to leave the river banks. Gathering all the courage she could muster, she turned to have one last look at that face on which her heart was transfixed. She did not want to leave but could not wait there either. With a heavy heart, she moved towards her house. She felt the same eyes following her. She turned around and saw a manly figure in a distance, in the dim light of the approaching dusk. Eventually when she reached her house, she could see the figure staring at her hut and slowly disappear.

Every day, as evening approached, the eager eyes followed Asya from the river to her home and then would slowly disappear from her sight. She was happy to be the centre of attention but did not have the courage to approach the young man nor gave him a chance by stopping in her way.. She did not know what to do. She could not bring herself to believe that such a thing was happening; that there could be a possibility to know someone but only as an unknown presence in a distance. As relieving it was to know the comfort, a corner of her heart was terrified by how much this new idea had occupied her mind. Calm but sleepless nights, happy but longing days went by.

One day, as usual, Asya went for her routine to the river bank, but the stranger who had caught her fancy did not come today. She looked around keenly to all possible places but was of no avail. Sadly she got up and left. All along the way she turned back to see, but today no one followed. Usually she felt his presence even if she didn't look back; but now he was gone.

She slowly dragged herself to her hut and placed the pots inside. Her mother rushed by her side. There was a twinkle in her eye. She looked at her daughter with delight and a look that meant a million things. Her father too came by her side and looked at her with a soft smile. This sudden reception stirred her curiosity and she asked the reason for their excitement.

Her father announced that they had a visitor while she was gone and he was expected to return the next day. Apparently they were happy at the arrival of the 'guest'. She enquired further but they told her that she would meet the guest the next day. She obliged dutifully and did not ponder on the issue. It did not matter to her; she just longed to see those beautiful 'eyes' that used to follow her.. She felt forlorn.

At night she lay without sleep. For the first time, she wondered about her mysterious 'stalker' whom she missed at that moment and wanted to know why he followed her. Why didn't she wait for him! If, for once, she had shown the courage to rest her moving legs, maybe then the eyes that followed might have revealed the face which she longed to see. Tears welled in her grieving eyes. What if she never saw him again? Was today the end of the small happiness that she had recently felt? She blamed herself for not stopping once in her path to let the person catch up to her. With this anguish in her mind, sleep slowly took over her unaware.

The next day, she was woken up earlier than usual. The house was abuzz with her mother's activities. Delicious aroma aroused the knots in her stomach as Asya felt hunger gnawing at her by the scent of the food preparations. It soon dawned to her that today the household was expecting a guest. But never had she seen her mother so merrily frantic and her father so ecstatic. Someone important was coming, she guessed. She got up clumsily with swollen cheeks from the lamentation of last night. She tried to ignore the sad feeling and hastened herself to immerse in her daily routine. She did not want the feelings of the night before to reach her.

As the day progressed, the hour dawned and the 'visitor' from the previous day arrived eventually. Asya had returned from the river after her bath and was getting ready. Her mother had given her clothes that appeared new and cleaner. She was happy to dress. Her mind was, for the first time since the previous night, a bit relaxed. She felt her nerves ease from the tension that had kept her up almost all night.

Her father received the guest and was heard talking delightfully. Asya could tell from the laughter that they had really someone important and dearly over for food. The other voice seemed younger and softer but clear and the tone showed respect for her father.

Usually the female crowd of the house is never a part of discussions of men, so Asya and her mother were busy inside their house attending to the details of the food. And because of that she was surprised when her father called her to the front. She did not heed him first; she thought she was hearing him call her mother, but later she heard him call her name clearer. She became nervous. She didn't notice that her mother, in between the preparations has left her side to join her father.

Her mother rushed inside, beside her and asked her smilingly to carry refreshments to her father. She looked at her mother and her mysterious smile – she was feeling uncomfortable and strangely suspicious. She obeyed her mother and took the tray of food and fresh coconut drink mixed in buttermilk and moved slowly towards the people talking. She could make out that there was only a single 'visitor'. And he was sitting adjacent to the wall where a direct view was impossible. She could only see her father.

She lowered her eyes and did not look at him, placed the tray and turned to leave. It was a little timorous with a tint of shame for her, when suddenly, she heard her father asking her to halt.

Her father said, "We have a guest today Asya, and he is not here just for me – this person has come for you."

Asya found it a little hard to believe her ears. Ever since she had lived here, no one had ever come seeking her. All the people in society would send some servant to deliver a piece of news. They were after all the rejects of the society.

Asya turned around to look at the person. Her eyes, still down on the floor, slowly rose up from his feet to the upper portion of his body. Fair but broad feet, rested beside each other and his clothes covering his legs, pale white kurta which almost covered the folds of his dhoti on his waist, a small shawl around his neck he sat on a stool that her father had made. Her eyes had moved quickly to his neck but when the chin came visible she felt a little bit dizzy. She knew every detail of that chin. She knew it. Her mind brought everything that it could and she felt her chest heave away a breath. She sucked the air in when she cast her eyes on that face. Those eyes she couldn't forget, those prefect instruments of vision that had taken the sleep of her pending night, the prolonged exhaustions from her mental deliberations that she had fought within to control herself from growing insane since the previous evening were all back. Those eyes had followed her feet for days and now there he sat looking at her smiling. The curve of his lips seemed to light the face as the cheeks gave a little tint of pink on the fair and clear face. She stood stupefied and aghast. It was the same person she had seen at the river.

She didn't have the strength to contain the flood of emotions, then, emanating within. All the confusion managed to ejaculate some clear liquid filling her eyes – a distorted glassy vision. It was very timely of her mother to intervene and hold her daughter's shoulder. Her mother said, "This is our only daughter, and it is our happiest hour to know that there is someone in the world who would love her and take care of her," looking straight at the young man.

Until yesterday, Asya did not have thoughts of pursuing the object of her affection and love, in the vaguest form. But today she was suddenly confronted by her dreams taking form into reality. From her childhood, she had learned to adjust her life to the likes and dislikes of others but never cared for what she really wanted. Last night, her thoughts for the mysterious man, towards whom she had developed a profound affection without even knowing him, had taken a deeper place in her heart when she realised she may never see him again. When reality presented the possibility of losing what she liked, she felt should have shown a little courage to pursue her desire. Her life would be a bland existence without any inspiration if she lacked the strength to go after her dreams. Now she understood what love was capable of – it was fragile idea but it challenges the core of one's belief.

She slowly moved behind her mother and stared away into the ground. She never thought that she would have the fortune to have what she liked, more precisely – what she had come to love. She, somewhere in her heart knew, cannot have what she liked or desired; so she had decided for life to act and let the feeling fade away which was in actuality reinforced by the events from the previous evening. She thought that she had lost her love and that she would grieve away with that thought until life would direct her. She had decided that that it would be her fate. She was never going to try.

But now, at this hour, fate had changed her circumstances. The person who did not appear for a day and wounded her with his absence had showed up at her door seeking her. The father and mother were overjoyed by the proposal when they found a young man at their door step, the previous evening, with news that seemed like a messenger from gods for a downtrodden family. The young man was new to the village, and was on his way to the country's capital. He was a soldier and had been offered a place of duty in a far away village. He was to get the necessary consent and decree document from the officials. Then he was to travel to the village he was stationed at by the authorities. But when he saw Asya, he decided to stay a little longer in their village. It took a few days to find out the details of hers and then he had come to their house. He had pondered what to tell her initially but was at the loss of words when he had tried. So all he could do was follow her. It was love for him at first sight and she too seemed smitten by the stranger. When there was no rejection to his moves, then alone he decided to come up with the proposal.

The previous evening, he had refrained from his usual routine of following the nimble lass, and waited for her to leave the hut. He knew her routine and he decided to take the opportunity to visit her house. He thought it would be appropriate if he asked her parents first, but in reality he was afraid to confront the girl he had loved from the moment he first saw her. She seemed beautifully fragile and he was hesitant to approach her, fearing the proposal from a stranger may cause confusion in her mind and eventually lead to a very painful rejection. So he decided to approach her family. It was very awkward and uncouth for him to walk into a stranger's family and ask for their daughter's hand; so he found out all the details about them and hoped they would agree to him. It had taken a few moments of courage to break this news to them but when it turned into a smooth flow of exchange, he relaxed. Her father was first a bit taken aback but later when revealed the nature of the stranger's visit, he listened keenly to the visitor's intention. The soldier laid out his proposal simply with no fancy display of affection for their daughter.

Her father was a simple man who believed in the hand of god and in his dull and hard life, he had seen the kindness of the Supreme. The childless couple was once very desperate, believing that they would never have a child; they had fervently prayed night and day for the gods to heed their plea but it seemed no avail. And when all hope seemed to seep away from their hearts, suddenly one day there came a child in the arms of a gypsy who had regularly passed through the village for many years and was familiar with the folks. The gypsy was looking for a trade and thought the couple would be a bargain for some useful goods. The pair found it hard to trust the nomad, but in all his years the carpenter had not heard evil about the passing group of the gypsy tribe. The gypsy showed him the cloth in which the child was wrapped and told them that she belonged to some people from the higher section of the society. The cloth was rich satin and a bright maroon in colour with golden embroidery. She 'could be' royalty. They had had the child with them for over a month but none had come to claim it. They had travelled quite a deal in the past month from the other side of the mountain ranges where the river began.

The gypsy was an old ugly fellow but his heart melted and all practical thinking went out of his soul when he heard the wails of the miniscule figure that lay in the forest with hunger. He gently picked it up and fed it with whatever milk he could find. But having a baby was a liability. He was soon knocked to his senses by his clan when they shouted folly to his act of picking an infant girl. He was too old to take proper care of her and more importantly the child was a girl – a big responsibility. It was not proper for him to have responsibility in the autumn of his life. If it was a boy then he would have kept him and after his time, the boy would still be looked after by the people of his group. It would be different for a girl; she would be looked on as a liability when she would grow into a woman and eventually be married off. So when he found about the childless carpenter, it was a relief for him as well as his tribe.

The carpenter, too, remembered his prayers; they wanted to have a child of their own but a child nonetheless. If god had forbidden his wife's womb to bear one then it was his will, but He had answered their prayers regardless. The carpenter could not show disrespect to the gods. He was provided what he was asked for. They silently took the girl and traded some pieces of wood work to the gypsy. He asked for the cloth in which the baby was found wrapped in when he first found her. The gypsy handed it over reluctantly when he heard the carpenter say that if one day, and god forbid, he would have to tell her the truth then he needed some proof to lay in front her. But in his hearts of heart he prayed and hoped that such a day would never arrive.

And today, just like the girl had arrived on their doorstep, a man had arrived seeking her. God, after all, had a plan for her. He was watching her, but more importantly he was watching the carpenter too. She was a gift and he did not own her. The carpenter remembered an old folk's tale which had been carried down generations. It was about a sage who once found a mouse in the cold. He took pity on the mouse and took him under his refuge. The sage, by his powers matured by years of spiritual development transformed the mouse into a young girl. He brought her up as his own offspring. She blossomed into fine woman and soon the sage was confronted with the reality of his child's marriage. He wanted someone to take care of her child as he had done, protect her and love her. So he asked the sun to marry his daughter. The sun said the cloud was more superior to him as it hid him from reaching the earth. So the sage went on to ask the cloud to marry his daughter. When the cloud heard the tale he said that the wind was more powerful than him as he blew the cloud here and there to his willing. Hence, the sage summoned the wind but the wind denied the proposal stating that the mountain blocked his path every time and therefore the mountain was stronger than he was. So the sage went to the mountain and laid his wish, but the mountain said that although he was flattered to hear the proposal, he still was burrowed through by the mouse that lived at its foot. If the vermin can dig through him, then he was stronger than the mountain. The sage turned his steps to the hole where the mouse had made his home. He asked the mouse and the mouse readily accepted. There were no adversaries or superior contemporaries that he knew or think of.

And then the sage turned his daughter back to a mouse and their wedding took place. Even after years of meditation, the sage still found that every aspect in the universe deserved a place and it was always destined for it to return to the rightful position.

The carpenter believed in this story more than ever now. He had told this tale to Asya many a times before she had gone to sleep. And even Asya felt the meaning of that story touched her. She felt the fairness in it and the feeling that decisions are not entirely weighed on one's shoulder as in the case of the mouse. Nature takes its course but still it is being controlled by something superior to it. What is meant to happen is meant to happen. And everything has its place. It was fair. As for the carpenter, he had done his role as a father and the gods had given him the opportunity to be one. Now it was time for his duty to give away his daughter in marriage.

Though, the stranger's arrival was unprecedented, the behaviour of the guest was genuine. There was no address of an over affectionate exhibition of emotion from him and the man had been honest in his pursuit. He had given the account of his purpose and action about the past few days of following their daughter and finding out where she lived. He was direct and simple in nature and this eased the parents of any suspicion though they still wanted to know more of him.

He was all alone in this world and looking for a suitable bride fell on his shoulders. His father had passed away when he was very young and was brought up by his widowed mother. He grew up to be a strong man but over the years his mother had grown old and passed away few years back. He had since then, been on the move to various places as a part of his duty. His experience had matured into a manner of gentle understanding and showed signs of a healthy mind rooted in principle. He believed in love more than any caste or creed that took away the liberty of understanding the fragile concept of affection. Only the ones who knew loneliness knew love well. So if he married a *shudra*, it was never a matter of concern. He loved her and no one had the right to question his love except for the people who had a right on her – her parents alone. So here he was for their permission. If they agree, then he has rightfully acquired what he wanted. If they were to disagree then he will leave in peace and that would suffice his mind. He respected elders and for that reason alone he had come meet her parents. Their consent was equally important and necessary for him.

He showed them the seal of the royal army and the scroll of his appointment to his station of duty. Soon they found themselves enjoying their company as the evening drifted to it dusky end. He took leave of the couple and asked them to ponder over it. He would return the next day for their answer. They agreed and welcomed him again to their house.

It was time for Asya to return, but today she was delayed by a few minutes. Her mother and father had found this time to be of use to discuss their thoughts. The wife understood the feelings of her husband and much was not required for him to say. She had trusted him and he had still cared to ask for her opinion over all these years. She knew he loved her and her daughter and she too had considered Asya a gift from the gods.

Though, it was sad to see her daughter go away – it was meant to happen one day or another. The young man had shown a desire in Asya and also hinted that she was aware of him pursuing her. It was for them to find whether their daughter too had the same feelings. If they knew she too felt the same way, then they could think further. In their hearts, they wanted this alliance to work. They were happy by the developments.

But Asya was visibly sad and a light sense of depression showed, so they had deliberately dropped the subject that evening. They decided that they would ask her in his presence and thus it led to the current scene where she stood shivering in surprise by the sudden revelation of affairs. Nothing much was to be told as it was evident that she too harboured the same feelings for the gentleman. She rushed inside with a tingling feeling in her feet and laid herself on the bed. She smiled broadly to herself and her heart swelled with happiness. She knew not, whether to thank the gods or was it just coincidence. She rumbled over many a thing but all the while she was full of adoration of the moment. She had given her consent and then she was allowed to talk to him – an opportunity which either of them never had until then. All she could think of was his eyes. They were clear dark eyes. She loved them more than ever and anything else. She thanked the gods profusely, all the while remembering the eyes in her mind's vision.

Although the couple rejoiced, they had one last duty towards their daughter. The parents revealed the truth about her birth, after he had left. She was sad but equally happy because all these years they had brought her up as their own child. She felt grateful to them and the thought of her actual parents did not bother to make an impression. They had abandoned her and this loving couple had fostered her into their home as their own. Her loyalty was to them but it was more than a bond of duty. She loved them. She wanted to be their daughter and she had the privilege to choose them.

Days passed in a blur and the day of marriage arrived much to everyone's delight. They were married by normal customs and the priest presided over the affair. It was an event with modest ado and the newly married Asya turned to her house. The couple stayed with her parents for a few days and finally the day of their departure arrived.

It was teary eyed farewell and the mother could not bear to see her child to go away. She consoled herself, remembering the day she was married and had set herself for her life with the man who was beside her. She thought of her duty and she had taught Asya well about it too. Asya too was in emotional upheaval but she had to go away. The father prayed for both and bade goodbye with tremendous restraints of emotion. When the sight of his daughter finally vanished from his vision, only then did his eyes bear warm tears of sadness. The father and the mother returned to their house. They had nothing to look forward to now. Their time was done. As long as their life prevailed, they had to live hoping to see their daughter again. All they could hold was the maroon satin cloth that came wrapped around a child years ago as a memory of their daughter.

Asya's sadness soon gave way and her new life filled her heart with happiness. They had arrived at a beautiful village and her house rested on a small hillock overlooking the entire settlement, where she lived today. It was just the previous day that the couple had settled into the new house which gave an incredible view of the entire village from their window. She could hardly sleep in this new place. The overwhelming exciting of a new beginning filled her mind with boundless energy and she rose earlier than usual. From her house, she saw the river shimmered in the saffron hue of the rising sun and the current carried itself slowly. The water mass rested as a smooth sheet giving rise to light ripples at turns and the sunlight sparkled on the wavering water while it flowed into the forest. The sleeping village, adjoining, was slowly coming to life to the daily commotion. The birds found it hard to contain their joy of the rising day, with their incessant chirping, and Asya felt that the flock of birds shared her happiness. The temple pond was full of blue lotuses and the priest washed his legs in the morning light getting ready for the morning prayers. The cowherd had finished his routine of milking the cows and took them to the plains adjoining the forests for grazing. The village reflected the joy of simple living and the flora ignited the beauty of the whole settlement that nature held in its bosom.

People were kind and helpful. They had enough to go on with and Mother Nature had endowed them her gifts of fertile soil and favourable rains. Farmers toiled and reaped their crops. The women, beautiful and graceful, carried their pitchers on their waist and head with water from the river. Children played gleefully and tugged each other into the water while their anxious mothers would raise their tone cautioning the young ones in between washing their linen amongst their gossip.

Asya was delighted and content by the new place. She was received and respected as the wife of a soldier and the women folk seemed to accept her with friendly intent. Asya did not mention being from a shudra family as she feared that she may again be rejected. Moreover, she was now the wife a khastriya. She is not a shudra anymore. She pushed the downtrodden girl into the dark recesses of her mind and tried to remember her as a person belonging to the normal class of people. It took bit of a time for her to cope with this idea because all her life she had been hiding and swaying away from the other sections of the society, but once her mind became comfortable with her new found status, she bid adieu to her past and resolved to be a wife but more importantly a woman with free spirit.

The village was content. And so was Asya, but the centre of her world was her husband. Her universe spun around the handsome young man with deep dark eyes. Everything was alive with him in her universe. The grass cushioned her feet and the stones sang to her their songs. The winds blew with glorious scents of the plains from far away and when the rain came, it was the perfect lullaby. The night parted to the day with a warm farewell and the sunlight spun a delightful tune in its beams as it fell on her. The breeze slowly blew on her face as if a light feather had alighted. Her luxuriant tresses felt playful in the waft and the wind seemed to be delighted with its entanglement. Her heart took flight with the wind and travelled over the deserts and forests to look if there was something more beautiful than what she felt now. Was there a dream that was so real to be truer than now! Her heart chose this precious feeling above anything and her eyes held the dream as a flower which had waited for its bloom.

When the early morning dew dripped from the leaves and the mist held the fragrance of the flowers, it felt that the trees and flowers and bees and birds and the sky listened to her heart. Her eyes swelled in this awareness and warm tears of joy and contentment brimmed to their edge. When they lay together, she felt his heart beat so lightly against her ears through his ribs soothing away any discomfort that may have been there, unknown, for ages. It dissolved her soul and the sound took her away from the world where there was nothing to think or say. It was the purest feeling that she felt. In her imagination, she built a world within herself filled with fragile things that she loved and would remain delicate throughout eternity because of the contentment that love had granted; she melted herself into each and every element which became the song of her heart. She knew that he heard her and she felt that as the warm tears streamed out of her eyes in joy with the assurance that came with love.

She remembered, now, her beloved longingly. He was gentle but intimate. The first touch of his hands on her and the way they trailed to find the small details and eventually the touch of his warm lips to the places where his hands had been drew her senses to rhapsody. He made it easy for her to shed her inhibitions and she followed him participating in the act of love. She never knew what the next step was but her heart always guided her. In the act of carnal contentment, their instinct took over and helped them to understand one another better; all they had to do was trust each other. The experience brought forth their sincere selves to one another and they slowly discovered the feelings closest to their souls. The moment was filled with completeness derived from tranquillity. She loved him and he believed it. There was nothing she asked in return but she received nonetheless and it filled her soul. She now knew herself in the eyes of the person she loved and surrendered without the slightest hesitation. She wanted to know more, swim more in the ocean of bliss of physical consummation and the sublime.

They looked towards their lives with promise. The small house grew into a home. All through the day, when he worked, he felt Asya wait at home for him. For her it was her days work as usual but her mind used to be at the path outside her home that led to the village. She often imagined him walking up towards their hut, his growing figure eventually reaching her. He was never away from her and lay rested in the beautiful abode of her heart and felt herself closer to him every moment.

Their joyful life went well till the day the news of war arrived. He was destined to go. He was a soldier; a good moral person he was. It was his dream come true and to be a part of such an event was the purpose of his life for a man who had devoted his life to his country as duty to protect it. Not every soldier gets such an opportunity; the majority just hears legends about wars fought in times long before them. He knew it would be difficult for Asya to comprehend so he explained to her his life as a fairy tale. When he was young and lived a life of playful existence, he had amused himself listening to the stories of war that happened a century ago. The names of the warriors were learnt by the children in schools and the praises of their glory sung and remembered throughout the country. He drank the idea of a strong persona that would defend the lives of others imparting some meaning to his own in the process. He, since then, had longed to be a part of the service that he can do towards preserving the unity, peace and happiness of the people around him. It was a simple dream. He was a warrior from his childhood, or so he dreamed, whenever he learned archery or when he trained himself in the arena. All that training and learning was now being given an opportunity to be put to use. He always wanted to be a part of something such as now, as life changing and threatening. Asya could see his excitement as the smooth contours of his throat collapsed and rose on his cartilage bones when he explained her. She realised that no amount of reason and love would stop this man from making his mark. He had already set the battlefield in his mind. It was only a matter of time to begin.

Asya never realised that a man could be so self-seeking in a dream that involved immense danger. How could a man construe so much meaning in something that could be an end to his life? Moreover the fear that she may not see him again troubled her. However she was ready to follow his dream, although she never understood it. There were more powerful elements in play and perhaps that is the reason why she could not understand. She knew he was skilled in his work and the confidence in him was undisputable for her to reject. But in a battlefield his display of skill and confidence are also a factor based on chance. This worried her a lot. She prayed to all the gods to end this war by some miracle. But the gods didn't seem to relent. She fasted, but alas the day came when he parted, and then her prayer changed to protect her love, to sheath him from every strike that the enemy intended on him and bring him back home at the earliest.

It has been more than a year, now, that the war was still raging with no news from him about his return. She received messages in between from him about his well being, which assured that he was in a fine condition and he will be back soon. In the beginning the news brought relief but as the same stale news arrived over again and again, she lost the feeling of any assurance of his return regardless what the truth was. It was always hard to hope in such a situation where she had nothing but to wait for the truth to be known first hand.

Sadness has a way of clinging to the fabric of the soul. No matter what we do to shake this repugnant feeling, it always sticks like an ethereal film. It attends the mind with determined adhesion but it also brings a sense of comfort in it. The feeling of misery from one wanting love so badly, shuts all the egress but also makes it meaningful to stay on course.

Asya was no different. She simply wanted him back. Her wanting set course to ravage her sensibilities but yet remembering him was obvious. She was quite at a loss as to what to do. But the body has a way for surviving from the onslaughts of its own mind; it gets habituated and moves along. Asya found the amount of sadness, agony and apprehension quite compelling but at the same point sustainable with the passage of time. The mind held her world while her body moved in another realm.

She tried to drown herself in activities that would take her away from the crashing waves of agony in her mind which spewed the vapour of desperation into her soul. She planted a garden which later grew into a very beautiful one. She knit attractive garments and mattresses and tried new delicacies. The village reckoned her skill with great admiration. Many came to her house for the beautifully sewn garments and mattresses. Asya felt the sadness go away for a little while, although it lay hidden in the back of her mind. The routine seemed to lighten her burden of heart at first but eventually that too ran its course. Although she did carry on, it turned into more of a rudimentary nature.

On one of the gloomy days, she decided to take a stroll into the nearby woods. She went a little farther than the usual path. She soon found herself in the untouched part of the forest where man usually did not seem to wander. It did not occur to her that the part may be residence to many wild animals until she heard small movements amongst the sombre foliage. She was startled and began to move away from there but soon stood halt after a few hasty paces when she heard a feeble human cry. She waited a bit longer. The silence of this forest was deafening and she thought she may have been misled. She was about to move again when she again heard some movement, this time, a bit more clearly but there was no human sound. She must have been foolish to move towards but she knew not why she did. It was a human cry, after all, that she heard. What if she was not wrong?

Finally she moved closer and reached the spot where the foliage hid her apparent dilemma. She slowly parted the leaves to find a young boy lying in a semi conscious state. He had bruised his shoulder and arm and there was a slight tint of blood flowing from his forehead. He wore dark, dirty gauze like drape around his tenders and had a pouch of water attached to him at his waist. She unfastened the pouch and fed him with water. She asked where he belonged and he handed to her a small amulet of wood marked with some obscure script and pointed into a far away direction into the wilderness. Then he collapsed to an unconscious state from which Asya could not revive him. She was frightened and looked around for some help. She hoped for someone to help her and the boy. Maybe someone who knew the boy may come looking for him and she can hand him over; she wished. She bent and felt his chest with her ears. His heart was beating steadily. She cleaned his wound with water and then tore a piece of cloth from the falls of her dress and wound it around his forehead where the slight wound lay. He had apparently hit a stone or something very hard. She looked at the wooden fragment that she had been given and folded it to her cloth on to her waist. She lifted the boy, who seemed light in her arms, and walked to the directions he had pointed. She could not leave him there; she quickly moved forward praying that there must be no wild animals around

After walking for a while the forest gave way to a beaten path which led her to an unusual clearing with smoke in the distance. The land seemed to slide down from where the smoke emanated. She reached the summit of the clearing and from there she could see a small settlement in the distance with a few huts, and men and women in the same muddy gauze–like draperies around them. She looked around and found a wooden arch and the same obscure scribbling on the posts. She assumed that the boy must belong here. As she approached she heard a hoot from the trees and all the members came frantically running and assembled very close to Asya mumbling in a dialect very foreign to her own.

Much was self explanatory then. The strip of cloth on his forehead, the affectionate way she held him close to her explained her intention was that she meant no harm. They took the boy and bowed many times to her but a mumbling continued till one of the oldest – the "Elder" of the tribe, by the looks of him – sprout forth to thank her. He knew her language very well. She was relieved and explained the whole incident to him which he later relayed to the entire assembled tribe. They raised their hands in the air and waving above her head, blessed her and thanked her over and over again. The bowing did not seem to end. In the crowd, the mother of the boy was relieved and she came forward taking Asya by the arm and welcomed her into their little hut. Asya was more than happy to oblige, although the boy was still in state of unconsciousness. The mother did not seem to stop from her incessant expression of gratitude. Asya was overwhelmingly embarrassed. She was not used to such attention but she accepted it. She was served some wild berries and pot of sweet liquid and some frugal preparations of rice. It was humble but very delicious. She ate it with much delight. Soon she looked around the house and the cloth in which the boy lay. He had developed a fever and the mother was finding it hard to keep him warm on the floor.

While entering the settlement, Asya had noticed piles of straw and hay. She went out to the Elder of the clan and asked for some of the straw. Then she broke some fine but strong twigs which could be used to knit. She knit them into a mattress which she then asked to lay where the boy was sleeping. The tribe was never used to such ways of living. They lived close to nature and had lives their lives on her sway without manipulating much. So this new addition which seemed novel to them added to Asya's importance. They were greatly impressed and Asya explained that it would prevent the cold ground from sucking away all the warmth that the young boy's body generated.

Later she asked them how the boy met with the accident. The boy had got lost in the forest while playing with his friends. They had tried to find him but to no avail until Asya turned upwith him. His worried mother thought that he must have become prey to some wild cats in the forest. She was relieved and delighted by Asya's deed.

Asya explained that they could use the straw to make mattresses and beds. They were happy to have such an addition if that would actually help them but they did not have the knowledge to knit one. So Asya offered her help to teach them and in return she would be provided with fresh straws for her own use at her house. The elder of the clan agreed to the bargain and from then on Asya remained their friend. They agreed to deliver the straws to her house and also came to collect the finished mattresses. She was provided with honey, fruits, vegetables and wax from the forest as a token of exchange in addition to her demand of straws. She learned their ways and slowly began understanding their dialect. The boy, after regaining consciousness, accompanied them every time to her house on the hill when the tribesmen set for delivering the goods. She and the boy grew fond of one another and they loved each other's company.

From that day on she made mattresses for the tribe. Soon the village too found that the mats she made were of good quality and asked her whether she could provide them in exchange of food grains or money. She readily agreed and was happy to have some work during her lonely time. Within a short span of time, she sew and knit mattresses for the village people and the tribal folks. That was the sole activity she engaged herself in, apart from her household chores. This helped to keep her sanity in check from the sadness that gnawed her mind.

There were times when Asya would keep knitting and sewing without being aware of the passage of time; the day slowly slipping into the nights. But her fingers never ceased to put the knots at the right place nor did the needles make a wrong stitch or a wrong weave. Her fingers had eyes of their own and always made sure not to interfere with the thoughts of their mistress. They knew their mistress's pain and how she would sit with the straw and threads to make the mattress but in a far away universe of thought.

One night, about a fortnight ago, after all the work of the day ceased and as she lay down only to wait for her swirling thoughts to rush back, she had heard soft thuds on stone. It was similar to someone working hard on stone with heavy blows. The sound seemed to come from very far from within the forest as it was feeble to the ears. The next morning, at the river, she received news about a man who had made his home at the far stretch of the forest on a rocky hillock that eventually overlooked the sea. He was said to be a 'monster' in appearance. Asya, as well as the other women, grew curious. They asked around and amongst the gossip one damsel blurted about the man having a damaged eye. 'It bled,' she squealed and all of them shuddered to their imagination of an ugly image in their mind. Asya on the other hand, did not seem to be taken for a trip along their naïve imagination. She was simply curious. But that spell was lost too once she left the banks to her home and her daily activities. Many wonderful and spiteful things happen in the world, but she had her own to mind. She let her mind her own business and let the 'one-eyed monster' mind his own.

The sound became a constant companion to the village and Asya. The stories of him being seen by men from the village, all of which in truth was hokum, varied along the days to come from the man being a flesh eater to the worshiper of the demons. His presence was just an amusement to the rest of the village, but none had actually seen him even once. The trading men who travelled from the far ends of the kingdom had happened to pass the news about a man on a nearby hillock with bleeding eye when their caravan paused through the village. It was an amusing story for them, but it did not generate any further interest in Asya as it did in her when she first heard about account. She was least bothered by their so-called devil or his dubious stories. She knew it was easy for them to judge a complete stranger, but none of them would ever investigate their curiosity.

However, for Asya, he became a constant companion through her sleepless nights. The thuds on the stone and the different tones, for the first time in many months, had managed to take her attention to some other imaginative playground. Her mind painted a very good picture of a person carving away in the rock. The change in the tones meant that he had changed directions of the blow and the stone was carved from a different angle. Her mind, not by intent, played along with it. She, unconsciously, forgot about the constant whimpering within her.. Every night she would lie down and wait for sleep to catch her but it seemed to evade her and she always felt helpless, but these new sounds gave her company. She felt her time pass quickly and slowly drifted to sleep. Many a time she resolved to sneak the place of his work and observe him. It was a novel thing and at night she would be quite motivated to go the next morning.

In the morning she would forget about the sounds of the night and move along, as usual, but was reminded of them when she heard it in the night. She felt a bit less lonely.

But it was until this night, when she had immersed herself in the river at this ungodly hour, that she did not hear the sounds of soft thuds on stone. The same old night crept and she had waited for it to hear but the winds had carried none of those to her. This had made her feel uncomfortable to the extent that she her insides flamed and felt she was about to burn away. She cursed herself for the weakness in her - the lack of control on her mind and thoughts. Her thoughts seemed to return, after a reclusive withdrawal, with much greater force provided there was no distraction today. As the sound in the night kept her company, at first, it felt that her troublesome thoughts had died away but today the absence of the sound let her mind unravel a single thought slowly which unlocked the floodgates of her melancholy and unleashed their fury.

It was early morning and the last hour of the night was giving way to the rising day. Asya slowly moved from the depth to the banks with her clothes draped on her like lees from a flood that sticks to a blockage. She felt the fine silt grind against her body as she walked. But all she could think was about the sounds that had been there for her company from the past weeks. She made up her mind to find out the truth. Has the personage known only to her imagination, divested his energies elsewhere and abandoned her nights? Never has she resolved with such conviction in her life. The absence of those comforting sounds made the old restless thoughts to resurface and once again her mind was in turmoil. She could not contain the surge of energy that coursed through her body and had to retort to submerging herself in a river in the middle of the night. Till then she never thought she was capable of such impulsive actions. In her desperation, she had broken a habit that had been a part of her life – the habit of thinking cautiously. With this unusual event, she found courage and a strong resolve that she too could bring a change in her life.

It is such resolve that unfolds the course of nature, brings time to its knees and outwits fate. This is where destiny unfolds. Hardly any meaningful event is required for this process to unravel. When time presents itself with it, nothing in the universe can stop it. Asya would later, too, find out the reason of meeting such an obscure mystery. Now she just wanted to know why this night had ceased without bringing the sounds that had given her a modicum of peaceful sanctity. However small or irrelevant the answer might be – she just wanted to know. She had allowed things to happen to her, allowed to be governed by situations, allowed people to decide her course. No more. Never had she resolved so strong. Never had her universe converged so intensely on itself that a random event would rouse her to find something she really wanted to know.

She decided to visit the god of her sounds – the one-eyed monster.

The One Eyed-Monster

Asya's feet felt the warmth on the grass from the early sun as she walked through the meadow towards the woods. The night had tormented her and now as she walked towards her curiosity, her mind was reluctant to do so. She had always prayed to stones that resembled the shapes of gods and goddesses, but never has she imagined that one day she would set out to meet someone who created the statues. She did not have the slightest idea as to why she is paying a visit to the *shilpi*. All she wanted to know was why she hadn't heard the work on stone the previous night! But for that reason, was she just going to bluntly walk to him and ask why he didn't do so! In context of entirety, it seemed very gullible for her to follow it. Yet she kept moving.

After she returned from the river in the morning, she did not lie down and rest. The night had burned her soul and when she returned to the hut she hurriedly completed all the work as fast as possible. She would ask the tribal folks in the forest to show her the way towards the *shilpi* – Asya thought. She had made up her mind to pay the 'one-eyed monster' a visit. Today was also the day when the boy from the settlement would come and exchange the sewn mattresses and raw materials. It would be a good company for her.

She prepared a frugal preparation of rice flakes with grated coconut and milk and put some jaggery to sweeten it; stirred till it became a semi-solid brown lump. Although she had decided not to talk to the *shilpi* much, it would be good to carry something sweet in case the sculptor has already completed his work, so that she can at least place her offering to the god or the sculptor. Meeting empty – handed would be a shame. She filled a dried leaf with the sweet and rolled it into a neat pouch. She had heard from the village folks that the sculptor has made his dwelling where the plains began outside the woods. She would just have a look and return. She only wanted to know whether he had left.

Soon the boy arrived with two young men from the forest. She exchanged pleasantries and handed them their lot of mattresses and set out. She had been kind to them and they were happy with the good natured girl who willingly helped them. They had plenty of new stock of straw and all of them were shown to her when they reached the settlement. Asya examined the lot and asked them to segregate it. Usually she would examine and leave almost immediately when she was sure she had all the things she required. Then she would visit them the next fortnight. But today she sat there waiting. Her legs could not muster courage to move ahead on her decision. Then she remembered the small pouch of sweet she had tied to her folds of cloth. It was still warm.

Finally she got up and went to the 'Elder' of the tribe. She asked them for directions to meet the sculptor. They were quite surprised by Asya's request. She explained her reason – she didn't hear the usual sound that happened for the last fifteen days, last night. She just wanted to know whether he had gone away. If he had, then she can see what he had been working on. It is very unlikely that the object of his work can be taken away so quickly.

The tribe too knew about a sculptor who had made his residence at the hillock a little further from their settlement. The Elder relaxed and called one of his fellow persons who quickly told her the path towards the east led to the place where the *shilpi* had made ground for his work. The elder told him to accompany Asya to the place but return back where the forest ended. He was not to wait for her. That was the rule of the tribe. They belonged to the forest and believed to be its children. They did not leave it unless anything threatened this norm. Asya agreed and left for the place.

Soon she found her way among bushes and thick forest with the person leading her way. He cut out the barks of the trees on his way to locate a return path for Asya. They reached the edge of the wood. The ground slowly descended into a slope and ahead lay a spread of green meadow. The person she was following stopped and looked at her. He pointed out to the eastern corner where a small hillock barren of any vegetation was seen. It was a rocky piece of land which gradually rose from the green pool of grass. She thanked him and he took his leave.

Asya walked towards the rocky patch and soon reached the foot of the hillock. A small breeze brought in the aroma of wet ground and grass along with it. The morning sun had started gaining its course and a small bead of sweat ran down her temple. The hillock was a gradual ascent. She slowly and cautiously climbed the ground up and noticed a patch of water that had flown on the place earlier. A fresh flow of water soon splashed its way down. Someone was pouring water. She followed it and eventually saw a young man with long black hair, turned away from her, washing a small stone with water and rubbing it with his bare hands at various places.

"So he had not left", Asya sighed.

He was muscular and wore a small linen cloth around his waist. The cloth was ragged and dirty with fine black lines at numerous places where the cloth folded. They were fine fragments of rock as the sculptor had sat down where the fine gravel fell. His whole body was dusty black and grey from the rubble and appeared very rough but it did not hide the definition of his musculature. His body was well built from labour and his skin had burnt itself into deep brown tan from the sun. His hand, like a pair of black film or glove, appeared to be in contrast to his entire body thanks to the water he had splashed earlier. The wind blew on her back and the sculptor suddenly stopped in his work. Asya suddenly became vigilant by the sudden change in the *shilpi's* movements. She was afraid but she couldn't run away from there. She would be seen by him and then he would follow, she thought. Maybe visiting an unknown place alone was not a good initiative. Her naivety caught up to her.

The *shilpi* turned around. He saw the demure figure of a woman, with a shy and timid face staring at him. A man in his prime, face was calm and had a bright radiance to it. Something lit his whole being and his entire posture reflected that of a learned man – Asya noticed. Perfect eyebrows below a serene forehead, broad jaws and the cheeks seemed to lay stuck to his bone. His left eye seemed to be disfigured, although his other eye was clear, big and gave a very steady gaze. The damaged eyeball looked pale bloodshot and there was no trace of pupil in it. On a closer look, Asya noticed there was some greyish content in them. Maybe it was the pupil. The beauty of his face and muscular proportionate body was only marred by the damaged eye and she seemed to be fixated on it. It rested so calmly in the eye socket that it seemed unnatural for a beautiful person to have such an ugly eye.

"If you have jaggery with you, then will you give some to me?" he asked with a smile.

Asya was startled by the question. She suddenly remembered that she had been looking at his eye without realizing that it might be rude. She got fixed on it without much thought.

He asked again, "If you have jaggery with you, then will you give some to me?"

"I do not have jaggery with me," wondering why this was man asking such an absurd question.

She felt he was making a way for some small talk. His voice was clear and gentle. It soothed Asya and made her less afraid. His tone was respectful and it showed no signs of threat to her. But why is he asking her for jaggery? She stood there confused.

"Well then it must be hunger that must be making me feel I smelt jaggery." He laughed.

Asya looked around. She saw a small cloth in a bundle, a few utensils and some ash in between rocks at the far away corner of the hill. The *shilpi* must have made food over that place. She suddenly remembered she had brought rice flake preparations in jaggery. The *shilpi* was not fooling her. He did really smell jaggery.

Realizing this Asya said, "I do not have jaggery but I have rice flakes prepared with jaggery and coconut. Would you like some?"

The *shilpi* smiled and moved towards a shade beside a rock which hid the sun. He took a dry leaf that he has folded inside a crevice in the rock and sat down with bowl of water. She sprayed some water on to his hands and the leaf and laid the food on it.

The *shilpi* nibbled on the brown lump of rice flakes with coconut bits on them but suddenly started taking huge morsels and started gulping down in frenzy. Asya placed what remained with her on the leaf and that too disappeared within moments. The *shilpi* ate like he had been hungry for days. Asya was surprised by his mannerism, but remained calm. He gulped water from the bowl and was soon finished. Heaving heavily, he looked at Asya.

"Thank you. I can't thank you enough. The food was very delicious. Thank you once again." Suddenly, with a tint of shame the *shilpi* looked at her and apologized saying, "I am sorry, I finished the entire lot without asking you." He folded his hands with his head bowed down.

"It is all right. I had made the food for the person who, I heard, lived here. So it was for you."

Asya said slightly embarrassed by this polite behaviour smiling sheepishly. She was not used to people folding hands apologetically to her. She knew that the *shilpi* was saying the truth. His voice and demeanour spoke that he was innocent in his words.

Relieved, the *shilpi* asked, "And who told you about me?"

"The people from my village; they heard it from a caravan of businessmen passing through our village," said Asya pointed to the way she had come.

"And what did they tell you?"

"There is a man who sculpts statues on the hillock far away at the other end of the forest. Few of them had seen you from a distance. They call you the one-eyed......." Asya's voice trailed off realising that she had spoken carelessly.

"The one-eyed ...!" exclaimed the *shilpi*. "Please tell me, what do they call me?"

"I am sorry. I have got used to hearing it from them that it came out without thinking. I am sorry but I did not mean to be rude."

The *shilpi* smiled politely and said, "It does not matter what they call me. I am not affected by it, but since you brought this up, please tell me what they call me. I am just curious to know."

"It is not pleasant to hear. Please don't force me." Asya looked away into the ground.

"I have heard my fair share of insults. It would not bother me. Neither would it make me angry. You wouldn't disgrace me even if it sounded unpleasant. Pray tell me."

Asya slowly said, "The one-eyed monster."

The man let out a guffaw and then his face lit up with a hysterical laugh that seemed to echo in the place. His abdomen shrank and expanded with the gasps of air he took while he laughed resting one of his hands on his chest and the other on a rock nearby. Asya was taken aback by this strange outburst. She thought that he would get angry and would hurl curses at her and the people from her village. But now she didn't know what to do.

Slowly his excitement came ebbed away and the laughter died. He had laughed enough to bring tears in his eyes. Asya saw the damaged eye had tears in them too. It was pale red in colour. She felt a knot curl up in the pit of her stomach. It was unbearable to look at. She slowly looked away.

The *shilpi*, by now, had returned to normal although his face was full of happiness from the laughter. It was like he had heard the most uproarious story ever. All seemed to fit the picture except for his bleeding eye. The *shilpi* saw the concern in Asya's eyes. He slowly adjusted himself to normalcy.

"Don't worry, it is normal. Nothing to be concerned about," he said referring to his bleeding eye. "The eye cannot bear the sun for long durations. As a result, small amount of blood clot in the folds of the eyelids and comes out with tears. But that was really amusing. Of all the insults and abuse over the years, this one seemed the most amusing."

Asya was still confused and didn't know what to do and say. To divert herself she slowly picked the bowl, filled it with water and handed it to the *shilpi*. He drank it and used some to splash his face. A small trail of pale red blood made its way on his face along with the water as it flowed on his cheek.

"I assure you, young lady; it's nothing to worry about. This is how it is. Over the years it has healed and now it's not painful anymore. Occasionally it bleeds but that is fine. For this reason, I work at night."

"How did this happen?" Asya asked.

"Once when making a statue I leaned close enough to carve a very minute detail on stone. Unfortunately the chisel slipped and a small piece of rock got lodged into my eye. It was a small accident many years ago; many medicines and many doctors later my eye has become like this."

"Where do you live? Are you alone or do you have a family or any loved ones?"

"I have lived at many places over the course of time. So the place I choose to rest my feet is my home and I don't have anyone waiting for me," said the *shilpi* without much attention.

Asya reminded herself to choose carefully what she asked next keeping in mind the privacy of the *shilpi*.

"So what are you working on?"

"A statue," said the *shilpi* abruptly.

"Why are you here? No one visits this region except for animals. But it is even rare for them. The tribal folk collect herbs at the river but they too do not come here. So tell me lady, why are you here? What is it that you are looking for?"

Asya explained that she had gotten the news of a sculptor who had arrived almost a fortnight ago and that she knew he had been working on something. She was instantly curious by the fact that there was only a single sculptor because usually sculptors moved around in teams. She had heard the description of the *shilpi* from the village folks and that had made her even more curious. She told him how she had listened to the blows on stones every night. But last night since there was no sound of the stones she thought that the work must be complete and the sculptor must have left. She was curious about the statue and wanted a glimpse of it and had therefore decided to pay this area a visit.

The *shilpi* was amazed by what Asya thought but he dismissed it with a smirk.

"We, *shilpkars* do not reveal our work until it is done. It is a part of our routine. We bind ourselves to austerity when we are working on stone, especially when the work done is from the heart," said the *shilpi*.

"I did not mean to intrude on your work. I had have always seen fully finished statues, but never a statue in progress. I simply wanted to see what you were working on. If it was impolite of me to barge in, then I am sorry. I shall leave immediately. I did not mean to cause you any discomfort," saying this Asya decided to take leave.

"No, I am not at all disturbed by you or your visit. It seemed unlikely, for someone to visit me. You are more than welcome to stay. You fed me with your food and I am grateful to you for that. Least I can do is to be of good company. Pardon me if I have, in any way, offended you. As for the statue, we *shilpi*s have our unique design in our mind in the beginning. It is usually simple but we keep adding details to it in our mind's eye before we bring it into reality or as we work along it. Every *shilpi* is an artist; he allows his imagination to fly and let it settle on simple aspects of the body which can be seen as beautiful. The slight bend of a lip, a thin eyebrow, broad forehead etc can make a great impact on the entire statue. This is the reason why we shun all the worldly activities and engage our minds in one single work. When it will be done, you will see it." The *shilpi* decided to change her attention to his work and not to linger on any further awkwardness.

"What kind of austerity do you follow during the course of your work?" Asya asked curiously.

"A *shilpi* takes his work on a metaphysical level. His work is meant for a specific purpose, but to generalise it, the purpose would be to create a sentiment in the mind of his audience. If I sculpt the statue of an *apsara* and place it in a temple it would be considered as divine, but if the same statue is kept in place like a harem, it has a different meaning. Our aim is to create the distinction in the image of the statue that it serves a singular purpose and the audience concentrates on the same sentiment. Through this we converge the thoughts of the masses into one single thought for a particular amount of time and that thought must be synonymous to our original aim while creating the *shilpa*. Then alone a *shilpi* can consider that he has succeeded in his work."

"For achieving such fine workmanship, one has to be concentrated on a single idea. Hence the mind must withdraw itself from all the activities that take up most of its attention. We maintain abstinence from worldly activities so that the body can be controlled in a manner that it does not affect the mind. Regulations in food, performing rituals, celibacy are some of the key actions towards this. And to maintain this consistently, sculptors usually come together as a lot. This makes it easier for one to be rooted and helps to maintain the decorum."

"Then, why are you alone? Where are your colleagues?"

"What I intend to create is for myself. All my life I have worked for the rich and thepoor, for the good of the society and I have contributed a lot of my skills in producing works deserving recognition, but never have I really used any of this skill to make something for myself without an outcome in mind. In my prime, I have done work required by people but as I grew old in age and experience, I developed the desire to create something for myself or maybe just create something – without the anxiety of audience acceptance. I really want to see what my mind wants," he said.

It was almost noon and the warm winds blew over the plains reaching the barren hillock where the two stood. Since the sun was at its peak, the *shilpi* led Asya to a small natural cave where there was shade. Both entered the cave but Asya chose to sit at the entrance. The *shilpi*, who had gone farther inside returned with some dried wheat cakes, salt, fresh mints in two dried leaves and two bowls of water and gave one of each to Asya. He said, "It's a very humble preparation. And since I wasn't expecting any guests, I made food that was necessary for my hunger. So pardon me for any shortcomings. It is the only thing that I can offer at the moment. If you would allow this old man a chance later, then I'd be delighted to serve you a proper meal."

Asya nodded lightly and tasted the food. It was quite decent in taste and freshly made from honey and some nuts. The *shilpi* must have made it from things that were naturally available to him. She told him that it tasted good and was not offended in any way. The *shilpi* thanked her with polite acknowledgement.

"Why didn't you work on the statue earlier? You said you worked on many things and places before, so there must have been plenty of resources. But now you are here in the middle of nowhere on a barren hill just for creating a statue!" Asya exclaimed.

"I did not create it earlier for the same reason that most people procrastinate in this world– the quest for survival. Like others I too required money for a living. In the hustle and bustle of life it was not easy to centre my attention on my thoughts. They were always fickle. Moreover, when you create something completely from the depths of your imagination there may be many intrusions from fellow companions and colleagues. Their opinions would taint what was truly my own creation. I refused to allow my work to become a topic of debate and so pushing it to a time when I'd be rid of worldly distractions made the most sense. As time passed, I learned and earned and eventually one day I decided to stop pushing myself away from my desire. I picked whatever my hands could hold and set out for a place where I would not be interrupted by the world. I travelled for a long time and finally arrived at this place. I felt at peace here and so I decided to settle."

"The sound of your blows on stone – I hear them every night but last night I did not hear them. Weren't you working last night?" asked Asya.

"I had outlined the stone to my desired measurement and form from the parent rock. I finished it day before yesterday. Now I can start working on my piece. Last night I washed the stone over and over again, and then lay down gazing at the stars. I got lost in time and spent the night without getting much done. The mind works on its own pace when you encounter some new idea. Many people fail even before beginning because they have only a vague idea to the work. If one persists, then the idea starts to unravel."

Curiosity began growing rapidly in Asya's mind. She was intrigued by the *shilpi* and the way he spoke about the creative faculties of mind which made her even more excited.

"How is a statue made? Are there any guidelines for making a statue? Is that why the tasks of making statues is reserved for an elite group?" Asya enquired.

"To say simply, anyone can make a statue. A statue is a replica of a human form in a material object. So it is easy to mimic the measure of a man or a woman in stone. But the size of a human form is difficult to place or establish at everyone's bidding and the cost of producing the work also increases significantly. Therefore to produce a smaller version of human form, we employ the method of quantifying the art by measurements.

A statue has to stay together as a composite structure to depict an image. Weight and proportion are two important factors that have to go hand in hand without annihilating the composite structure so the balance by even distribution of weight can be achieved. Also proportion plays an important aspect in the aesthetic value of the form. After all *'prati'* meaning copy and *'ma'* meaning measure which makes up the measured form called *'Pratima'*. So to quantify the icon, the human body is studied for its anatomical clarity.

Providence has designed the human body aesthetically but body proportion also have a mathematical ratio. Anatomically the proportion of the entire body can be broken down to scale in relation to one particular body part – the palm. It is the most convenient scale to measure our body. If one is to observe closely the distance from the forehead to the base of the chin is usually and approximately the length of one's full open palm – from the tip of the longest finger to the base of the palm," the *shilpi* pointed to his open palm explaining to Asya with gestures.

Pointing to the depression below his neck, the *shilpi* moved his hand saying, "The length from the centre of the collarbones to the navel is twice the measure of the palm. Likewise the length of each arm from shoulder to the hand is four times while that of legs is approximately five times of the palm's length. Anything replicated in this measure not only projects a human form but also accommodates its proportion automatically. If our bodies can be stable so can a statue, within the same proportion. This is classified under a system called *Talamana Paddathi*; the system of measurement by *Tala* – the palm of the hand. The statue used is usually the measure of the palm of the *shilpi* or the *yajamana* who had sponsored the work."

The effect of words from a learned man about his craft only increased the enthusiasm in the young girl. Like a child eager to know more, Asya leaned forward with excitement.

"What is *Talama Paddathi*?" she asked without making an effort to pronounce the word properly.

The *shilpi* smiled and corrected her. "It is pronounced *Talamana*... not *Talama*." Asya withdrew sheepishly on the remark but when the *shilpi* started to explain, she listened carefully to his words.

"According to this *Paddathi*, each *tala* is further broken down into nine or twelve divisions called *angulas*. Such division enables to engrave details on scale within the stone to mark proportionate parts. A grid is usually drawn over the area in which the statue has to be engraved and is broken down to the simplest scale - *angulas*. However to depict an entity of importance, the height of the statues are varied. For example, when demigods are portrayed they usually have less height as compared to the statues of gods while dwarf figures are used to represent some inferior entities."

"The basic type of measurement which comprises the nine or twelve division *tala* is called *Madhyamatala*. This is the referential unit of measurement in generic terms. Figures which are represented taller to the referential unit are generally four *angular* taller known as *Uttama Tala* and similarly shorter figures are four *angulas* shorter known as *Adhama Tala*."

Though Asya understood the explanation, she still looked confused.

The *shilpi* looked at her. Asya was quick to respond – "Why to complicate a simple design with such complex system?"

The *shilpi* explained:

"A measuring system helps to quantify work; makes it easy to construct even complex figures following simple rules. As I explained before, the human body has a mathematical ratio that gives the body an aesthetic appeal and the measuring system helps to carve a beautiful statue to gain the same appeal in stone."

"The guidelines, rather known as canons, on which we structure our work is encompassed in a school of thought that has evolved over the ages known as *Shilpashastra*. The work is mainly divided into two parts – the inanimate and the animate. Carved pillars, lamps, beams etc. form the inanimate part and usually is part of the architecture while idols, statues, animals represented in stone becomes part of the central attraction or icons according to the entity's importance. Statues and idols are different from other creations like a stone lamp, or a pillar. The former is a container of emotional value in stone and hence it is not always possible to follow the rules of measurement due to its diversity in representation; hence additional care has to be taken while adding minor details which are deviant from the standard procedure as a result of the *shilpi's* thought pattern," said the *shilpi* with a smile.

"Does this science have an origin?" Asya always seemed ready with a question.

"*Shilpashastra* has its origins in *Sthapatya Veda* which is a subset of *Pranava Veda*. *Pranava Veda* shows the connection between the gross and the subtle nature of manifestation in the universe. Simply put, it shows how the invisible or unmanifest part of the universe forms a part in the gross manifest of conceivable reality. It encompasses of four streams of knowledge and their relation between the gross and subtle. These four subsets are *Sabda Veda* dealing with poetry, *Gandharva Veda* dealing with music, *Natya Veda* dealing with dance and lastly *Sthapatya Veda* which deals with architecture."

"*Sthapatya Veda* details the sacred doctrine of construction of temples and iconographic sculptures. Tradition pays tribute to an entity called *Mamuni Mayan* believed to be the son of the celestial architect of gods – *Vishwakarma*. He was a scientist, sculptor and architect who had mastered the principles of *Sthapatya Veda* and believed to be the progenitor of *Vastu Shastra*. Legend has it that he, a native of a faraway place to the south of Indian continent known as *Jamboo Dwepa* in *Kumari Kandam*, arrived to the southern part of our land just before the great deluge as mentioned in the scriptures for which *Vishnu* took the form of a giant fish to protect the righteous. His homeland is now believed to be submerged under water as the aftermath of the flood. He then spread his principles and knowledge for the benefit of the society and till today he is revered as the progenitor of *Vastu*," explained the *shilpi*.

"What did *Mayan Muni* teach that gained such importance and how did this affect man?" Asya expressed herself with the curiosity of a toddler gaining interest in a story.

The *shilpi* seemed more than happy to entertain Asya with an answer.

He continued:

"According to *Mayan*, there existed an order in the universe – a regulation between the subtle or unseen and material or conceivable world. Both these worlds are accredited with consciousness. When this consciousness attempts to express its own feelings, it causes vibrations resulting into a 'force' in the network of energy. This resultant force momentum of energy is called *Kaala*. In simplified terms, *kaala* is the same force of energy rising from the inner consciousness causing vibrations which man utilizes to make his outward developments. Hence *kaala* which was formed by the initial expression of subtle consciousness got converted or manifested itself into another form as gross elements. Thus the primeval force exists in another form – i.e. gross manifestation. So, *Kaala* is said to inhabit all living beings. This is how the cosmos was created. *Mayan* took these principles and defined creation, simply as an expression of consciousness on energy."

The original idea of the absolute existed in spoken medium prior to the creation of science like *Shilpashastra*. This spoken medium was carried on from generation to generation but when the contemplative hymns ceased to reflect the *lakshanas* or nature of the absolute, they needed to find a way to re-establish the connection. When confusion arose among the perception of the original idea, interpretations became variable. This prompted the necessity for a medium to aid the process of creating a lasting impression of the idea through material means that can be commonly agreed upon. For instance, a tree gives shelter; hence for the idea of shade the original inspiration for shelter might have been a tree which finally resulted in the construction of a house. This might be one of the reasons why the idea of an image was considered best that actually had an impact on man by its presence. And, by nature, species belonging to the same class has a proper understanding so it was ideal to create the image of the absolute in the likeness of man. So using the flexions that the hymns conveyed, the material equivalent anthropomorphic god with numerous arms, weapons and ornaments came into existence portraying the supra human form to the human intellect."

The *shilpi* truly knew how to represent a subject and there was a sense of satisfaction in Asya's mind because she received a complete explanation on an unfamiliar subject but the person who explained took the effort to make it easy for her to understand it.

"So, in that case what existed before creation started?" Asya asked. She could understand what the *shilpi* had explained but she did not want to leave the scene with missing elements. She wanted to know more and pressed further keenly.

The *shilpi* stretched his legs and then spoke:

"According to the *Vedas*, when there existed nothing, Providence was conceived as an egg called *Hiranyagharbha*. It was composed of energy without form and had the potential to create the universe. Any particular aspect that has a tendency to create or evolve has 'Will'. As a child in its mother's womb, this energy lay nascent for eons. With the passage of time this 'Will' manifested into the so-called universe we are in, as an 'expansion'. This expansion is what is called as evolution. The two events of the energy staying stagnant and the subsequent evolution were not possible without a stimulus. The 'will' itself formed to be a stimulus and the resultant was existence as we see today. For the sake of our understanding, the potential state came to be denoted with the masculine nature of things sustained and was responsible for the life or *prana* and the material transformation is referred to as the feminine became nature or *prakriti*.

Asya seemed lost. She could not see the connection between the description in the *Vedas* and a simple statue. She wanted to gain more insight.

"If statues are simplified forms of the absolute idea, and this being a science, how can it deliver us to the divine?" Asya questioned.

"Statues are a medium of one's expression which comes from experience. Experiences generate emotions that convey some relevance to one's being. When an emotion etches itself in our consciousness along with an incident we tend to remember it. This is the reason why we have memories. A beautiful dancer would be remembered for her grace and movements. Objectively, she is not remembered because she was graceful; rather she would be remembered because her grace created an emotion and had an effect on the human mind. It forms a convenient medium to depict expression through statues. To create a 'subjective residue' that would nudge man towards his goal is the prime motive for creating such a science. This science is therefore of clever design. It slips into the mind without much question. The entirety of the prospect is to create a fulfilling and lasting belief without the inquiry of doubt. An emotion which is questioned is not likely to last since it will be subject to logical reasoning and feelings cannot be always reasoned with," explained the sculptor.

"What do you mean by the subjective residue?" Asya asked with a million things pacing too fast for her mind to comprehend.

The *shilpi* smiled and looked at Asya. His grin below a damaged eye was irritable to bear. She slowly lowered her gaze and tried to look at the half finished stone.

"Let me tell you a small story. There was once a farmer who used to visit a saint once a month at his *ashram*. He would bring the sage, produce from his toil as a token of his gratitude and devotion. Notwithstanding the age difference between them, they were great friends. One day, as usual, the farmer visited the hermitage and after his ritualistic obligations sat down for a chat with the sage.

He asked, 'Gurudev, how are you able to maintain such serenity? What is the secret for this calm demeanour of yours?'

"Child, I meditate," said the sage.

"What actually happens during meditation O great one that you are at peace? Pray tell me. I too want to experience this peacefulness," enquired the farmer.

"It would be difficult to explain what I do, but since your desire is to experience peacefulness then I will give you a method. It would be different from what I follow but I am sure it will help you."

The farmer listened attentively.

"Take into account the most treasured possession of yours and try to imagine it in your mind. Choose a single valuable thing. Keep your imagination intact on that and let not the loudness of your mind interrupt it. Practice this daily and you will achieve peace."

The farmer had faith and devotion towards the sage and he absorbed the advice that the teacher had given. He went away happily."

However the next month, the farmer did not come for his routine visit. And a few more months went by. Concerned, the sage decided to pay a visit to his friend.

Reaching the farmer's house, he called out for him. There was no answer even though the door was open. The sage called his friend again but still there was no response. Finally when he entered the farmer's house, he found his friend in his haunches, lying on the floor in a very strange manner. But he seemed to be serene in his bearing.

"What happened to you, my friend?" asked the sage.

"I am sorry I could not come through the door to receive you. My horns get stuck in the doorway."

The *shilpi* paused and looked at Asya. Although the *shilpi* spoke about matters regarding his work with great flair, this explanation seemed to be confusing her further. The *shilpi* seemed to enjoy her confusion.

Finally she broke the silence, "I do not understand."

"It turns out the most valued possession for the farmer was his ox. He meditated on his most valued asset and finally merged with his idea."

Suddenly all the pieces of the conversation started to make sense. Asya recollected her original question regarding the subjective residuals that impresses on the mind. And when it became clear, it was a revelation in itself.

She remembered she had looked on statues of gods and goddesses before and never ever doubted its purpose. Despite the image of god she saw in stone, the significance of a self higher to her was the sole idea. It just created a form to the 'god' she used to commune with. That was the impression she had created in her mind without inquiring. She understood how a statue influenced the idea of divine in her mind and also the working of the science that the *shilpi* explained. She remembered her prayers and the expression of the so-called forms in her mind at various times. When she was sad, there was an increase in care and affection from her gods and when she complained, the gods reasoned with her. All the way along she had created 'her own god.' The images were impressions borrowed from the material world that had left a residual impact on her mind. But it was her mind after all; all that she felt was her own creation. If this was a product of her imagination, then what was the real form of the absolute? Or is there really a form? Was her emotion at that time, true since she had prayed many a time in fervour? Was it her mind alone which created the answers to her prayer or was it really something divine? After all it was a lifeless stone. She wanted to know.

The *shilpi* said, "Subjective residues of the mind are feelings or emotions or collective knowledge which affects the mind and its process of action. The state of development of mind is called *bhavana*, which itself is a derivation from *bhava* – the subjective becoming of the mind. It is purely the action of Gross and Subtle manifestations. As they make a registry in our minds; the resultant is a thought. Thoughts usually arise and subside as long as there is a contribution from the senses. It would be logical to say, if analysed closely, reducing the action of stimulus would be the step to come closer to know the actual nature of things. If the attributes refuse to have an impact on our senses, the mind is free of any thoughts. So detachment from the attributes of the object and concentrating on the idea is the right step. The goal is to merge completely with the idea of the absolute. The gross manifestation just forms an aid in the merger. Rest all happens in the subtle world."

"Is that all for what this science was created?" Asya asked. "If there is anything more to this science, pray tell me."

"The real explanation of this is of dry taste to man. He is not interested to monger his mind in arid philosophical discussion or treatises. Many of them are usually uninterestingly tedious and mind numbing," said the *shilpi*.

"But I wish to hear," she insisted.

So the sculptor continued:

"This science was a result of a need – the 'need' to establish a union with the absolute. There is a tendency of human mind to question, when continuity between man and the divine is broken. Man, who had remained subjective until then, was also studied as an object and the composition of man with a mind was evidently found. 'Man is the product of his abstract thinking' was one of the finest points of revelation in this study. All that man desired existed in a realm that cannot be touched but what he felt. This led to the detailed study on what external factors affected this realm. Finally the masters arrived at the conclusion that the senses were the conduits to the intangible territory of the collective consciousness called 'mind'. All they wanted was, now, to find the things that can affect the senses collectively and create an impression on the mind that would guide mankind towards the absolute. Thus man followed the image of gods in stone for his pursuit of higher thinking and moral living and since then, this science found a way to be a part of the human lineage. It is one of the greatest inventions to guide mankind."

"But now as I understand that statues are mere props, how can one believe in God? There seem to be no logic in belief." Asya said pondering.

Impressed, the *shilpi* sighed with the contentment of a genius and pride welled in his demeanour. How he could stimulate a common girl's mind into superior thinking! Amazing!!

He replied:

"An event supported on facts that explains it becomes more reasonable, because, at any stage of transition within the event, man can trace his steps forward as well as backwards in context to the occurrence. This gives a sense of completion to the idea and the security that he is on the correct path. His emotional participation comes from the satisfaction derived from successful fulfilment of logic. Otherwise there is no celebration of his idea. Belief, not always but primarily, is devoid of logic because it is solely a part of emotional expression or experience. Logic is what we create to support what we believe, not otherwise. Idols are such a piece of manifestation. Hence when we read the scriptures we 'feel' insufficiently informed that a dormant but powerful energy suddenly decided to transform into a universe. But it is too simple for the taste of man for the universe to be conceived simply because a "Will" decided to create it – because there was no logic in it. What if it was meant to be in this way! All through his life man tries to connect the events but to his dismay is unable to find some of the missing links because he is limited by the thought that belief can always be understood logically."

As time passed, the original reason and meaning got lost in translation except for those which were commonly agreed upon. The material expression of the abstract thoughts outlasts the meaning and we see them as statues. If one has to understand the reason for creating a particular statue then the events that led to its creations are also to be taken into account. That is why the history of every individual creation is worth knowing. It gives the scheme of things at that point of time."

"If this is the case then not everyone will understand this." Asya interrupted

"True. But what you have to realise is that this method of communion came to relevance when man shifted away his attention to what he involved himself with. This is a part of the evolution; entirely circumstantial. This is a medium that would cater human understanding till he can develop his mind where higher truths and realization can be accommodated with understanding. Like a child who requires elder's assistance for him to walk initially, this 'nudge' is the assistance that tunes oneself to divine. Once its purpose is served, man would no longer rely on statues for assistance. Their existence will be regarded as props which just aided in one's ascension to a higher level of understanding."

"In that case, understanding of man too evolves over the passage of time." Asya piped as much as she could fathom.

"Yes"

"So if understanding is evolutionary, then what is the last stage of understanding? Is it infinite!

"No, evolution of understanding is not infinite. Understanding only evolves till the right attitude for perception sets in. However, understanding too can be, for the sake of study, be said to be of three types. Do you wish to hear?"

She nodded.

The *shilpi* cleared his throat and continued his explanation, "At the beginning level, man with the lowest level of understanding knows himself as a body who can think for himself and the divine resides outside him. He relies on the scriptures and philosophical or anthropomorphic and sectarian concepts of "God". This approach is useful as allegory; literal interpretation cannot be extracted from them.

Then there is an intermediate level of understanding where understanding itself is a belief. It is justified by the presence and experience of a subtle world within oneself and that "God" exists within oneself too, as it is perceived in statues and sacred texts. It is at this stage that one realises the presence of divine within oneself, but at the same time is in conflict with the beliefs that one has as a result from the lower level of understanding. Words and concepts used to represent the divine gets in contradiction with actual experiences and the point of conflict and chaos erupt. This is the stage where one feels the 'need' to know the truth instantly, becomes strong. Feeling of renunciation, to do something substantial that would make way for faster progress becomes a pressing urge. This is the stage when an aspirant gets stuck in rationalising the dualities which only can be removed after one ascends the polarities by discarding the anthropomorphic "God". The metaphysical and esoteric faculties govern the understanding at this point of transcendence.

At the highest level of understanding, the subject and object becomes singular in thought and action. There would exist, no difference between the aspirant and the divine. This stage happens when the conflicts of dualities give way to total acceptance and realises that there is no relevance of words, because it excludes whatever is relative. All words would be able to hint it but only experience would convey or encapsulate those realities. This is the state of being."

Asya, listening to this, analysed her own mind. She was in a state of conflict herself everyday owing to the unrest her life has set into. She wanted god more than anything else but at the same time she wanted to reject it for something powerful so that she would get what she seek. But she was unable to find the right balance. She found this entire explanation too exaggerated. Nothing really helpful came from this for a girl like her. The more she understood, she felt confusion and an immense need to solve it instantly. Somewhere even she was searching for answers to her own question relevant to her own life, but this encounter suddenly started to fade its sheen, when reminded of her grief and her inability to find a solution. She wanted to know simply how to commune effectively so that the absolute hear her prayers. She wanted to know a way that her prayers were received and it will be fulfilled and be united with her love. She was not interested in knowing the working of the universe and the science to trick mind into believing a normal thing like prayer something more of repetition of belief. No man would want to exert himself with heavy philosophy when he is surrounded by grief and dullness. There was a change in Asya's thoughts and as struck by some power she quickly found herself in between her grief and the recent understanding of god through the *shilpi*. Numerous thoughts passed in her mind and utter confusion clouded her.

"The science you say of is intricate in nature. It means that understanding the idea of absolute is just not enough. Man has to believe too. How can he believe when he does not understand such science? I did not know of this until now but I too had communed with my idea of Absolute in the past and found solace in it. Knowledge of the science is not necessary for everyone." Asya managed to say.

The *shilpi* could read in between her thoughts. He had lived long enough to know what one actually expected. He was sure that Asya was searching for something in midst of his answers. Only a person in need would propel his mind to such rapid pace of thinking. The questions she put forth could not come from a dull mind. The *shilpi* made a mental note to answer her further questions in a manner prominently relevant to her. But for that he had to know what she was seeking.

"Man usually does not follow himself. He is a follower of some higher idea to his own thinking. And the idea of being 'higher' should be represented in his image with some minor modification to symbolize the higher attributes. In simple words, like the farmer who merged with the *bhava* of his valued possession and 'became' an ox, statues with four arms and numerous heads are props to merge with the idea of a higher self. The sense that Absolute, so vast, can configure itself into the form of man is assuring to the development of man. Hence, temples are the homes to the statues we call gods as it is an extension to the idea that man too lives in a home. So wouldn't a greater entity, but in the image of man, require a home too! The satisfaction from his 'higher idea' helps in his security of beliefs. And only by believing in what he sees in higher idea, is man liberated from his attachment from its lesser counterparts."

"And this science exists regardless of what man feels, my lady. To pursue it as a school of thought or belief is purely a matter of choice. As I mentioned earlier, one of the goals of this science is to slip the idea without much question. I can see that you have your idea, which means the science has already done its work. If there is any other thing that is hindering the working, then the quandary is in your belief." replied the *shilpi*.

Asya was taken aback by the sudden reply. Her eyes turned moist and her mouth clenched a sob. Somewhere the *shilpi* has hit a raw nerve with the right answer.

"I am a person who infuses some sense into lifeless objects by making it a piece nearer to human understanding. I am required to understand expressions as a product of mind because I have to engrave it as humanly as possible on rocks. Naturally I had to study the root – the emotion behind an expression. A man who can understand expression well is a man who can understand the thinking of other people. I can see the sadness in you but I do not know the reason for it. And if your questions have an underlying inference to the gloom inside you, then I may prove of little help to be any good to your original dilemma. So, pray tell me what is that you are looking in midst of stones?

With tears welling in her eyes, Asya took one look at the disfigured face of the sculptor and looked down again. She poured her heart out. She narrated her story – her childhood, her youth and the events that had made her forlorn and how she was trying hard to know the manner to set all this in an order. She told of her prayers and the way it made her existence even more painful. Why had her prayer gone unanswered? Was she equipped with the lowest of understanding like the *shilpi* had explained? Did she need progress so that God paid a little attention to what she had to say? She wanted to know this more than anything else.

The sculptor raised his hand and moved it across the stone he was working on. He washed his hands and got up from his place. Moving to a ground closer to Asya, he sat down beside her.

"So you think that the order of things is unfair to you!" he asked.

"Isn't war a way to destroy people? Isn't life more important? Then why does such a thing happen? If He is the supreme controller of the universe then why can't God stop the things that destroy his beautiful creations? What is the meaning in it and what is the truth behind it? Is it so easy for God to just discard this as a process of good over evil? Doesn't it affect the people around the event?" Asya asked.

"What you ask of is from your own experiences in life, so the answers which you are looking for would not be readily acceptable to you. It will take time for things to make sense to you. If you have already concluded on the fact that life is unfair then it wouldn't make any difference about what I say because those will be in contradiction to your conclusion. You are looking for a missing link that is evading your understanding in the whole process. Promise me your patient attention and I will lay down your answer in a manner that you can understand."

Asya looked down and nodded in agreement. She wanted to know what the *shilpi* had to say.

"It is an untrue conception that the entire universe works on the principle of good and bad or right and wrong. In the real sense of understanding, there is nothing that is good or bad. Even though the scriptures attach importance for morality as one of the pillars for a society and its subsequent benefit; it is only a part of it. Existence is a process of cause and effect. All other theories and dogmas become redundant in light of this doctrine. The distinction of good and bad exists for easier co-existence, and man is the only species that can be looked on upon as good or bad. Animals and plants are not concerned with the good and bad of the universe; rather they are affected by the effects and its causes that an event has on their existence. How can humans be excluded from this paradigm?

A system, in the first place, was created to ensure the smooth co-existence of numerous components in a single realm. When that system becomes inefficient then a new system arises that succeeds the older one and the motive of existence is continued. All the organic and inorganic components follow this without exclusion. When this process of substitution is viewed with a sentiment, one tends to overlook the meaning in it. That only happens when one has developed an attachment to some particulars in the system. When one is free of this attachment, things are viewed as they are.

As for the war, it is necessary. It will restore balance to the order of things and life will resume its natural course. Your beloved is in participation of a very noble cause that is in line with the evolutionary steps of the universe. It is remarkably astounding to think that the entire creation could act out in such a manner to represent its presence. This struggle will only cease when the two imploding forces achieve balance.

However, you are sad because you did not have a chance with what you had decided in your life. You are not able to find out whether you will have your chance in your life to be happy –whether the object of your love will return or not! But your sadness deepens when you think that you have been denied an opportunity to live a simple you desired."

Asya was amazed by the way the *shilpi* explained her-'self' to her. Until that day, everybody she knew showed pity but no one had been so upright. When she heard it, she had to admit that even though she wanted him to come back, she was more concerned about whether she will have the opportunity to do and be what she had decided. She just wanted the future to come out as she had intended it to be. She felt ashamed and angry; she felt she was selfish. And it was not a good thing to know in midst of her sorrow.

As the confusion flushed its way through Asya's face, the *shilpi* interrupted her thoughts.

"No. It is not selfish to think that way..."

"How can you say that?"

"Because, it is the truth. Human mind accustomed to love and care does not know what to do in its absence. That is the nature of the mind. And when it encounters facts that are in direct opposition to the efforts taken while in love, confusion arises."

"But out of this one must be true alone. There could not be more than one possibility. Either I loved him or I did not love him at all." She sobbed realising that she had been selfish thinking it was love.

"It is amazing how the mind can be so weak and yet if there is something that has to be accomplished the same mind does it. You are spending a lot of energy in wasteful thinking. Don't you see your mind needs a certain sense of security about whatever happens to you?"

"What do you mean?"

"When you found out that you were selfish, you immediately needed a speedy conclusion about the things happened and so you ended up feeling that you may or may not have loved him at all. This pace of thinking will always elude you from the real nature of things; infuse you with insecurity and fortify the feeling that the efforts you took were worthless. You loved him at the point of time when he was beside you and when he left you still love him across all the distance but just because of an uncertain future and the absence of an assurance, you are questioning something you wholeheartedly did once."

"Then why do I feel selfish?"

"It is you who 'want' to possess your part in love. But you are denied of it because of circumstances. Wouldn't a child be just as sad if his favourite toy was taken away suddenly without the possibility of getting it back? How would he react! Tell me."

Asya tried to think an answer, although she felt a little sarcasm in the sculptor's voice, there was nothing illicit in what he asked.

"He is sad because he feels that his fulfilment of happiness is in playing with his toy," said Asya.

"And what happens when the child is given the toy afterwards?"

"He will be happy."

"Good. You can think through your sorrow and confusion – signs of a reasonable and progressive mind, young lady. There are many people who are going through the same situation but very few can reach clarity about oneself rather than forming a conclusion to support the meaning in their sorrow. They would feel that they are suffering because it is their fate and that there is no reasonable explanation to it; some would put it as god's will, other few would have said that it is because of their bad karma... but no one will accept that their sorrow is because of their own thinking. People who understand this so-called suffering as a product of their thinking can easily find their way out of it. Do you want to stay in love with your sorrow?"

"I do not know what to do, that is the most discouraging thing." Asya said dejectedly.

"I agree it is difficult. There is a simple way but it won't be easy."

Asya looked up in hope.

"When you are ready to receive you will receive, but prior to it you must be fit to receive. Then alone you are worthy of receiving. The entire answer will be there in the same things that you work daily, but unless you are ready to see it, you won't understand it. Change is the only constant phenomenon that supersedes every other aspect of life. When the object of your affection changes, it forces you to undergo a change too. Since one becomes attached to the happiness derived from the object in question these changes seem unnatural and unnecessary. The logical mind would question the change and will tend to see it as an unfavourable outcome. All through time it is satisfaction that is the motive for any and every struggle."

"You long for your love and you feel that if he was here you would have been happy. As an individual who is concerned about her own happiness, have you ever thought the happiness of your husband? Have you ever tried to find what satisfies your husband in being a soldier! Even when his time is laden with the possibility of losing his life at any moment, he pursues a path that he consider true to his ideal. His actions would save many wives, like you, even when he may not live to see you. It is your love that has delivered him to a greater purpose. How can he be crude to let that go and come back to you? Love never takes one away from his desires. It actually finds a way to liberate people. Such love becomes stagnant and stunts growth of the soul. You can be in companion with him, even now, across the mountains and seas and one with his battle."

"People often feel insufficient, when they have no or little participation in the lives of the people they love. They begin to agonize themselves with thoughts that destroy their value. They begin to doubt their actions and indirectly it begins to affect the people they love. The only thing that you can do is in the 'present'. Keeping focus on an uncertain future will erode your strength and when you, in reality, have an opportunity to act upon, you may be filled with doubt. This usually happens when you wait for happiness from other people. You bind yourself with the people whom you like and expect their presence to complete you. In this moment, you never think about the aspirations and intentions of the person you love. You would like to believe that being with the one you love would make you happy," reasoned the *shilpi*.

Asya remained silent.

"A free and happy mind is free from doubt. The prayers of such minds are easily answered. All desires are immortal, even if you choose to neglect it. Desires are stones that fall in water. The water has no interference with the nature of stone, but the stone by having weight sinks to the bottom. Desires are weights that pull you towards your goal. Prayers laced with desires are relentless. It does not even require faith. You could choose be with your husband, right now in your mind's eyes, feel him with your soul and fight his battles with him. That could be your prayer. Such prayers produce forces beyond any comprehension and manifest as miracles. All it requires is patience. Be stone that falls in water."

"One last thing" continued the *shilpi*. "Learn from fear. There is no great teacher like fear. Be motivated by it and each time your fear surfaces replace it with your desire. Allow fear to find you. Feel it and experience how it paralyses your thoughts. When you stare right into it with your desire, it will start to fade out because fear was composed of varying thoughts and it did not have a clear foundation. That is why the root of fear seems untraceable. It is just a thought which you created unconsciously that did not complement to your desire. Remember, to have strong hope one has to know despair. Without despair, hope finds no fertile ground to bloom. Many people are unaware of it and unconsciously set themselves upon a course that makes them feel like a prisoner."

Asya became more gloomy and distraught by this sermon. There was no comfort in those words even though she wanted to be like a person as the *shilpi* has expressed – one with her love so far away.

All she could muster to say was, "It is easy to say this when one does not have anything to lose. Nothing of theirs is at stake, so one can be as much objective as one wants to be. You are not a soldier and you do not have a wife waiting for you back home. So I do not expect you to understand it."

She got up; looking down on the ground folding her hands. She was trying hard not to look straight otherwise the tears that have glassed her vision would be a spectacle for the bleeding rascal. She wanted to leave.

"So you think that I am alien to your grief and I have not experienced anything my life synonymous to yours?" asked the *shilpi* unmoved.

Enough was enough for Asya, She showed respect but this scoundrel does not relent from mocking her.

"What possible adversities have you been through? All your life had been spent in between piles of rocks. You can preach sermons because of the profession you follow but do not consider wise to preach in matters of heart. The grief can only be understood when one goes through it and a person like you who had lived like a nomad cannot comprehend its depth and how it wrecks oneself."

"Please do not be offended by my words. I beg your pardon for what I have said. I have grown old and it had been a long time since I had been in a company. Please do not leave feeling depressed. I understand your endurance because I am familiar to it in my own way," said the sculptor in a small voice.

"I was never like this. I too had a life like yours. But now that is a far away reality."

Asya stopped in her path and turned. The *shilpi* began his narration.

Reflections

"I grew up in the north from where the snow clad mountains could be seen while the sun rose behind them," began the *shilpi*. "Born in a *brahmin* family, my father had excelled as a learned scholar in his youth. He therefore would advocate gatherings where learned scholars and economists met to exchange views. Soon he had become the part of the royal advisors in the court of the ruler. My father had struggled with poverty in his youth but he converted all his labour into a fruitful life. Wealth was hereditary for me. My mother was a lovely housewife. She was the dearest to me and I was the apple of her eye. She was a pious, devoted wife and a caring mother. Life was abundant and joyful.

"As I grew to the age for academics, I was admitted to the finest *gurukul* that the kingdom had. People from far and beyond came to study, research and produce new theses atthis coveted place of learning. It was a school for thought, reasoning and philosophy. That place had, in the past, generated poets and philosophers who had a great impact on society. Although it was very painful for my mother to leave me, as a woman who understood society she too wished her son to become a great person like her husband or even greater. The *gurukul* system required the student to leave the house and live at the place of his tutelage till his education was completed. It took years till we met our own mother and father. But that was the system laid and hence everyone one was to follow without exception. This took me far away from my home but plunged me into the world of knowledge.

"I had a natural curiosity, a flair for new things, and a contemplative mind which enabled me to methodise whatever knowledge was provided. The education system in the *gurukul* was designed in way to groom the students for their future contribution to the society. Academically, the students form the different castes of *Varna* would be given a common tutorial foundation and as they matured in their understanding each candidate was taught according to the caste he belonged to. A *khastriya* would be trained in all means of warfare while a *brahmin* was taught the nuances of philosophy and intellectual reasoning and for the *vaishya* sect – the finer aspects of trade and economics," said the *shilpi*.

"The enjoyment I derived exclusively from my academics filled my days with the fruition, reinforcing my determination to seek more and more, to know what lay behind every principle, from every verse laid out in the ancient texts. I was loved by the teachers for my penchant for understanding and respected amongst my peers. 'The knowledge, the revelations from the mystical texts to the effects on man' – I wanted to know it in its entirety; to unveil the mystery of the words written by the masters of lore.

"It enriched my foundation and I was received as perfect model of our academic institution. Teachers prophesied my future to be a great and learned man and compared me to the finest jewels that their academy had produced. Many loved and hated me for my excellence but none of it mattered. None understood my work, my effort – neither my teachers nor my fellow people. Everyone had their own version ranging from a lunatic bookworm to an egomaniac who would not leave any stone unturned until he was accepted as a unique and exemplary student.

"I, however, had no interest in the exultations of my fellow companions. I was on a quest of my own. I wanted to find the missing link between theories and experience. The texts dictated theories about human life but seemed surreal and beyond grasp, like astral worlds and the subtle energy within our body. This fuelled me; the objective was to find a practical application which would lead me to the disclosure of these worlds and the meaning it held. 'I must know...so I must learn...but learn with clear understanding' was the sole purpose. What my teachers and contemporaries failed to understand was that my motivation lay in the mystery of things. And that was the singular unison of the state of affairs – none understood me as I was, but only as much as their imagination allowed them.

"I devoured information from any and every source. I contemplated and studied and observed and never let any shred of thought wander. My ruminating mind swallowed, collecting in all the pure and impure thoughts alike and in my leisure spend retrieving it from the gut and masticating into a assimilative form for the insatiable being in my cranium. I was fixing a maze or a puzzle that lay extinct to the eyes of the uninterested, but lively and genuine to the eyes that needed to see reality.

The trait in me, to look for every detail and its implementation, took my learning to new levels. I was able to distinguish the nature of rules as said in the scriptures with my own personal experiences. Initially, my progress was hindered by many obstacles- like the difference in experience and the information mentioned in the scriptures or emphasis on ritualistic worships which in some cases I considered unnecessary. Since I was pursuing a path that purely relied on one's efforts with no points of reference, I found myself surrounded with doubts and at times an overwhelming feeling of insufficiency crept in mind which distracted my attention. All the text provided a glimpse of the experience that I was looking for, but at times I felt myself pursuing an abstract feeling that was a result of my thoughts after reading the texts. The only relief I felt was when some of the fleeting references mentioned in the texts coincided with my experience and instantly seemed to motivate my depressed mind back to action. I tried to gain insight from my teachers and peers but they were of no help to me. Any attempt to question the objectivity in practice of a method was pacified by giving references from scriptures that hardly related to my question; others looked at me like a scholar who had gone crazy. All offered their answers, none of which suited my expectation. I just wanted them to share their experiences, if any, with me and help me distinguish the shortcoming in my efforts.""What kind of experiences are you referring to?" Asya interjected.

The *shilpi* for a moment caught his breath and realised that he had swayed with the memories in his mind. He had spoken with the same vigour that he once had in his youth, but even now people failed to understand that his struggle was to understand his inner self. The memories that surfaced still held the enthusiasm of his young age but he rambled on with the expectation that that everyone would understand what he said. He had to make Asya understand with a relevant example.

"In the ethics laid down for man, the practice of penance and its effects intrigued me. It is a vast field and one has to rely on his own experiences. When I started on course, my efforts did bear results but it differed in some areas. Also if the real nature of the soul lay in deep penance then why were so many rituals and obligations to be followed? Why did the mind clutter itself to the practices of offering and pleasing the gods materialistically?

"I was always seeking perfection so I compared it with the threshold set by the ancient masters. I could concentrate in the wee hours of the nights to contemplate on the hymns and meditative techniques, but still longed for the answer at the end – the mystical and esoteric state of fruition. I always knew that hard work would pay its due and one day I would find it. What I did not know was that it took years of patient application of the procedures to reach it. So naturally the hunter in me would question, debate and argue over the methods that I practised. . But I did not reach any satisfactory answer. I took it on my mind and overburdened it with thinking and exhaustive implementation. Who was to tell me that the thing I sought lay in the matured years of spiritual penance rather than the objective questioning of the methods?

"Anyway, I finished my years of schooling and returned home with accreditation of my knowledge, but yet a thirsty mind. The eyes of my parents filled with happiness and their bosoms with pride. I soon found my so-called academic success elevate the position of me and my family to the league of elite. I followed the footsteps of my father and so became the part of a small kingdom's most elite cadre, responsible for setting and executing the highest rules and regulation. Important decisions governing the morals and ethics of the society and people's benefit was the field of my study. I was to find the most generic way of enabling people to imbibe ethical conduct in the society without imposing any stress on the psyche of the masses. For that purpose I travelled into the heart of the people and their ways of living and found their way of life and means of survival. All the theories and dogmas learned in my childhood found practical relevance during that time of work. It was a very responsible and tiring part of my life where I exhausted all of my emotional resources to depletion. I loved to see my hard work bear fruit when I was able to convince the court about my thesis and their support for its implementation. Riches followed, accolades bestowed I became a respected person in society.

"Then dawned the important and the most happiest moment of my life. I met the person I was destined to live with. My parents found their last discharge of duty towards their son when they found a very pious, soft but beautiful woman for me as my better half…and she was indeed a better one. A whole new sense of perception pervaded that period of my life. The sensations and the revelations it brought made it a magical moment to exist. She was indeed the purest description of a human being that one can come across. She had lived by every rule laid down by her elders as a part of her nurturing. Her obedience and faith in the things she followed was indisputable. Her soft nature and temperament was indigenously compelling that made even a person of violent temper and action atleast to mellow down and connect him to a thought of calmness and reason. She never burdened herself with overwhelming thoughts and feelings that could put her in a state of apathy. Life is to be kept simple because it simply was simple; she knew this.

"I was, in many things –in knowledge, in learning, in position – superior to her, yet I respected her more than I loved her. I could look to her and learn everyday from her perennial well of tranquillity and still wonder what secret made her the person she was. None of my education had ever been given an idea of such beauty that could emanate from a steady mind. And such energy is powerful. It has the most potent form of penetration...the power that could penetrate and change the heart of a person...and she did change my heart. To this day I have only loved her, still long to love her. She didn't need me, yet she wanted me...I needed her and I wanted her. All luxury seemed non-existent in her presence.

"My mind wandered for a more serene life without having to battle 'learned minds'. I wanted no more to know –but to *believe*. My mind no longer yearned for appreciation from work or the betterment of the society. When love came I became a little selfish for my self-worth. With all the accomplishments my mind grew, but with her my soul bloomed.

"Much to the dismay of my parents and shock of the noble community, I left the 'elite' and started a much more meaningful life. I started teaching in a *gurukul* and moved away into the arms of study and nature – to a more peaceful way of life; unlike the chaos within the administrative strata of the country."

The *shilpi*'s eyes turned moist. Asya looked away as she did not want to see the eye bleed again. But she couldn't resist looking. But this time it only produced tears.

Asya saw the *shilpi*, an individual so prosaic – adorned with the confidence of intellectual learning; the man who gave an aesthetic appearance to his mathematical calculation into a sacred geometry of statues which he created resonating the idea of ancient knowledge, developing signs of being a human for the first time. Love indeed was powerful, she thought. And to receive it freely was the greatest privilege. For an entity that dissipated the aura of logic and reasoning from every atom of his body – emotions surfacing on his face was hard for her to comprehend much less offer a word of any consolation. She felt best not to speak.

The furrows on his forehead disappeared, the skin on his face straightened and all the other elements resumed its state of prior tenor in a blur. Even his unattractive oculus ceased to squirt and took the state of placid calm. It must be a house of a very sound will that controlled the reigns of sadness efficiently that it replaced all the marks of agony with tranquil and indifference. This must be what the *shilpi* might have learned from the woman he loved, Asya thought.

A moment could hold a distinct but varied array of things. To plunge into a state of misery and to spring back to the former state of acceptable civility – it would be easy if one understood how to cover the grounds of such quick transition so easily. It would help to know more of this wretched muddle of a genius felt Asya.

He continued:

"We lived happily; prospered. Every day was a feeling of true freedom, never to feel time command any aspect of life. To feel the sweetness of my love waiting at the end of the day and to be with her, it was indeed magical…though I never wondered what mystical force created such abundance in my life. I loved the small elements that made my life simple. It was an epoch of pure joy and elation for everybody. But we only understand the difference when that force, is taken away. And such a time came.

"Unrest in the country set in when the unification of many small divided pieces of land created tension. Though it happened at a faraway place, it soon reached our frontiers. Superstitious terror frowned the living of the common and danger lurked. I had confidence in the defence system of the country and always expected the enemy to make a respectful battle for the acquirement of land. But that was only my expectation. The enemy had other plans.

"Our small village was raided by dacoits and the help from the provincial administration seemed far away. They looted the nearby village with stealth and precision. No one came to know about it till someone found out their belongings were missing. But this heightened to a new extent when the wave of unification of kingdom struck them and they resorted to new means for their expression of power.

"Villages on a whole were attacked, looted and people were killed. An entire night would mark the end of a settlement and with such efficiency that if historians sat down for a revision they would have to work continuously for creating new maps every day. This was to mark the hostility of the territory for the invading forces. It spread contagiously to all the nearby territories and the people just formed an instrument of brutal display of bloodshed for the ones in power.

"On one such eventful, unaware night the legion of barbarian horde cast their feet into our peaceful village. It was, to my confusion which I am unable to decipher even today about my absence that night at my house, destiny.

"Morning arrived and the wafts of smoke from oil, hay, wood and flesh penetrated my nostrils in my sleep. I woke up suddenly and my cart had just made it to the outskirts of my village. I was returning back to my village after visiting my parents. It smelled of a pyre. I sensed someone must have died. I anxiously looked out from my cart to witness, in the distance, inverted canopies of smoke at various places in the direction where my village stood. I tried to recollect of any auspicious quality for that day; maybe it was a sacred day and offerings were made. But the smell of burnt flesh in the drift was irrefutable. I urged the cart to go faster. The sound of the wailings, which I initially discarded as a humming, seemed to get stronger and reinforced it wasn't my imagination.

"As I entered my village, seemingly difficult to comprehend, it looked as if the entire village had one pyre for every house. The ground was laid waste to blood, property of domestic nature like clothes, utensils, pottery all destroyed without any sign of hesitation. My heart winced. I covered my ground fast not paying attention to people who wore the same look as the ground of our village did.

"The door seemed quite stable without any signs of forced entry and not a single shard of elements were out of place in the outer décor. But the door was not locked. I opened the leaf of my door and stepped into my house. All my humble belongings were shattered to pieces and I rushed inside. She was no were to be found.

"I ran out and looked around; around the hen coop, around the goat's pen. She wasn't there. The cows mooed and for the first time in my commotion I paid attention to them. I ran to the stable and found drags on mud as if something was dragged. I went inside and the cows, terrified, ran into a pile amongst themselves to a corner. In the corner of the hack stay lay a glint of dried reddish-maroon ink which had flowed from the body of my beloved. They had bludgeoned her head to a side and her soul had left without requiring any further force. Except for a soft red trail on the side of her forehead above, there was nothing of physical cause that could indicate murder. She was frail and peaceful as always. And she was asleep, still, with the same grace that she had brought to my life with her devotion. I did not know where my tears hid. She had never made me cry and her countenance had always taken my sorrow away. There was nothing for me to believe that she had gone because this life-like body that I had loved so deeply still took my sorrow away. I sat with her head on my lap and looked at her.

"People who had seen me move rapidly earlier, rushed in to the stable when I did not come out for a while. The *vaidya*, who had a torn forehead too, moved along with his apprentice to check the pulse. She was gone and I did not need him to tell me that. People took the lead and moved her away from me and some helped me to do the affairs of her last rites. It was later, which the *vaidya* sought to think, that it may be a consolation to tell me that she had passed away even before the registry of pain in her brain. She passed away purely from a blunt force but without trauma. She was blessed to have such death to have spared her pain, given the circumstances. I stood still listening, but none of it aroused any emotions. I did not feel anything…numb and deaf to the surrounding expect for the occasions when someone came and spoke to me near my lobe.

"She was laid on the pyre and I touched her skin. It was still smooth and soft, but today it missed its warmth. She was cold and I wanted to ask her why she was cold. I was asking her already in my mind as I always did when she moved around in the house. I always used to communicate to her in a subtle way which even she didn't know; when she moved around as she did all the chores, I used to watch her but never speak to her, except in my mind. I would talk to her about how beautiful she looked when she moved gracefully. How her hands would reach the folds of her clothes on her hips, how she would tuck it and to see her beautiful body beneath her translucent clothes and flirt with them, to tell them they belonged to her and she belonged to me!

"And each time when she would turn around on the premonition of my subtle messages, I would be looking straight at her, into her eyes. I wanted to ask her how she knew it, how I always looked at her and she always knew. She would smile and I would smile back.. I had the satisfaction that my vibrations had penetrated the surroundings to reach her and she knew that I had called her. My humble house was the filled with the vibrations of love and it permeated everything in our presence. I had the enormous contentment to know that I filled her mind as she did mine. She had conveyed in all its essence that she did really love me. I was just a man, she was greater to me... and I always wanted to know whether she loved me for the man I really was. She humbled me by her humility and that was her greatness.

"And today she had gone away with the same dignity that came from her humility. The gods had seemed to make her pass easy considering the way she went without knowing pain. I thanked them for this gesture of kindness and I could have, for all my life, went onwith this single thought of contentment, if I would have not known the truth which was revealed to me later. It was this truth that led my life to the new appointment of consequence with my destiny.

"I lit the pyre and bid adieu to my wife. I prayed for her and in midst of her final rites I heard the garbled voices of women with sobs and wails.

'He should know...' trailed off a woman's voice.

'It is not necessary, she is gone,' said another strong voice.

'But it is his right to know," said a third feeble voice.

"The priest guiding me with the sprinkling of offerings, for a moment looked daggers at the women folk and the entire assemblage hushed a vacuum of silence with occasional hisses and sniffles.

"I noticed the priest trembled a bit; and I suspected the suppression. After the rites I asked him what he was hiding. He negated my question with a forced amount of zeal and smile of a plastic temperament amongst his angst. I persisted. He looked at the *vaidya* and lowered his eyes. The *vaidya* stepped forward and took me by the arm into the house. He looked at me with the eyes of a man who had treated many a diseases, whose heart and brain was stable even against the worst appeals of human discomfort and diseased state. He kept his arm on my shoulder and revealed that she was pregnant with my child."As I recollected – it was only last week that I had left for my parent's house and she had seemed radiant with a new glow. Unlike every time, she was happy that I was leaving. I had asked her about her mysterious shine and happiness. She had smiled and laying her head on my chest told that she had a surprise on my return. I imagined a nice evening with delicious food and a night of romance.

"It turned out that would have been the greatest day of my life if only the events were not the same as it had occurred. She was pregnant and knowing that would have made me cancel my trip to my parents; so she decided not to reveal it to me till my return. Her silence saved my life but it would have been better if I died beside her.

"Rage seemed to capsise the shores of my mind within and all the calm disappeared. I didn't even have a chance to know it before I burnt her. What sin would I have done not to know when I had the chance! I flew into an uncontrollable rage of madness towards the doctor and blamed him for withholding the news. I barked insolence, insult and curse. The entire scenery changed with my voice rising through the burning crackle of pyre which I had set a few moments ago as the vice of longingness gripped my heart and tried to take over my sane mind.

"Time passed. The sun rose with a sickly golden luster rendering its phosphoric radiance lighting the entire morning mist which once gave joy to me. Nauseated and bereft, I was beside myself in my empty house which once cooed with the sounds of her flirts and shy retreats. The pigeons freely hopped and ran berserk in the house. The ungovernable hurricane steadily cast its unabated violence on my mind and I shrunk away from the world.

"I was immobile as a tree, as insensitive as a stone, an inanimate as anything deprived of life with one exception. The thought of loss - instead of all the usual vibrations of the body, there was now only one single vibration. I was stiff as one single mass with my thoughts focused into a tremendous, ferocious regret. I just wanted my chance to know, to hold her and feel the new life that had grown within. There was nothing else that I could want."

The narration turned Asya sad. She had thought that her pain would never be understood by any other but here she was in presence of a man who has dealt with the same anguish, as her own, which churned her heart. Yes, it was in another epoch, another era; but it was pain indeed, nonetheless – the pain of longing. She looked at the man speaking, a man revealing the place of his heart that had been degraded by the vicissitudes of the human mind. Yet he was stable and no mark of pain or anguish, now, showed within him. He had crossed the mighty ocean of his aching heart, and triumphantly.

The *shilpi* continued:

"Then came the counter measures for the victims. The idea of unifications and their ambassadors slowly brought relief work to the villages that were victims of pillage and plunder. They needed willing people, ready to carry on the work of rebuilding this phase of the world into a unified kingdom and that no other people were met with such fate. It was a cry for a new beginning to end this tyrannical and murderous rule of callous power."

"I cared nothing of this till the words of a man rung close to my ears. I do not have the memory of his form, but in the midst of the chaos raging in my mind this particular voice penetrated. 'You will have a chance to redeem yourself–you can prevent it from happening to a father who doesn't know that his wife awaits home with the news of their baby. You will give them a chance to share the news. Rise and help us in eliminating this injustice. We need able minded people for this movement. Be a part of this cause.'

"There was a new thought. I didn't care about myself but I would not deprive another man of the chance to know, to his right to live. I just got up and joined the procession of people willing for the cause. And I was willing to fight for it. I did not care for the motives and rules for the new society. I had my own motive. I would not enable a man to be shunned from his right to know the news of their yet to be born. I will fight for such fathers and mothers and children from whom their shade of support had been taken away. I will become the most fearful, terrifying thought of evil for my enemies. For the first time in my life, I had enemies.

"It was easy for my rage to take control and turn me into monster who resided in the temple of a humble *brahmin*. Those who saw me immediately said I was unrecognisable. I trained within the league of people with the idea of ending the power of the ones who considered themselves above others, who considered that other's life are a mere fickle of fiction to satisfy their needs to be superior.

"I trained in the ways of swords, spear, archery and hand to hand combat. Motions became fluid. It came naturally to me. I did not need to tire and coax my mind. I was immune to fear. I was fear. I was an idea so terrible that even my comrades feared me as my enemies. Like a blazing army of *asuras* and *devas* combined and my once feeble composure of a *brahmin* changed into a *khastriya*. People around me felt that I might be a lonesome warrior who died in my past life reincarnated to fulfil my past obligations to redeem myself of my own karma but was wrongfully born as a *brahmin*. During the day I trained and struck blows and in the night I penetrated the heart of my enemy in my mind. Anyone who stood in front of me was my enemy. I could not touch the belly of my beloved, to feel the new life developing a body and you have taken away this chance of mine. With every movement of my weapons, every thrust I wanted my enemy to carry this thought to his next life."

"Were you not afraid?" asked Asya in the pause that the *shilpi* managed to take in his recollective narration.

"The element of the unknown was the most favourable for me. Others were terrified by the thought as to what the next moment would bring, but I did not want the next moment to be known or anticipated. I just wanted the next moment to be mine – mine alone; when I would strike the most powerful, humongous enemy whose glory they sang to strike fear in our hearts. I learned from fear. To not know, to be arrogantly cruel helped me to fade the fact that my enemy was stronger to me. I only relied on the knowledge that I wield a sword and my enemy can be cut by it. I *will* have to find the place and - *cut*. I never bowed to any other thought and the loss of my beloved gave me power to live this thought, to breathe it and guide me, to end the power which took her away from me. I was cruel because all that was innocent was taken away from me without any discrimination. My wicked, cruel and grotesque thoughts sprung from the forced abduction of the innocent things that I had come to love.

"The war brought forth many realisations. Many fell and many were alive wounded. Many changed their minds and fled while many stood their ground to their monumental demise. I did not care. Breathing a fire as possessed by thousand suns, I killed thousands, travelled many lands and spread terror to their hearts. My comrades gave me greaves and a golden armour of a lion embossed on the chest for the valour I displayed. I had the resolve to travel single handedly into the heart of the enemy and take their entire squadron down to ashes. There were no prisoners and I was always sent to crack the resistance of the unbreakable and invincible. I put their names to the scroll that *Yama* would have to carry back to the nether lands. I had given them a message to remind the gods – 'you have taken away from me what I wanted, here I take away your life for that. I will not stop till the last of your remains ends up for the gods to sort a new beginning for your next life.'

"On one particular incident they saw the golden armour of radiant persona, with a silver blade glinting in the sun and striking into the hordes of enemy. Blood, splinters, roars, screams, spears, arrows, dishevelled organs, bones with remnants of flesh, carpets of corpses, broken chariots, terrified horses and elephants, split helmets, smashed penetrated carcass with foreign objects lodged in them. All, anything, everything in my hand was a weapon. The *vaidya*, the *tantriks*, the priests of the enemy – I will never give them any opportunity to do their duty – nor to save any wounded, nor to bring a force of divine intervention or an opportunity to offer the last rites. I will serve them with mutilated bodies with severed parts which will take an entire *kalachakra* to identify. They will have to be burnt like many a hay stack that they had carelessly set fire during their plunder. The departed enemy will have to carry the mortal markings of my torture on their souls till the eternity of time and yet not be released from the pain that I felt. I was the weapon, a lion who was forcefully caged for amusement, now released. I wanted my fangs to feel the last pulse of their arteries beating to feeble immobility. I cut their breasts from which the milk of cruel passion flowed on to this world and by which their young ones annihilated their fellow beings. I will end their race and castrate them to impotency. I was born to do this –many sung such praises in my honour.

"There was nothing poetic or glorious about being on a battlefield. I wanted revenge. I did not crave for respect or the credit that followed for my actions. All knew it. I had made all the reasoning with my mind. There was no mental dilemma. I only needed to act. And so I did.

"The time came when the objective of unification came to an end with the founding of the new empire that spread, now from the slow clad mountains of the north to the glinting sea of the east and west and mountain ranges of the south. All the small kingdoms were dissolved into one nation. And the epoch of my sword had come to rest. I was offered a great place in the kingdom and for the valour placed in the battles. I was honoured with great respect and power. Among the counsel of men, who still feared me for a man I had become, doubted my sanity could be entrusted with anything of delicate nature. Ignorant of my past before the war, they considered me unable to hold a peaceful and functional society. I did not feel the need to display my credits to them. Nonetheless, I was added to the group of founding members that required to lay a governing mechanism for the country.

"As a part of the new found government, issues like basic amenities and a strong moral foundation for mutual trust was given priority. But to execute it was not an easy task. Discussions and debates followed. I, too, was asked for my views and opinions to which I presented a simple working method to begin with. I was given a chance to elaborate on my theory and the knowledge that I gained in years of tutelage came in handy at this juncture. Many of my views were accepted and so did the perception of my colleagues changed.

"Soon the structure was set into turn and found promisingly smoother than anticipated. People wholeheartedly contributed and co-operated. The war had a tremendous effect on them and they strived to their core to set forth a system together that would never ever give to the possibility of a new war and destruction like the one they have witnessed. I was also given a place of honour and an opportunity to service for the betterment of the people.

"However as time passed by, and the task I was entrusted was delivered beautifully to its execution, the person in me returned, in memory, to the time when I once worked among the administrative strata of then kingdom. I had no doubts as to the reality I had created and the will with which I had strived for the betterment of the society but I felt the same pangs of uneasiness set in before I had resigned to a peaceful serene life of a teacher. I had chosen this path just for one reason – to end the atrocities done to me and any other person that stood in my place; and now I had fulfilled it. I had done my part of joining the people together and contributing to society so that they may live a peaceful life. I had done enough; this life of a nobleman or warrior was not for me, it could not drowse the effect of my past. I decided to resign to much more peaceful way.

"I bid farewell to the life of a nobleman after handing over my responsibilities to others within the new rule and soon travelled to many places by sea and land. I saw deserts and lakes and trees and mountains and the parts of the world a man would feel unnecessary to visit in his lifetime. I kept on procrastinating the idea of a renouncing active life, apparently for no understandable reason. The possibility of a tomorrow with a life retired to the peacefulness of my mind and penance gave me strength, but lacked the longingness to take me away from exploring what held in a day of today. I felt insufficiently arrived to the stage for a resolve that was needed to live a life of an ascetic. The resolve in a strong tomorrow but not today, made me feel sufficiently inadequate to start over the decision of renunciation. I looked every day in tomorrow for a day to start but continued my travels.

"On such a day of travel, after a tiresome trek over an unknown region, I reached a shrine built in black stone and the floor felt so soothing against my tired feet that I almost collapsed on it to embrace the cold and feel my heat drain away. I drifted to sleep and after a long slumber found lazily resting my back on one of the pillars of the great temple. I was woken up by numerous sounds of objects clashing and clanging on stone with deliberate and varying intensity. I walked to the side where the sound emerged and I soon reached the place where many people were engaged in activities of cutting stones of huge and small sizes. Hammer, mallets, chisels etc. lay beside them in numerous quantities.

"I walked further and the number of men reduced to a countable few. These people seemed to be entrusted with the task of shaping the cut stones which were passed by the earlier group. Some polished and some washed the cut stones. After which they moved it to a place where few members fewer than the second group sat engraving designs, faces, hands and legs on them. Some were round and three dimensional all around its area and some images stood embossed on a thick slate of rock. They did all the fine process of giving the minuteness to the carved images or designs finally fit to use and see. It was indeed a great display of art and skilled labour combined. All seemed very busy to see an interloper had entered their private area of work.

"On further prodding along the path, I reached the back of the huge temple which to my dismay looked like a quarry attached to a mountain or a hill. Unfinished rocks of irregular sizes ranging from boulders to fragments lay there. The skilled people had managed to shape the entire mountains into a sanctuary of devotion. However, it was astonishing to watch a highly excited group of half naked old men clad in ochre clothes with sun burnt skin sitting and arguing profusely. They were deeply starved to reflect their bones even when their skin lay folded in luscious quantity on their bodies. They communicated in a frenzied manner with many gestures of their hands each time mentioning a portion of their palms.

"I stood there for a long time immersed in their exchange and could identify some of them were measurements and that it coincided to the sizes of statues. Finally after a long and deliberate conversation they seemed to arrive at a common ground of acceptance, did they notice my presence. They all soon dissipated and made themselves scarce except for an old man who smiled warmly. He was the eldest and the most experienced amongst them and obviously their guide for this entire activity.

'Young man, you seemed to be impressed by our work. Are you here to learn the art of *shilpashastra* from us?" asked the old man.

"Before I could say anything, he continued, 'but I must warn you – many a young men like you have fled in the dark of the night after they worked here. Seems easy, but it took them a while to realise it was not. Some stood for years, some for months and some for weeks.' I understood the mild neglect and snare from his fellowmen earlier as they left, as the reason became clear with this description. For their eyes I was one of those enthusiastic young men who had come in hopes of making quick money.

"I smiled at his humour but I stood there with respect and answered him about my curiosity and how I strayed in to their area of reserve. I apologised for any violation of rules.

'Care to sit down and give this old man company if the hour doesn't demand your presence elsewhere?'

"All I had was time. I sat with him.

"Soon I was engrossed in the tales of this old man's youth and achievement as he regaled the incidents from his prime. It turned out that he was man of high respect and admiration to many. He had travelled all the highs and lows of earth and could gauge the depth of the ocean and a star faraway in the sky. He learned the math of dissecting the anatomy of man figuratively and creating the anthropomorphic part of him to be revered.

'Why this barren mountain for a temple! Why did you choose this place instead of something nearer to any village or city?' I asked.

"He smiled. 'No matter where I carve it people will throng towards it. And the longer the journey the more sacred it would be to them. Anything easily available soon loses its lustre. Moreover this barren piece of adjoining land too will hold meaning for new people.

'But the important reason, the one I give credence to, is the same as mentioned in the texts which this whole ritual follows. Have you ever wondered why the ancient always turned to stone to carve! Why not any other material?'

'Because it is available abundantly,' I said.

'Hmm, but that alone is not the answer. Do you wish to know the metaphysical fashion of things in this order?'

"I nodded. He continued, '*Prana* or energy has one innate property – it is composed of vibration. This vibrational property is known as *tanmatra* – the property of being; as it is. Tanmatra is derived from two words 'tat' and 'matra'. Tat meaning 'self' and matra means 'only' – the Only Self – The Absolute. During transformation of prana, the singular vibration in it transforms itself into multiple vibrations of varying frequency. Due to this the possibility of different vibrations at different areas in a given space arises and the resultant is different elements of varying frequencies.

'And as universe has been created by the process of expansion of the Primordial Will, *prana* is primordially a 'will' which itself undergoes expansion and because of the preponderance of the 'stimulus form the will' that led to the transformation, gets divided into attributes and then converts into elements. The elements then have their own individual *tanmatras* which are different from each due to the variation in their resonance. Thus formed *akasha* (ether), *vayu* (air), *agni* (fire), *jal* (water) and *prithvi* (earth) in the ascending order of density. Each of these elements is progressive in its nature and the further expansion would be the next element. For instance, the result of *prana* on *akasha* gave rise to *vayu* and the further expansion gave rise to *agni* and so forth till it reaches a stable state where further expansion was countered. Thus the final element was *prithvi*.

'Due the relative differential resonance of these elements all had their own attributes, like *akasha* becomes space, *vayu* occupies the space, *agni* has heat, *jal* cools and earth stabilises. So the original energy gets converted into matter maintaining the expression of prana as their attributes. Thus the single became dual – Matter and Energy. Matter form the Gross Manifestation while Energy forms the Subtle Manifestation. Matter, the female component of the polarity becomes part of *prakriti* and *prana* was the masculine energy.'

"As a part of my schooling I had already studied this. I knew what the old man was referring to. The entire universe is the *prana* playing with prakriti. The masculine and feminine tend to be entities of individual properties originating from the same source. Even with dissimilar attributes, the masculine and feminine coexist and are responsible for evolution. And when evolution reaches its pinnacle these individual properties that aided the ascension becomes stagnant and then the decline begins. However I did not interrupt him. I wanted him to continue so I could find how this process was related to the profession he carried. I listened to him.

"He continued, 'In deep states of meditation, the masters found that *akasha* can only be heard while *vayu* can be heard and felt on the body; *agni* can be heard, touched and seen whereas *jal* can be heard, touched, seen and tasted and eventually *prithvi* had the property of odour in addition to the other sensory qualities of the *jal*. Each sensory aspect had at least one or more tanmatra that can be felt. This was the result of varying frequencies of *prana's* expression on our senses. When man came into existence as a part of evolution, he was closer to the truth so he understood it - uncorrupted. Providence and its ways were never questioned because there was nothing to ask. That was simply the way of it in its being. But with evolution came mundane activities in tow, so man had to create a means for his existence and as time passed; the truth he once knew was left unattended. In times of distress, he wanted to return to the original idea from his worldly activities for higher guidance, but the chain was broken in a quest for his survival. All that remained was the knowledge of a history that once man communed with the truth. So the element which had an expression on all the senses of man was ideal for creating an impression in his mind. All sensory organs that distracted him were given equal stimulus to concentrate one single idea and be in unison. After all, man too is the composition of all the five elements in proportion and hence he could associate on a metaphysical level even without his conscious understanding.

'The Gross Manifestation was easy to comprehend without much explanation so *prithvi* was the easiest element to understand. Hence statues were universally made in stone. Later on statues can to be made in metal but it was still a subset to the earth element.'

"I was surprised by the unique explanation he offered. I had never thought about it but I had followed this paradigm nonetheless. All the rituals and obligations that I once questioned and thought to be a hollow practice did hold meaning. Except that in time, since the explanation was lost, none could actually answer the practice properly. This man had relieved me of the questions I once abandoned, without actually having to ask again. I thought to myself, maybe asking the question is important, time will confer its answer to me. But what was worth knowing was to be asked. We will get all the answers we want – in time."

Asya too was equally astonished and some relief, unknown to her, found her. She could not explain it but she felt it regardless.

The *shilpi* said, "I prodded him further. 'You said that man too is composed of the five elements. That is why he can easily relate to the elements without proper understanding. So metaphysically what is the composition of man?'

After all, in a short time I would be on my way and it was after a long time that I had encountered someone who rubbed my intellectual side. I decided to pull something more from the time at hand.

"He was happy to hear a question for it was my first. A slight satisfaction showed in his smirk. He picked up a fairly square rock in his hand and pointed to it.

'Imagine a composite thing like this,' he said. 'If I was to break it into pieces and examine the pieces individually, all the fragments have a structure and an appearance on its own. Some look beautiful, some reflect coarseness, some are just worthless. If we were to fix all the fragments, it would fit itself back again into the right places into the same composite element. Similarly, prana is without any attributes. But when the expansion in it happens, polar opposites are created – say, one with the fine attributes and one with awful attributes. On observing objectively, the attributeless prana has converted into fragments of attributes or *gunas*. These *gunas* are as a result of the preponderance of the will due to which the expansion of prana happens. When clear black stone is broken down, its particles would be grey; a combination of black and white. Have you ever wondered where the white came from in a black stone?

'The design of things by providence is such that both the polarities exist even in the atomic level. Like I said earlier the important point was the 'attributeless' becoming the 'attribute endowed'. So the *guna* which form the negatively passive polarity is called *Tamas* and the positively dynamic is known as *Rajas*. When these two attributes nullify each other and exist in harmony the quality is known to be *Sattva*. You may be familiar with these terms. So, metaphysically speaking, due to the preponderance of *Sattva* and *Rajas* the perceptive mechanisms capable of detecting the subtle vibrations called the *Jnanendriyas* are produce which are the cognitive senses, the *Antahkarana* which is the collective mind where the cognitive information is received, the *Karmendriyas* which is the apparatus for human expression, then the *Panchapranas* and finally the *Upapranas*. These instruments in the course of evolution when composed together into a *Pranamaya Kosha* came to exist as *Vyashti* or an individual. So in true sense, all human beings are dynamic because the *Tamasguna* does not exist unless it is received by the sensory organs. Only the faculty to understand the tamas guna exists in us. That is why detaching ourselves from this aspect automatically propels us to our dynamic quality by default because there is nowhere else our consciousness can return. Thus detachment is a prophesised tool for spiritual development.

'As for the rest of the tanmatras, they undergo quintuplication – the fivefold multiplication, where due to *tamas* quality, each of the five elements gets divided into two equal parts of which one remains intact and the other part gets further divided into four equal parts. The intact half of one element gets joined to one-eighth portion from each of other four elements. For simple explanation, space gets divided to half and it is attached with one eighth of air, one eighth of fire, one eighth of water and one eighth of earth. So does the other halves and one eighths of the elements follow the course. This process is called *Panchikarna* according to the Vedas and explains how the gross body was produced from the elements. These five elements form our gross body along with the subtle consciousness and the original potential from which we are created. And earth, being the most stable and capable of influencing all senses, naturally became the suitable option,' the old man said.

"I was impressed by this simple explanation," the *shilpi* said. "He had explained brilliantly how stone can influence man although they never really wait to think of it in such a way. "This earth has so much to give and tell us. It is abundant with riches and fertility. As per the *shastras*, we being composed of these vibrations of elements can detect the concentration of subtle telluric currents in earth. Such regions generally have the ability to absorb or exude energy in a quite detectable fashion. Temples are built across these regions to accumulate this energy at that centre. That is why geometrical shapes of temples have relevance. Pyramid, cones and domes have the ability to maintain the flow of energy into stagnant pools. This energy when accumulated can be harnessed according to our body's nature. That is why people visiting temples feel a sense of calm and refreshment because they are in touch with the natural frequencies of healing and harmony. That is the real objective of building a shrine. And the mountain like this is a natural pyramid. Moreover the area surrounding it had been untouched by man and therefore the flow of energy is uninterrupted. This makes it an ideal spot for constructing a shrine as compared to the ever bustling villages, towns and cities. Coming here is a matter of revelation to everyone,' the man concluded.

"This elderly man was mature and understood the laws of the world and also lived closer to it. I was naturally intrigued by him and so I asked, as anyone would ask an old man, about his greatest personal achievement from this field of work. 'None,' he said.

"I looked at him, puzzled. The man said, 'Son, as time and age had passed, one thing remains clear. All that I do is a farce. I have not done anything but worked on an idea that went away unreceived. And just because I did that well I was rewarded very well. This is the realm of men and one lifetime is not enough to live and understand it.'

"I was still confused. I started to find him slightly eccentric, but he seemed to not be joking. I implored him, diplomatically, 'You have to make a lot more sense from that. I am unable to deduce any wisdom from your words.'

"He replied, 'I have created so many statues and pieces of entire architecture that would for last centuries to marvel. But more importantly, I have created all these for mankind who are just thirsty for an idea for them to believe. I created gods in stone and laid a stone clad shrine for them to reside. Millions flock to creations of mine and bow at its doors with respect and reverie. My statues rise in height and people had to build ladders for the ritual obligations. And they bow to a dead stone. No one can take their right to devotion, but if they bowed to each other with the same reverence wouldn't mankind live a much peaceful life?'

"I understood what he meant by his earlier answer now. *It is in our nature to destroy what we have come to love – to drive it or to be driven by it. Without this feeling man would never feel that he has lived.* I concluded without wanting to get into any philosophical soiree. I had no taste for any logical understanding on this subject. My understanding was plenty. Man does what he can but he did that on whatever his belief held.

'But is it fair for a stone, the face of which my scrotum touched while I sat on it to carve, receive faith respect and love when the people offering it doesn't have it for each other?' he said excitedly.

"It was hard to resist a smirk at the notion of his bony posterior on the face of god and the rewards he received for doing so. Before he created the statues from stones he was the person who stood in the sanctum sanctorum. How can one give credit to a creation that made man bow to a worthless object on the pretext of divine intervention? It indeed sounded like a farce. If the statue inspired devotion in people, would the creator of it be inspired to bow in front it? He had made it with indifference and mathematical accuracy. His logic would not allow him to bow his mind. Is belief so deceptive that it takes away truth?

'We do not want the truth in its real from. All we are looking for is the things that happen to coincide with one's beliefs. One's perception always confuses and corrupts the truth. As for the truth, it gets lost in its own translations. The human mind is incapable of accepting a complete truth,' said the old man.

"I looked pensively at him at his last remark and he responded to my perplexity, 'If he understood the entirety of it then he would not remain human, would he now? If you cross this end of the river to see how the other end looks, looking back you see that the earlier place of your start in all its composure. Some elements add to the picture that you could not identify earlier due to your position. But when you started from the place of origin, you move thinking that you knew the place well enough to be left. That is the whole idea of moving, isn't it? One would not move from a place if he has not understood it. And in that way a small amount of truth always remains undiscovered in our belief that we know what we have seen. We have to cross over to look back for the absolute scene.'

'So you are declaring that every man dies with arrogance,' I said, 'And the men who dedicated their lives to the pursuit of the absolute truth, are their lives futile? Do they, too, die in arrogance?'

'Have you met any person who says that they have found the absolute truth? Will any man of such pursuit confess to finding it? When they climb the pedestal of self realisation, do they feel that they have found the truth that they can extol?'

'I don't know,' I said after pondering but admittedly my mind was in unison with the old man's words.

'My son, if they found the truth wouldn't they stop looking for it? But do they stop? No, because there is still truth to be perceived. The journey extends this life, this plane of existence. Like I said earlier, why would you move ahead if the place you arrived at is sufficient?

'Entire lives of men have gone to waste because they find this idea of denial, renunciation and penance alluring to a higher idea,' he continued. 'Even the greatest yogi will never agree that he had found the absolute truth. He still pursues to find an end to the infinity of his experience. Do you not see the deception in this? The person who looks into his experience of self realisation for the truth never finds it because the truth is the experience. He stops looking for the truth that he thought he eventually is going to find what he was bred to believe. So in reality there exists no such absolute truth. That is why the other side of the river seems so different when you set foot on it, unlike the way you saw it from its original place of departure.'

'You mean to say then, that the truth is in being?' I asked.

'Yes. And in this life of man, a man will never find the completeness of a truth unless he finds in him the state of being; untouched by the position he is in. Therefore whatever he wants will never come in the way he expects. He has to cease being a man to see what lies behind him, to know the complete truth. And when one ceases to be a man, he is transformed.'

"There was something hidden in the old man's witty remark. All our security lay in the thinking of what we have accomplished on the basis of the belief we hold and all our dismay and regret lay in the opposite of it. If we would 'look back' and accept it then all the disappointment would disappear.

"I was happy by this exchange but also aware of the time passing. It was twilight. In this conversation time had flown. I was still spellbound by this old man's simplicity and verity. An absolute truth can only exist when there is the acceptance of completeness to any entity. An absolute entity never needs to be believed on. But man can never stop believing the things he understands. And man cannot believe a truth that will destroy his identity – his ego. The great masters of lore who showed the world their pearls of wisdom and teachings had claimed to be seized by their ego even after realisation. So it must be true that man indeed is incapable of knowing the absolute either by the lack of the faculty to perceive it or being human is just a milestone in journey towards the truth. There must exist a path ahead to the absolute and being a man was just one small place of existence towards higher understanding. Being a man was just an experience. All hindrances will be cleared if man accepted all the events in its wholeness. "The old man smiled as these words sunk in. He was indeed a wise but unsatisfied man, unhappy by the 'farce' of his life. Maybe in his youth he may have believed that he could change the world. A man unhappy about world in his old age can only be an idealist when he was young. I smiled at this thought.

"It was after a long time that I had met a man who stimulated me in an intellectual way and provoked one to think on their own. I surely was in a presence of a person from whom I could personally learn a lot more than I could find in years of travelling. I wanted to stay.

"As I was taking my leave later in the evening the old friend invited me to stay for dinner. I considered that it would be a nice place for rest and for the first time in many years I would be in a company of people while I slept at night. I gladly accepted. I was introduced to many of his colleagues and contemporaries over food. They discussed work and then turned to fun and a bit of merriment when they put together their small musical instruments to use. They prepared a small bonfire enough to warm the place and slowly slept beside it.

"It was nearing midnight. I could not sleep. I pondered and pondered. Maybe this is why I instinctively kept my procrastination alive. There may be something more to this. Many thoughts crossed my mind. Why would I stop here and why would I be involved in a interesting conversation with a stranger if I had the desire to quit this world for monastic purposes? It would have been a calamity. I would never be at peace and all I would achieve would be the result of some mechanically followed spiritual path. I did not want to wade into those waters deliberately and invite a self imposed loneliness. This confrontation of fate was no accident. I was destined to be here till I knew what I wanted.

"Finally I got up and went to the edge of the mountain look at the view below – an entire mass of darkness, without the faintest light. It looked purplish black – even blacker than the sky. I heard the wood crackle in the fire behind me. I made up my mind."

Thoughts

The mention of twilight reminded Asya to look around.

The sun had begun to travel west and the birds flew in front of the blazing ball towards their home. She too had to return to her nest. Unlike the swallows, that had built a nest in a niche in her house which now lay abandoned, humans have a single place to return. And that cannot be forsaken.

The distraction in her caught the attention of the *shilpi*. He waved to her. Suddenly Asya realised that she had spent the entire productive time of the sculptor, that day, only making conversations. Although the *shilpi* had been kind, he was there to do his work and she had distracted him from it. Though the tale had been interesting, Asya felt responsible for steering the conversation to a personal note, which hadn't been necessary for the *shilpi*. But now it was time for her to return and the awkwardness she felt to initiate an exchange of departure was clearly visible as the naïve nervousness of a woman.

Much to her relief the *shilpi* pointed that she should not delay and she could come back tomorrow. Asya playfully said, "Only if you complete the rest of your story tomorrow."

This retort brought a smile to the weary face of the sculptor and the white teeth in countenance with the rest of his face lit him. He acknowledged the request. It was nice to see the naïve playfulness in a person who barely knew him but had taken the right to demand a story from him. It made the departure feel a little more intense. A streak of delight gushed in the poor man's heart when he felt an elderly affection that one has for a child, surface. His eyes saw a child amble away content with a half story waiting curiously for the rest to be heard.

Asya crossed the plain grounds of grass which now appeared greyish green in the fading sunlight of the dusk. She looked at the far end of the horizon and saw the smooth ball of saffron-red luminance dropping to the ground. The sky too had prepared itself and had cleared away into a mix of violet and blue with saffron red maroon hues. The volery of wings rushed towards their nests with anxious hearts. Asya looked at the flock and felt the rise of euphoria; the freedom that the birds held and the strength they had in their wings. The atmosphere filled itself with the ceaseless wavering chatter of chirps from far and near. Asya was happy to have met the *shilpi* and know a person of great knowledge and experience from a different era.

She walked on till she reached where the forest began. She looked back one last time, before the view behind her would vanish in the engulfing dusk. To her disappointment, she could only see the outline of the hillock. A shrill unexplainable chill surrounded her being; she wondered how the *shilpi* would survive the night in this cold, lonesome abandoned place alone. How his days were forlorn of company and people! In the distance Asya saw maybe the last flock of birds to return homeward. She could not help thinking about the birds that didn't have a nest to return to; where would they go! When she saw the hillock for the last time for the evening, a flame had lit on its corner where she had been earlier – her heart told her even she had a place to retreat to, but what about the people who lacked a place to lie and rest their back on? Home was a place where man could return after battling with the world for his living, where his worry about his existence can be limited by the warmth of his loved ones within the four walls. She felt sad for the *shilpi* who lay on barren forsaken rock in the midst of wilderness. The empathy of being alone overwhelmed her – a familiar ache woke her heart and made her eyes moist.

To know that one can feel so deeply and be aware of the feeling was indeed unique. What would have man done if he was to live and live life without feeling it. Though those moments brought in torments of insurmountable proportions, it also gave manthe courage to pursue his aspirations against the opposing current. As it dawned to her, Asya realised that she had a long way to travel in heart to reach the place where her sanity remained in equilibrium; to join the pieces of what she felt, to the portion of what was conceivable in reality. The *shilpi* was one such person who had succeeded in making his life worthy; a person who can say that he has truly lived as he ever has wanted. She was indeed lucky to meet him.

Asya walked slowly through the forest, but she was not afraid of the approaching dark, nor was she afraid of any wild animals contriving to eat her. Those things had ceased to bother her. She was in a world of her own. She met a magnificent persona who through a casual conversation has endeared and imparted a great deal of courage to her. All her usual worries seemed faraway. How many people in the universe are capable of such intimacy! To mean something so valuable in such short time! She felt a new sense of energy. Her experience had changed her perception. She thought back to the morning when she had set out, hesitant, seeking the help from the tribes, but now she felt different. And the people, who saw the *shilpi*; who waited for no second chance of inquiry and concluded him to a demon worshiper. He was the one-eyed monster to them. How in the world are people going to understand each other when they can't wait to draw a conclusion for their own satisfaction?

She was about to launch into a hysteria blaming the world for its apparent short-sightedness and lack of humility when she suddenly remembered the state of gloom she had once. How she had wanted her righteous grief to be heard; how she wished the world to know her aches, how she wished to tell him that she loved him; how much she wanted her gods to understand! All that time she pushed hard to make her impression felt but no one really understood. She suffered without recognition. She was no different from the people in the world – all were lost in their own glum. How could anyone look beyond his own suffering and understand what others are feeling? It was her decision to meet her curiosity that had rendered her this insight and courage and wellness to her being. In reality, nothing had changed in her life, but she felt some of her wounds healed. The few ounces of awkward courage made this change come through. That was the difference between her and the other on-lookers who judged the sculptor. Answers came to those who had the courage to take the first step.

Her mind, though calm, wanted to investigate her sadness and if possible cure it forever. She recollected the dark times of her nights spent in longing with a question as to why she suffered so much. For once she wanted to know the source of her happiness and what made her sad. It dawned on her the chaos that ruffled her soul had the genesis in her own thoughts. In the confusion of sadness she had actually strayed away exploring her melancholy rather than finding a solution. How devious can it be when we realise that we love and that we are ready to suffer for it and it actually cripples one from seeking happiness? Self righteous grief had a way of justifying itself with grace.

How could one abandon the thought that the one we love is in danger? There was some comfort in it to endure and stay unlike the crippling nauseating feeling from inaction. It is easy for one to say to let go, like many had advised Asya initially, but the suffering and pain had a way of demanding to be felt. In such a scenario when logic fails to present an answer, one is compelled to sway in the turbulence of one's pain. The absence of a powerful comforting thought that assures the well being of the problem in question drives one's sanity to precipice. Are we really beings of logic or beings that feel? Asya wondered.

Peeling away her thoughts one by one – she wanted to confront the elusive idea of her sadness. Trying to find the truth about it was like catching the rainbow – the more we run the farther it was. No. She wanted to know. She pushed herself in the mind – Why was this sadness unbearable in spite of being righteous? What has love given her that she never had before?

She pondered and then realised how her life blossomed when she met him and how her mind build dreams of them together. All the way along, she did what enriched the beauty of her dream. This is what dreams do, she guessed. Her heart and mind became creative. A silent but powerful motivation had crept in. The world she had created was dear to her and the sudden changes dissolved it in a spur. All the dreams got smashed against the changes of time.

Maybe this is what happens when a creative force meets an immovable stagnant object. She felt passion is what causes life to have its momentum along with beauty. She and the *shilpi* had the same force within them. We all want to be the part of the creation – the reality we create and the comfort in knowing that we can do what we want. This thought was completely liberating. She felt a large blob of heaviness heave away from her chest making her feel light. She at least had something to hope. She could still create the life she wanted – in time.

She felt her beloved to be the part of the dream that he had nurtured in his childhood and living it. She felt proud to be the wife of a soldier. Earlier it was just him she had loved. Now she could accept him for what he loved too. It was cleansing and relieving. Selfishness swept away from the pores of her thinking and for once she began thinking of herself with her love over the distance. She felt her presence beside him, beside her weary husband who had toiled and fought with his life. She nursed his wounds and kissed his lips with all the power she harboured in her thoughts. All seemed possible to her. *No. He will not die – not when I can be beside him like this. He needs me and I will be there for him.*

It was more than wishful thinking. Sometimes intense thoughts can transcend time and space and be a reason for instant manifestations. Asya felt the ripples of her thoughts touching her husband and comforting him. She too had a role now to play. The entire vacuum was gone.

She resolved never to let this spark of energy die away in her heart and guard it against the onslaughts of her own mind. She had suffered much and now she hada way; she would not neglect it.

Her thoughts once which roamed and rampaged and ravaged her mind now happened to open the floodgates of thoughtful thinking without much stimulation. She wondered… the *shilpi* was a gifted person with such contagious enthusiasm and passion that some of it might have transferred to her. Otherwise who was to be given credit of this sudden revelations that she was having!

The days of her past shined in her memory. How great were those days when comfort filled her heart; everything was worth loving. The sun, the moon, the wind, the rain – everything deserved to be loved because they were the part of her life. She, at that moment, felt that she could love anything. Her heart was happy and her mind was full. She smiled at the thoughts and looked at herself as a person from the past walking beside her filled with delight and joy. How she loved the idea of the beautiful past that filled the gap of the present! We are actually in love with the dreams that we build and so everything in it becomes worth loving – she thought. We love ourselves for loving our perceptions so dearly.

With these thoughts she reached the village and walked towards her house on the hill. She felt her universe shimmering by her own presence. Her house now filled energy and self sufficiency. She went outside and lit the lantern and looked at the flame through the weaves. It did not flicker – she would not flicker.

♦ ♦ ♦

The clear sky of the night showed the star that shimmered brightly enough to cast their luminance on the black canvas of the universe painting it a pale white. Lying down on the rock, the sculptor looked at the roof of the universe studded with sparkling celestial beings. A moderate fire warmed his body. Memories rushed to him. Recollections spread across his consciousness. He then tilted his head to see a tiny speck of light that showed in the night. He had seen that light every day before sleeping. Somebody lit a lamp in the dark and it had always made him endure the night. Somehow he felt the light gave him an impetus to endure – to live.

He had climbed here, a fortnight ago, after bathing in the river late at night, having travelled for many days. He ate what was left in his bag and laid to rest like he did today. As he turned his vision around in the pitch black darkness, nothing seemed visible except a dot of light in the faraway distance. It swayed with the wind but still burned. He felt alone, like the particle of light in the dark. He too would endure like the light that passed through space of blackness to reach him. That was enough for him to decide. It was later the following evening that he realised that it was from a lantern when a house became visible behind it on a hill.

He slowly closed his eyes taking in the life he had lived and looked at the stars.

Faraway, Asya looked out from the window to the star studded sky and her mind drifted into peaceful slumber.

Karma

Asya rose early, well rested in mind as well as body. The early birds had just begun their routine of chirps. Her heart felt light, strengthened by some force unfathomable. It was different from everyday, all the gloom had faded; like she now knew what it was made of and it no longer prodded her. She opened her door and found the cloud of morning mist hanging over the village below. It had been a long time that she had ignored this view. The flowers were heavy with dew and the earth smelt pleasant like after the first rains. She just wondered how god must have created all the elements so complimentary to us; how he made the flowers and its fragrance that inspired men, how the sun rose and it yielded the crops, how the rains fell on the hot soil and released its scent.... All the elements had their way of conversing with us. It was, maybe, their way of greeting.

She made some food, today, in a little larger quantity for the sculptor.

As the horizon shed its maroon hue and the shades of yellow became bright, she closed her door behind her and left for the forest. She now knew the way and did not need any help. She picked an alternate way that she had made a mental note of the previous day. She did not want the tribe to know her intention or be the subject of unnecessary questions. It was easier to hide truth than to explain it.

The beauty of the forest with the rising sun was simply alluring. The smell of every tree, distinct from one another, the wet ground from the heavy dew and the settling mist and the cool breeze spoke of freshness. And the mud smelt sweet; sweet enough one make bizarrely hungry.

When she reached the summit where the forest ended and the plateau began, she saw the greyish hillock almost white by the surrounding mist. She walked the ground, over the wet grass. She smiled as she felt the ends of her dress touching the ground getting heavy due to the seeping of the dew. She felt a fancy to play in the grass; somehow harbouring the fantasy that the earth wanted to play with her.

She reached the place where she had met the *shilpi* yesterday. She searched for him and soon found his work untouched from the previous day. And nothing much was changed in the scene – ashes from an extinguished bonfire, a cloth covering his work, some clothes in the cave; but the sculptor was not to be found.

She just waited curiously thinking he may have been to the river for a bath. And her doubt was proven right when the *shilpi* emerged from the other end of the hill, wet. He smiled at the waiting girl and greeted her. He told that he did not expect her early but welcomed to stay anyway. Glancing at the parcel she had carried, he smiled and said, "I am fortunate today."

"Today you have to tell me the rest of your story. Only then you can have it," Asya said impishly.

The *shilpi* too laughed. After the usual pleasantries, both of them settled down. Asya laid some food on the leaves which served as plates. It was early to have a morsel but somehow the aroma of the food tempted both to have some.

♦ ♦ ♦

"The much awaited morning dawned," the *shilpi* began.

"All night, I spent my time contriving the moment when I would ask the old *shilpi* to accept me to their group as a student, so that I could learn their ways. It was after a long time, after many faces and places I had arrived to some interest. I could not contain my excitement. The earlier day was worth watching. The way their hands moved on the stone and the care given to it was almost like a young one in the arms of their mother. The stones seemed to adhere to the command of their tools and they easily unhinged from their parent material with ease. The scene just kept playing all night. It brought me the memory of my days in school, where I used to fantasize about a subject I was learning and imagined to be the learned scholar, one day I would become who reasoned with others in contradiction to me. A similar spur of enthusiasm had surfaced after a very long time.

"It was time for me to meet him. I finished my morning obligations early and waited for the *shilpi* to resume his work. To my astonishment I found the old man already at the place of his work on my return.

"I went to him and stood there in complete silence for his attention to drift towards me.

'So my friend, are you bidding us farewell,' said the man as soon his eyes found me.

"I laid away what I had in mind without giving much of my past and the reasons attached to it. I simply said that I would love to learn the art if it was not a trouble to include an additional member to their group.

'I think I didn't scare you enough. Even though I was jealous of your muscular arms, which I could have put to good use considering the amount of work and pile of stones we have, I thought you would be on your way after the talk we had yesterday. Many people are scared to lose their self to the talks of an intellectually indulgent old man. But you seem to be drawn to it. It had happened earlier but this is the first time that man had been drawn to an eccentric argument so quickly,' mused the old man.

"I smiled but kept my silence. After a small pause, he asked…. 'Why do you want to stay?'

"I said, 'I simply want to learn.'

'Is that it? And what happens after you learn what you wanted?'

'I don't know,' said I without much thought.

"The entire time he was looking at me. The old man paused and mulled on it but his face showed no expression. We were having a very direct conversation but he did not show even the smallest amount of emotion to give away his intention.

'Okay. If it is your will then you can stay and learn,' he said finally.

"I was happy to stay, but I had some decorum and discipline to learn. I was not allowed to touch the tools till I was initiated into the work by an elder. The benediction of a higher learned man was necessary as part of initiation in this area of work. And I was to follow a vow of celibacy and abstinence – as long as the task of the temple was at hand. I was to follow a routine of rising early in the morning and offering a ritualistic prayer and ablutions to the gods. Only then was I to begin my work.

"I had no qualms in following the regime, but for the first few weeks I was only a labourer to carry huge and heavy pieces of stone within the construction. The remainder of my time was spent in observing and studying the movements of hands and tools over the stone. To grasp in memory, how one turned an ordinary stone, to a *shila*; to learn, first in mind the uses of various tools and other aspects of the art.

"In the evening I would sit and converse with the old man. He never asked me about my work or what I learned. We simply sat and spoke about how good the wind was that particular day or how the nearby forest from the distance looked like a region full of spikes after the trees shed their leaves. He would remain indifferently enthusiastic about any topic. I was unable to decipher his silence on my progress. Didn't I matter to him? On the first day it seemed that he was my patron and now he seemed so distant and the initial connection seemed to be lost.

"After a few days, during the usual chatter, I asked when was I eligible enough to start using the tools as the others. He smiled and said that I was free to use it since I was already initiated into the stream. No more obligations were needed. I was surprised by it and asked why he hadn't told me then!

"He said, 'For a newbie, the initiation into the field is our obligation but to move ahead and get initiated is the student's duty. We can only show you the path; it is up to you how fast one wants to cover it. Only a man of true yearning can progress and when he is dissatisfied he can have the thirst for knowing the right way. Discontent is the only fuel that motivates a true learner. The mystery that eludes one propels him to push further and harder. He would want to be clear in the process rather than being worried of the result.'

"He was correct. I must not have stayed diplomatic in my approach and should have showed my interest unabashedly. I remembered my fervour during my childhood, but as I grew old I became cautious about my behaviour waiting for an opportune moment. After all, conduct did not matter while performing one's task. I joined my hands and bowed him to take his leave.

'Soft things loosen faster than hard objects. And so does one know how to co-ordinate the force required. An efficient hand on stone is a practiced hand on wood,' said the old man, looking away into the fire he was warming himself with. That was a good advice.

"Carving on wood is easier and can be discarded easily in case of mistakes. Here stone is precious and it cannot be wasted. Moreover with wood, not much energy has to be utilized and made the practice much easier.

"Dry blocks of firewood that we burned at night; I used it for practice during the day. The earliest work of mine was genuinely childish. The initial confidence I harboured burst like a bubble, as it vent itself away to scribbled and broken work on wood. I looked at others who learned on wood and asked for their guidance. They were menial workers who lacked etiquette and bluntly ignored me while they chafed away on their craft. I was disappointed but somehow I was not angry with them. I patronised them in my heart and consoled myself of them being devoid of any formal education and manners. They were bound to act like that – to act superior to an apprentice. That was the only way to wield their importance.

"I waited patiently to have their attention. Then one of them took a little pity on me and sufficed my query with an answer. He was already adept in that technique and displayed an enormous speed in delivery of its completion. I was confused and looked puzzled at him. I was not going to learn anything like this. He was quite satisfied with my bewilderment and guffawed loudly. Other amateurs joined in too. He had established his superiority; rest did not matter. I was dismayed by their behaviour. Anger rose and almost showed itself in my eyes. These puny uncouth miscreants didn't appreciate my humility. Don't they want to complete their task faster? Isn't working together and helping each other an easier way to finish the given work and be on their individual paths? Why did they like to torment a person who has a willing heart to learn?

"I was dejected. Clumsily I sat at a far way place under a tree. I could hear the roar of their laughter as I started to move away from their place. It soon died down and they went back silently to their work. I was gloomy over their behaviour. I was a student once but this didn't happen to me. I was equal in all respects to my contemporaries then, but now as grown adults people seemed less educated on how to behave with others which didn't require any schooling. Anger closed in me with its burning grip. I pondered about my decision of staying there and learning their craft. I couldn't get along with simple workers, how was I supposed to spend a long time with them? I was free and just to learn a new art I was not going to face disrespect from them. They were mean. I felt alone, unlike the free heart of a drifter I once was.

"I lowered my head and closed my eyes and breathed deeply. My mind went adrift and I did not impose control on it. Various memories played and then it automatically went to the recollection of the first impression of a sculptor carving on stone when I reached there on the first day. I played that vision over and over again. I felt each and every move of his hand and focused my mind on his work. It was easy for him and he knew what he was doing. Nothing was random and his hands made the right grove, the appropriate cut and then chiselled away the excess. His breathing was steady even making the intricate curves, I recollected. Sleep took over and I did know when my consciousness faded.

"After some time I opened my eyes. It was about noon and all the workers had gone for lunch. Memories of the earlier events of the day rose in my mind once again and without any further thought I took the piece of wood and started making the design of my imagination. I did not care if it was of correct measure or according to the texts. I just made small grooves, cuts and nicks till the image in mind coincided with that on wood. Finally I carved a beautiful design similar to that on the pillar but in my own unique way. I felt happy. There I did not feel the need of reassurance from anyone. I had completed my work and it was better than how I had imagined it. Application of one's imagination releases graceful ways to a rigid method. It becomes aesthetic along with being functional. I sat there breathing calmly – the same way the sculptor did in my vision.

"The old man came looking for me. 'Are you going to feed yourself with that piece of wood?' he asked.

"I smiled at his mild sarcasm. Usually the group of sculptors joined together for food but today I was not in the company. The old man had tried to ignore my absence but when he heard the worker's gossip about what had happened earlier he came looking for me. People could be mean and those not accustomed to their life will not understand crude humour and fun. Though he considered me a good man, he was yet to be assured that I was a patient one. That notion was dispersed from him when he saw me and the piece of wood.

"He examined the wood closely and then threw it away. 'Come, let's have food,' he said.

"I was neither angry nor sad that he threw away what I had worked on. It did not matter to me. I saw him, now, in the same way as I considered the workers who had made fun of me earlier. As long as I was careful in my actions I could always deliver good quality work. As for the beautiful piece I finished in wood, I would have discarded it sooner or later. A product of excellence ceases to be of a marvel for its creator after it has been appreciated Soon the appearance of beautiful things diminishes to the level of any other natural object. Close examination of any art will reveal some defects in it. Art is meant to savoured, not scrutinised by logic; there was always some amount of imperfection to any piece of art, I realised. I had no interest in it since I had accomplished it. Creating a much more complex challenge did bring momentum in my mind. I looked forward to it.

"I realised another thing. I am what I teach myself. I am my own teacher.

"We sat down to eat. After having our full, the old man said, 'If you are interested in studying the iconometry of statues then don't go back to carving wood today.'

"I was thrilled as there were more things to know and I was actually getting the boost. I noticed all things flowed once

I made a deliberate effort of staying my ground. I consented but before sitting down the old man took me to the group of workers that carved the generic patterns on pillars. It included the people who were sarcastic and mean to me in the morning. Overlooking them the old man said, 'Tomorrow onwards, he will supervise your work. He will decide what is acceptable and what is to be rejected. All of you are to report to him.'

"I was surprised as were all the others. Jealousy beamed out from the miscreants. Some people cooed at them, 'Stupid in the morning, master by the evening.' It was their turn to be made fun of. Regret and shame showed in them.

"Why me? And why so early? I have many things to learn. I just carved my first design this afternoon," I asked the old man after we sat down for conference.

"Do not feel misinformed when I tell you that you can supervise them. You do not need to convince yourself by practice what you can do as long as your hand follows your vision. Rest falls into place and everything comes to age with value. Some of those workers are years older in their craft yet they cannot deliver more than what they are doing. They have no passion for growth and not all people have the appetite. It has taken them years to perfect what they are doing now, but they do not respect it. One should have the aim to move forward then alone does circumstance play its favour on him. Moreover, if you stay in one place skills become stagnant and how are you supposed to learn anything new there? It is part of my job to find such people and provide them with an opportunity,' he said.

"But I am not ready in practice," I argued.

"Knowledge does not come at one's convenience or bidding. If you can learn how to carve on your own, then how to practice it depends on your managing your time and skills. Will you delay your next lesson, just because you are not confident in what you just accomplished?" he asked.

"I understood what he wanted of me. He knew that I was different from the ordinary folks and he recognised that I could be harnessed to a better level. So I paid full attention to what he taught but also practiced what I learned. It turned out to be a favour from the old man as the stint with supervising the workers kept me in touch with the skills and lessons learnt when time to practice seemed short. From that day on he laid down the charts and scrolls for constructing a statue and taught me the ancient treatises.

"I still remembered my first lesson. I was very impressed by his presentation of knowledge. All that he spoke could be easily associated and related to. He was a brilliant teacher because he did not just rely on the principles laid down in the books but also had a panache to show its actual application. He had explained, 'There were thirty two principal or *Mukhya Adhayas* and thirty two *Upa Adhayas* or subordinate treatises. In all, they sum up the sixty four arts that we follow. Almost all of them have interrelation to each other. Some of the mechanical arts which formed parts of *Upa Adhayas* had the emergence of its parameters derived from the *Mukhya Adhayas*. For instance, *Natya Shastra* is a *Mukhya Adhaya* which dealt with the tenets of expressions and dance while the tools to make dancing possible like the musical instruments formed the subordinate part of that art form. All arts had a natural origin and all of them were studied and categorized by our ancestors. Music, dance, medicines for healing as well as for personal care, sewing, painting and all the random activities that we follow and do are a part of these scriptures.'

"He laid down treatises like *Manasara, Mayamata, Kashyapa* and others. All of them had valuable information on construction, carpentry and creating sculptures. Most of these literatures were consulted by artists for gaining a solution on contested points of art. I enjoyed the lectures and discussions stretching out into midnight, fun and frolic, extensive story-telling and their arguments on actions of the prominent mythological figures. We relayed objectivity on their actions and criticised gods. We were drunk with mirth and favoured the actions of *asuras* over *devas* in our frenzied talks."

Asya became curious. She raised her brows when the *shilpi's* excited movements made a reference to the defaming of the gods. Why would learned men mess themselves with some higher power just because they know something about the creator! Her naïve mind could not understand why we should wrestle with the unknown. Even in her misery she had always maintained that one day God would listen to her and fulfil her wish.

The *shilpi* could feel that in her glare so he turned to an incident that actually happened between him and his old teacher.

"In my childhood, I have learnt that Vishwakarma, the celestial architect of the gods was responsible for the architectural creation of the universe. He primarily existed when nothing was created. He is said to have scarified him to himself so that the universe as we know could be born. Some versions state, as his progeny he had five sons; *Manu* – an ironsmith, *Maya* – a woodcutter, *Tvasta* – a metal smith handling brass, copper and alloy, *Shilpi* – a stone carver and *Visvajna* – a jeweller who worked with gold, silver and gems. The five sons later flourished themselves and history had seen them grow into an independent castes based on the work as we do now." Asya listened very keenly.

"I and the old man argued on the details of this particular story. According to him, *Maya* or *Mahamuni Mayan*, as he was believed to be called later, is the progenitor of *Vastu Shastra* which he gained from his father as *Prana Veda* was revealed to him. On earth, he is believed to have resided on a now destroyed ground called *Kumari Kandam*, south of Lanka. He was believed to have meditated on the science of sculpture and architecture and their conjunctional importance by mastering the principles and doctrines of *Sthapatya Veda*. That is why he has graduated himself to the level of a *Brahmarishi*. He is said to have lived on *Jamboo Dwepa* in *Kumari Kandam*. Now, the continental landmass is believed to be submerged underwater after the universal deluge for which *Vishnu* himself have taken the incarnation of a giant fish. As a part of his destiny, before the floods Maya left *Jamboo Dwepa* and travelled to Lanka and then from there he came to the south of our country. From there he set up his own school of thought and focused on the architectural progress of the people while his brother Manu laid down the rules for mankind. *Manu* travelled to the north but *Maya* stayed in south but many of his work were in conjunction to the treatises and principles preached by *Manu* for the betterment of mankind. Many temples and rituals came to existence and so did the role of architecture turn into a grand area of importance.

"I, too, had heard this story, but a different version of it. Though the personage entitled *Maya* remained the same in name, he was an *Asura* according to me who have lived and outlasted himself over the *yugas*. According to me, He was the son of *Kashyapa* and *Diti* and *Maya* was the father of *Mandodari*, the wife of *Ravana* – ruler of Lanka. He too, was a king and his subjects were adept in architecture and had a unique insight in creating magnificent, impregnable fortresses. They even had the knowledge to liquefy stone to form the complex singular shapes.

"*Mayasura* as he called, was the designer and the architect of the 'three flying cities' known as *Tripura*. Legend speaks of his unquestionable faith and devotion to Lord Shiva, which was the reason he was saved when his three cities of iron, silver and gold burned by a single arrow. And he later built the *Mayasabha* or the grand assembly hall of the Pandavas in *Indraprastha*. So a demon that had lasted the *Tretayug* and *Dwaparyug* must be the real *Mayanmuni* and not the old man's version. Not all *asuras* were fools. There were learned and great devotes in their lineage.

And moreover the death of *Mahamuni Mayan* is not mentioned in any scriptures. All the knowledge appeared to reach out as a facsimile out of the *Vedas* or *Puranas*. *Mayasura* and *Mahamuni*, according to me were one and the same.

"I was dim-witted to have put this in front of him but he countered me without losing enthusiasm. 'You are a brainless twit,' he said, 'The knowledge along with many other boons was conferred on *Mayasura* at the end of *Satya Yuga* after having performed many austerities. However, *Mahamuni Mayan* was one of the personalities who existed before the great flood while *Vishnu* took the *Matsya Avatar*. *Mayan Muni* predates *Mayasura*,' he snorted.

"He was correct. Both happened in different periods in the same era – one at the beginning of the epoch and the other at its end; yet I did not have the common sense to look back on what I had studied. And usually humans have the tendency to vouch for the things once learned; we are ready to defend by the little known knowledge, however ambiguous, which comes as a result of unfounded information. It starts converting into belief and one seems so ready to flaunt it when an alternative version casts its shadow on our version. Somewhere in me the student and his impatience still lay dormant and came out with the right stimulus. The age of the *brahmin* was resurfacing even after a life I had led and retired as a *khastriya*. I realised that there is much knowledge in the universe; facts about its origin quoted or believed maybe different, but its function remained the same. Like the primordial energy is known by many names but it always had a function based on cause and effect.. Nothing matters as long as the results derived are up to our benefit. I must keep an open mind and let the polarities exist to atleast derive a proper solution and a sound understanding.

"Such nights followed and we indulged in many more stories and its controversies. It was a blessing to have a person who appreciated even my occasional stupid, naïve arguments without countermanding my value in his mind. It helped me shed my prejudices and automatically programmed me to keep an open mind without questioning at the first sign of doubt. He cleverly sharpened my analytical attributes and helped me clear my thinking through this bout of verbal exchange."

Asya's attention sharpened. She asked the *shilpi* to narrate all the stories that he had heard from his teacher. It was informative and entertaining unlike his usual sermons. Moreover people relied on stories from *Puranas* rather than the *Vedas*.

The *shilpi* smiled and realised that despite becoming adults, people still have an indulgent ear for stories. They are still children within.

"Very well then, do you the story of *Karna* from *Mahabharata*? The story behind his birth?" asked the *shilpi*.

Asya nodded. "When *Kunti*, the mother of *Pandavas* served the sage *Durvasa* to his satisfaction, he granted her a boon that could summon any god to her bidding. After the sage's departure, to test the boon she invoked the sun god. *Suryadev* appeared and enquired about her welfare and the reason for the summons; she gently replied that she was just testing the boon she had received and she desired nothing as of now. The sun god explained to her that the boon did not work this way; she had to ask him for something. Reluctantly *Kunti* agreed to accept anything from the god. The sun god gave her a child wearing flaming golden armour and earrings already pierced to his lobes."It was how Asya had heard the story from her father. She wondered if any alternate theory to this version of story existed that she was not aware of.

"Hmm…the story is correct. But do you know that *Karna* – the child given to *Kunti*, was in reality a demon in his earlier life?"

The hair in her ears stood at its end. It was getting interesting. "No," she said.

"As it turns out, there was once a demon called *Dambhodabhava* who mediated on the sun god for a long time. Impressed by his penance, the sun god appeared and asked his request. Initially he asked the boon for immortality. Refusing it, the sun god explained that it was against the law of nature. So the demon requested for a thousand armours that he could wear over his body. The peculiarity in this case, was that as long as at least an armour remained on his body, he could not die or be killed. To break a single armour from his body would require thousand years of penance and another thousand years of battle. Another condition was that once a person has succeeded in breaking an armour from his body, the warrior would die instantly. The sun god reluctantly gave this boon and disappeared.

"Drunk with power, the demon wrecked havoc to the people on earth. People called him *Sahasrakavacha* – the demon with a thousand armours. His terror drew the attention of gods. Vishnu, who is the preserver of the universe, heard the suffering of people from *Murti*, daughter of king *Daksha* and the consort of lord *Dharma*. She desired to put an end to the menace of the evil *asura*. Appeased by her prayers, Vishnu appeared to her and blessed her with two sons – *Nara* and *Narayana*. They were inseparable in duty and devotion to each other. They loved and trusted each other implicitly. They learnt warfare and mediated on *Shiva* for a long time and generated spiritual powers by their devotion; one of those powers they had the ability to bring any dead person back to life.

"When the demon attacked the place where these brothers were staying, *Narayana* went and challenged the demon to a battle while he left his brother mediating. He fought for a thousand years while *Nara* meditated during that time. When one of the armour fell from the body of the *asura*, *Narayana* died and was instantly revived by *Nara*. He then challenged the *asura* for the next thousand years while *Narayana* meditated forming a loop. They fought with the *asura* till there was only a single armour remained on his body. Realising that the brothers could end his life, he fled to sun god and hid behind his throne. *Nara* who was fighting the demon ran after him to the sun god and requested his return. However, sun god could not hand over his devotee for killing, so he refused. At that time, the earth was also under the phase of time descending to another *yuga* which also forms the reason for the escape of the demon. *Nara* and *Narayan* declared that they would be born again and *Nara* would kill the asura. *Nara* cursed the sun god that he then would not be able to protect his devotee and he would have to suffer the pain of his death.

"Thus, *Nara* was born as *Arjuna* and *Narayana* was born as *Krishna* in the next *yuga* and, *Arjuna* killed *Karna* in an eclipse that *Krishna* conjured to take away the shielding powers of the sun – *Karna's* benefactor. Also the last of his armour was given away as charity to *Indra* who disguised himself as a brahmin and begged *Karna* for his armour of gold. This was how Karna got killed in the battlefield."

"But how is the past of Karna revealed to us? No one knew about his past, then how is this story relevant?" asked Asya.

"After killing *Karna*, *Krishna* reveals to *Arjuna* and his brothers about *Karna's* identity as their elder brother. In grief, for hiding this as a secret, *Yudishtira* curses *Kunti* and the entire woman sect that they would not be able to contain any information that has to be kept in confidence and eventually reveal it. Then *Krishna* intervenes and pacifies them with this story of past about *Karna's* previous birth. He reminds *Arjuna* of his vow that he had fulfilled by killing the demon relieving them of the lamenting they were in."

"If Karna had a past like *Arjuna* and *Krishna*, then *Nara* and *Narayan* too must have a past prior to the episode of *Dambhodabhava*," observed Asya.

"Brilliant observation," quoted the *shilpi*. "*Nara* and *Narayana* are two different forms that originated from the famous incarnation of *Vishnu* as *Narasimha*. The lion head split from his body to form *Narayana* and the body to form *Nara*. Thus man is also known as '*nara*'."

"Are there any more stories that common man does not know, like this one which explains the past of an entity?" asked Asya.

The *shilpi* noted that it will take up much of his time if he was to entertain Asya with stories. So he asked her about the stories that she wanted an explanation on; that would be much easier.

"Is there a reason why, the father of *Kauravas* was a blind man?" asked Asya.

"Yes. It is believed, as legend quotes, that *Dhritarashtra*, the father of *Kauravas* was a tyrant king in one of his previous births; One day, when the king went for a stroll beside a lake, he saw a beautiful swan and hundred cygnets swimming. Just for the sake of fancy he ordered his servants to remove the swan's eyes and kill all the cygnets. After the war of Mahabharata, in his despair *Dhritarashtra* asks *Krishna*, for an explanation of his terrible fate. Krishna explains as this being the part of his karma from his past birth; he too faced the same fate as that of the birds he once slaughtered," said the *shilpi*.

"So how did your life continue after your work with your teacher?" Asya asked.

Relieved, the *shilpi* returned to his life's incidents. He continued:

"The day arrived when I myself sat for work with stones; initially I was to carve lamps and floral designs. I practiced it on a wooden block and then set to finish it in stone. After many mistakes afforded by a newbie, I carried on with the resolve to make every curve destined for beauty. In a few weeks I learned to deliver a quality of work like an average *shilpi* would. I lacked finesse and the elders always showed me there was always a scope for improvement on my work. I kept on moving forward not afraid to make mistakes but also carefully using my imagination and bending every thought with action into pieces of art.

"Once a task was entrusted to me, I wasn't given any new work until I finished it. Initially, the great amount of energy I squandered in the deliberate practice for finesse was now replaced by a more relaxed pace. Still my mind did not derive the satisfaction that comes from the accomplishment of my work. I wanted it to be perfect. I observed my fellow workers who worked on a similar pattern and mimicked them. It became easy. There was no deliberate rambling of the possibilities to create a curve in a design or search for a better way to do an existing type of work. I just allowed my work to flow without the interference of reason from my mind. Speed and accuracy increased and so did the coordination of the two help me to deliver faster and the lack of clarity in my work disappeared. My work began to resemble the refined form of art delivered by skilled people. There was less to correct in my work and I gained fluency. I did not push hard and never let any new work intimidate me.

"Soon the pace of my work increased. I worked faster and soon found assisting people around in their work after the completion of mine. I slowly gained a small acceptance among this new group of simple people.

"One night the old man took me to his place of recluse amongst the pile of rocks behind the temple. After the general pleasantries, he casually put forward, 'So would it interest you to learn how to carve a statue if you feel that you had sufficient pillars to taste?'

"I was delighted. To carve a *murti* was reserved for the elite and a low worker was seldom given a chance to work on one. It takes years of practice and care and devotion to the tribe and then does a man of low beginning rise to such a task – it was the general practice. I said, 'I am glad to accept you offer and I am delighted to learn, if you consider me eligible for the task.'

'Don't worry,' he said, 'I have not chosen you out of any sympathy or affection. You have learnt what you came here for and it would be unfair not to test and give you a chance when the time to ascend comes. Your skills will get stagnated if they are not honed by further challenges. One fact remains indifferent to you and me – you and I are still going to make mistakes regardless of the greatness we achieve. It will be the same piece of stone and it will be the same doubts that will recur every time you set for your task. The wise would clear their uncertainties earlier when the work is small. That is what differentiates one from others. You become great when your quality of learning is greater. Remember, the child is always afraid of the dark. If the fear is not removed at the early stage, it will also grow with your skills. He will always fight the same fear on a battlefield as he once had while being in the dark. Today's mistake of yours is the one you ignored yesterday when you first set hand to the task. Never forget your first fears. You will be battling it for a very long time although it will change into various forms throughout your lives. Nevertheless it will remain the same old fear.'

"Like always my teacher made another true and honest delivery. He had trained me but it was I who can control my work. The limit I set for my work is the only limit it has. I had always remembered those words of his and never ever had forgotten to apply it to my work.

"From that day onwards, I surrendered my mind to learning. I learned the applications of the canons not from texts but by guidance from my teachers. I learned to carve and soon became an expert. And the fear I had encountered in my new works due to its complexity and the fact that I have never attempted such work disappeared by the memory of how I overcame my fear during the initial attempts at work. I felt encouraged and charged into every endevour and finished it with tremendous zeal. I developed my signature styles and soon people around me too appreciated and recognised my work.

"As time passed we finished the work of the temple and after its inauguration to the people, we left the place for new work. There was plenty to work – new temples, statues for palaces, entire buildings for higher officials etc. I soon graduated to higher levels and conducted the execution of bigger tasks and projects. But still I enjoyed carving statues and design myself although now I mainly made statues that were the centre of attraction or the most important of all. My work made me famous. People flocked in from far away by recommendations of the people who had seen my work. My stature rose and so did money and luxury. People perceived me not only as a talented sculptor but also a privileged guest. Kings and noblemen honoured me with coins, gems and precious stones. My life as a *brahmin* and as a *khastriya* seemed to me from another birth. I was far away into a world that seemed real enough to forget the earlier part of it as a half remembered dream.

"My benefactor, the old man, also gained his accolades through me. He never had to venture out for new work on his own. My mere name was enough to bring a flowing abundance to him. He too rejoiced my success and congratulated many a times for the position I had acquired.

"It came to a time that I was thoroughly satisfied by my progress, work and place in life. The rise of my vocation had reached the place where anything higher seemed to be only a hairline difference in my mind. Everyday was the same. The current of stagnancy set in. The well built body of a warrior had undergone many changes and it suited much to one of a businessman. I enjoyed the satisfaction in my accomplishments but it did not make me happy. I needed a new inspiration that would fuel my mind. A lull came upon and nothing seemed to interest though business and work flourished. Restlessness of mind grew; nights got deprived of sleep and the only sleep I managed to get was when the mind exhausted itself from work.

"I thought of leaving this work and going back to the ways of the wandering life I had before taking this occupation. All night I would be filled with the resolve that the next morning I would launch into a journey and be gone from this place of dullness. But the next morning, I would rise late and the resolve of the earlier night would be gone. So I would wearily start my day looking for the work to be attended.

"My mentor soon intervened, to my good fortune. I shared with him my phase of mysterious disorientation. I explained about the lack of clarity since I could not understand the reason for this state. There was no help for it; so I submitted myself with good grace, and listened to what he felt about the situation.

"He said in simple words, 'You lack interest now because your task here is done.'

'I do not understand. Please spare me your wit, my mind is unable to process much less understand any rhetorical quote. I am here, depressed, thirsty for some simple wisdom,' I said.

"He smiled and said, 'You came to me to learn and learn alone; if you recollect your answer to my question before you were initiated in to this field. It was not a general question. Your place in our group and the nature of work to be entrusted depended on that answer. Many people flock to me so they can learn from me and earn a great deal of money. They want a respectable and famous position in the society and afford all luxuries of life – that is their primary objective. . They gauge their greatness by the amount of money and fame they can accumulate after they learn from me. But you were not bound by any of those mundane objectives and were unaware what would happen after you would learn the art to perfection. You were not bothered about what followed once you learned it – and you said the same when I asked about it. Money, fame, exclusive works – none of those was your aim. You enjoyed it, so you worked. There was not a plan of further action while you learned. It was pure zeal that had driven you and the accomplishment of greater challenges was just its buoyant effect. Now that interest of yours had run its course like any other occupation. There is a limit to what a pursuit can offer. You have reached the peak of this pursuit but you are not ready to be stagnated by it. And hence I said it and I quote again – 'You lack interest now because your task here is done.' I was convinced by your answer, that day only for one reason. I knew you would stay with me for a long time, travel many places and have great accomplishments because you had no other motive than to learn. That is one of the main factors why you graduated to creating statues so early in your progress.'

'So what should I do? You understand me so well as if you yourself had been on the same path as mine.'

'Yes, the grounds of your unrest are familiar to me,' the man replied,'I once found myself seized by throat by this stagnation. But I found my own way. I am not a good guide to provide a glimpse on this as one has to make his mind and choose the path ahead of him. What one had chosen is applicable for oneself.'

"I begged him for a more unambiguous and understandable answer. To all honesty, he did not seem to have an answer.

'Atleast tell me what you did?' I begged finally.

'I looked for inspiration. I dissociated from my practice and wandered around for a long time till my mind found its enthusiasm back. It did not inspire me to come back and work again as a great *shilpi* or any other area of interest for that matter but it showed me a clearer picture of my own self.'

'Pray tell me, what exactly did you do?' I repeated.

"He replied, 'I told you and I tell you again; you are my friend, but the path I walked myself is not for everyone. And you may not want to travel it...'

"I felt the urgency to do something, even though I did not know what. So I interjected without allowing him to finish. 'Show me. Reveal what you have done.'

"The old man held his silence. Staring into my eyes, with an enormous amount of concern he said, 'Tonight, after the sun sets, await me at your doorstep. Keep your horses ready and we will take a trip. You are much younger, but you are my friend; and a friend always cares. But I see that you are in desperation to find a catharsis. I will show you what I did, but I would refrain you from walking my path. Think and choose wisely. Do not judge me for my deeds and remember that you would be solely responsible for your actions and choice.'

"I paid no heed to the advice and the mystery he had created and dismissed his theatrics as the vanity of an old man. I was not taken away by his discourse, as always. To my opinion he had flair of glorifying things with elegant and tasty words. My frustration got the better of me. What can this old man possibly do in this past? I was sure he would not have done any heinous acts in his life. Atleast not as heinous as mine, taking the lives of many. I was sure that this simple person may have engrossed himself in some activities that brought him back his mental vigour which he deemed unfit for normal people to pursue. I was anxious and looked forward for the night to arrive.

"The appointed hour arrived as the servant rushed in to convey the news of arrival of the old man. I hastened and soon found myself on a road along with him in the dark. We did not chat except for the initial pleasantries. He rode in front of me leading the way. The night showed a half crescent but had ample light to show us the path. Nature filled the ambience with sounds of crickets, owls and occasional distant flaps of wings. I veered around to look at the beauty of the night as the meadow, which we crossed, stood bathing in the soft moonlight. My inner artist was at play in my mind and I conjured new thoughts and designs for future. There was nothing else I could do to push the excitement of the journey to the corner of the mind. The old man had visibly held restraints to the description about the nature of our destination. Curiosity just could not be contained so I indulged in many fantasies just by looking around and savouring the night.

"We stopped at a lake, very far away from where we had started, after a long time. It was almost midnight and the bright curve of the moon cast a velvety illuminating blanket on a lake before us. The old man got down and allowed his horse to drink some water. I too got down and steered my horse to the other mare at the lake.

'We will have to walk from here,' said the old man pointing to a dull path on which only two people can walk. It trailed to a winding curve in the dark and none of it could be seen. He then held the reins of his horse and pulled it towards the path. I followed him.

"We walked for quite a while. The road was mushy and the horses found it very irritating for them to keep up in the soil as their hooves sunk every time they tried to move quickly. Sweet smell from the bushes filled the air and tempted the mares to swing around for the green foliage. The old man however was not at all perturbed by the events. Soon we reached a clearing and a very well-constructed path began. The path lead down on sloping ground and from the distance I could see brilliant lustre emanating from the depression in the ground. It was of huge expanse and lay hidden to sight because I was not aware that we were standing at the edge of a hill due to the dark, which gradually rolled down. The crescent had disappeared between thick black and grey clouds.

"The lustre grew in intensity with each passing step. At first, it seemed like a well full of light but later as we moved towards it, I was filled with awe at the settlement that stood in the sunk earth. It was brilliantly lit and was surrounded by hills on three sides and the open front of the city lead to many places and eventually the sea. The entire expanse of the area could be seen from above. All the buildings were white, magnificent and large, built from expensive stone and lavish. The descend was gradual, and the path winded around the city to give a tour of the major areas. There were shops, wineries, gardens and gathering grounds. People thronged the streets even at this hour of the night. Men and women were dressed to their best. Even the pot-bellied businessmen were dressed in their finest with great care. There were no signs of poor people around. Smell of various incense filled the streets from different houses.

"The buildings were carved in a very delicate manner. The contours on the carving and the depiction of statues in sweet romance filled the place. Two beautiful statues of women bearing pots with water continuously flowing out from them were placed at both sides of a garden and the view was simply splendid. . What taste! What architecture! I was spell-bound by this mesmerising place. Truly the old man was amazing. He had hid this place from me for so long. The conduct of the people and their way of approach to each other was visibly different and affectionate. Women spoke with lowered eyes to men and none could resist the sweetness in which they conversed. They were plain men and women but somehow they had conditioned themselves to delicate mannerism which was hard to miss. They must have been taught well to maintain this candour amongst themselves.

"The old man was watching me intently as I tried to take the surrounding in for my mind to assimilate. His gaze was impassive but his smile was warm with affection. There was a feeling of pride in him that aroused when he saw me smile broadly. This place looked indeed marvellous and the old man had hidden this from me. I felt a little envy creeping. Who knows what else this gauche held under his self! I followed the old man and soon reached a building with a large entrance.

"We reached the door step where stood two well-built guards with beautiful faces looked at us smilingly. They only wore a dhoti and a piece of cloth tied around their heads. But their bodies were perfectly built, symmetrical, oiled and tanned. They could have proven to be a muse for my work any day. From the negative space behind the door and the building, a glow emanated from the lamps inside like the luminescence of sun behind the horizon. It was an overwhelming feeling. All the events and objects were made with such care that raised even the ordinary to the extraordinary.

"The guards looked at the old man and paid a small acknowledgment. They opened the door and we stepped into the courtyard. The courtyard was filled with flowers and the scent filled the air. A building which housed three storeys stood in front of us. White arcs of marble with intricate carvings, carved pillars, brightly lit corridors with soft and translucent curtains at the pillars ran throughout. It was a splendid piece of architecture. I felt I could improve my work if was in constant touch with a predecessor like this.

"We entered the building and were greeted by the sound of someone singing - a scat singing style. I have never indulged in music or lavish entertainment of any likes. Apart from the dance and music performances that I had seen in my youth in the court of the king I served, I have never treated myself with any forms of indulgence. My only closeness to music was the music that the sculptors sang, gathering around at night during their period of work.

"We crossed a corridor and walked towards a thick curtain hung in front of an arcade. The sound became clearer and finally when we brushed the curtain aside, a hall filled my view. It was lavishly built and opulently furnished with large string of lamps on pillars, chairs and mattresses in a fashion that all of them pointed their view to the direction of a stage ahead. The roof of the hall extended high above to form a dome shape and at the centre laid the hold of the attachment from which hung the array of lights. The centre of the hall was left empty to have a direct view and the sides were filled with ornamental chairs and pillows and mattresses for people to sit and watch. Brilliantly lit stage with deep dark maroon carpet over the sprawling white floor was a sight of beautiful contrast. Care was taken on each and every detail of the hall.

"There sat a man, the singer, with a huge body in the centre of the stage with his shrill high voice and sang the scat words that went high and low at times. On either side sat two men who sang the same style of song in different tones at regular intervals blending with the main singer. On the ends of the stage on both sides sat two men – one with the *mridanga* – the barrel drum with it ends tapering where the hide produced the sounds and one *sitar* – the egg shaped lute with a long neck with strings and frets. They just kept their instruments on their lap and seemed to enjoy just the singers involved in frenzy.

"There was hardly any music but involved a rough exchange of rhythmic syllables accompanied by the clapping of the singer's hand on his other hand or occasionally on his thighs. '*Takita takita takita dhimi takadhimi ta, ta, ta, takita takita takita dhimi takadhimi taa...*' The singer enthusiastically swayed his head with raised brows looking at his co-singers.

"The others chipped in to add a different verse of syllables and finally the third for a different verse eventually collaborating into one single style of syllables and tone. It was amusing to watch them and I couldn't resist smiling to myself. My heart felt happy to listen to the brilliant collaboration of instruments and sounds.. The night that the old man spoke of was beginning.

"I looked around to search for the old man. He had vanished leaving me alone to this musical feat. Except for the singing and clapping of the singer's hands, no one talked in the room. All enjoyed the event. Suddenly the picture on the stage ensued into an argumentative style of singing – singers visibly teasing each others with intended puns of musical display with the same syllables. One would engage the other while the latter would return in another style as his answer. Then the singer would turn to the audience and appeal them as if the answer received was irrelevant. They jested on their pride and made fun of each other as we would argue and debate to show superior talent or knowledge. The audience couldn't, in the moment, resist a chuckle.

"As the performance ascended, the *sitar* and the *mridanga* joined in to create the high and soft consonants. They progressed and all of the instruments and vocals joined into a frantic excitement of sound. It encouraged to focus more and could feel the same excitement in me and the audience. Finally the clash of sound climaxed to the roar of the audience and the singers were showered with praises and flower petals. They bowed their heads in respect and rose to depart from the stage. The audience, some, congratulated them while others indulged in sweet wine and betel leaf spread with slaked lime, sliced dry nuts, cardamom, and cumin seed folded at the centre within the leaf clipped at the centre by a single clove into a roll as refreshments.

"The old man reached quietly and placed a hand around me. He too was chewing on a betel leaf. He raised his brow in a gesture asking my reaction to the performance. I was visibly full of glee, amused by the show and he could read it. This was a place of indulgence and my mind was thoroughly refreshed by it. 'This is the place that I hold close to my heart and I have learned many lessons of my youth from here,' said the old man gesturing outside to the city. We came out of the palatial building on the street for a walk.

'This is really an amazing place for music. What else does this place teach?' I asked.

"He replied, 'Many things. There is no teacher here; there are only students. The entire city works on that principle. People mingle around and they learn from each other. There are no boundaries. Only one has to have interest. This not a centre of art alone,' the old man said with a mysterious gleam in his eyes.

'Oh the old man is yet onto one of his tricks,' I thought. I asked: 'What am I to learn here?'

'You are surrounded by new things and you ask me what you want to learn? Do you need me to tell you what you want?' asked the old man.

"He wanted me to explore and find my own vocation of interest. I could not forget the happiness that I had, just earlier, by the musical piece. There was mirth in it that I have never enjoyed in my work. All was a rudimentary procedure and the little satisfaction that I had was only at completeness of a statue. I understood the subtle hint from the old man. He wanted me to enjoy and find something that made me happy. And it was difficult for me to say that in one night. I have just arrived and the old man would not tell me much about the place.

'Then I will have to come here often. This place is marvellous but I still need time to understand what this place offers,' I said.

'Why don't you stay?' asked the old man.

"For a moment, I went back to my own life and pondered. Should I leave behind my routine and stay in this place? I was not the free drifter anymore. But then I remembered the passion I had while I learned sculpting a statue. I had totally abandoned other routines and followed what was necessary and was not deterred by any other means. If I have to learn I will have to stay here and find what I liked. The decision lay on me and I made up my mind to stay.

"The old man was happy about it. He suspected that I would stay back so he had already made the necessary arrangements. I was to stay at the place where we had been earlier. They accommodated the people who wanted to stay and spend time in the city.

"The night slowly drained away; we strolled and talked to each other. Unlike a guide, the old man showed me the place but did not describe much about the place. He showed me the grand buildings and garden and places which made the finest pastries and sweet cakes. All the people there were rich or well bred. We soon reached the harbour and saw the mighty sea in the dark of the night. To the left there were huge ships, foreign and native and many people thronged around it. There were light skinned people, like the ones I had seen in my travels from other parts of the world. They ambled away with sturdy and fast strides. Everything was new and a fresh feeling surfaced within me.

"I breathed in the moist salty air of the sea and walked with the old man along the sandy mass adjoining it. The crescent, hasting away with the night, held its view in front of our vision above the sea as we gazed away to the horizon with the green water mass touching the sky. There was a lot this world held and the same things I had seen once now held a different meaning for the person I had become. The feeling of tenderness from the universe and care made its appeal in my heart as I held the spectacle in my view. I felt blessed for the life I had and remembered my beloved in this hour. After a long time I had remembered her. It was she who had sent me on this journey; otherwise I would not be here. I thanked her and the gods in my heart and felt the soft hands of happiness reach in me. I was full. My work was done. There was nothing more to ask for. This place would be the last that I would visit. I would draw all the happiness I can derive from this place to my heart's content. Then I would wait for my time.

"It was a good decision to stay…I believed."

The Harlot

"The morning brought rich rays of yellow light penetrating the city," the *shilpi* continued. "I enjoyed the scene of illumination by the rising star. The light moved away the shade of the night as if it was uncovering a hidden dwelling of richness and abundance as I watched it from the shores, where I stood, and behind me the sea brought the tranquil noise of the waves. I watched the sun rise behind the mountains in which the city hid and leaned towards it inwardly soaking all the energy. I had a new sense of enthusiasm which flowed from the place. The clumsiness which clinged as gritty slime in the recesses of my mind simply vanished. I watched the rays of the sun penetrate through the leaves and eventually casting itself as a shadow on the ground. I felt good and thoroughly refreshed. "We walked back to the city, to our lodging where we both retired to our respective rooms for my morning obligations.. The bath was soothing and warm and I spent my time recollecting the endeavours of the night.

"We chatted as we were served the morning banquet. Many people joined in the hall where the old man interacted and introduced me to others. 'Do you know all these people here?' I asked enthusiastically since the old man seemed to know everyone. He wasn't shy while conversing with them. 'No. I hardly know any of them,' he replied.

'But you speak to them like you have known them for ages,' I said. It felt strange to show apparently immense cordialness towards people of slight acquaintance.

'I spoke to them as one would, or must speak when we meet for the first time. Wouldn't it be awkward if we introduce ourselves with a little hesitation for the first time? Wouldn't that uneasiness become our first impression? When you are amongst people whom you don't know, atleast be firm on who you are. Let them know what you are made of so your reputation will come across as a confident man. That is the best asset that you can flaunt to attract the right people,' said the old man.

'You are sounding rather pompous,' I said, 'as always.'

'Sneer as you like, my little fellow, but here all of them are distinguished in some form of skill. The unique quality of having a skill is that you are vulnerable to flaws even after having practised your craft and achieved great finesse. People would judge your final result and they will not care how many hours you toiled if your work shows even a minor flaw. This can overshadow ever your greatest work if you are looking for perfection– you and I know that. Look at them and tell me aren't they susceptible to such an error!'

"I looked around at the people. Some were tall, some short, some fair, handsome, ugly, fat, slim, hefty and so on. They were common people except their face showed enthusiasm about the things they talked. Their lips had a smile and their eyes had a sparkle. I hadn't seen so many seekers of arts in one place before. And most interesting part about them was they did not seem to be bothered about any sluggishness from their rudimentary stream of work – unlike me. The old man's sarcasm made sense – they were indeed confident. It was gathering; one of a kind.

"Pride blossomed in the old man's eyes and his broad grin spoke about a taunt which was to mean 'how silly of me.' I would have kicked his pompous behind if it was some other place. He took pleasure in agitating me. But I decided not to spoil the moment by arguing with him. I was at a new place – a new experience awaited me so I pushed the annoying grinning picture of the old man behind in my mind.

"I overheard someone say, 'There is a brilliant drama at the end of the road.'A stout man in ample silk clothes spoke jauntily to another person. His voice was loud enough to make a few people turn around to look at him. It turned out that he had been to this place, not far from here, and had witnessed a drama enacted by a brilliant group of artists that he was tempted to visit again. He divulged the location of the place with a big arch at the entrance and a beautiful garden of water lilies at the end of the road that passed in front of our lodge.

'The music is enthralling. It almost moved me to tears,' he said. His voice lowered and the group around him hushed and looked at him. There was some empathy in their looks for a silly fat man who had become emotional over a musical; it seemed unnecessary; artificial, I thought.

"The previous night was quite delightful. I had enjoyed a show of music by elite singers but I did not get emotional about it. I reserved a mild sense of disgust for people who exaggerated a subject. Such people find pleasure in starting a conversation, for the sake of gossip and eventually end up with nonsensical portrayal of the topic. The sudden emotional change in the fat man's demeanour simply took the enthusiasm away from me. 'You should pay a visit to this musical and see the drama,' said the old man.

"*Shut up you old twit. I will do what I want. Don't patronise me,*" screamed my inners to the old man in inaudible words. Here I am looking forwards to learn and explore the place by myself, but he wants me to visit some musical drama and waste my time. But I did not make my thoughts audible. I did not need an argument now. 'Okay. Sure,' I said without much expression.

♦ ♦ ♦

"The girl ran to the god and cried till his feet were wet," the *shilpi* narrated. "The bluish gray body sat immobile unaware of the wail from the distressed dame. My heart lurched with the pain. 'How could he ignore such a cry? Is there no mercy?' I felt anger. Are gods such merciless beings! I wondered.

"The stage was opulently set. Brilliant lights illuminated the area where this commotion unfolded by expert artists and their delivery of experienced portrayal of the story. It was the story of *Rathi* – the consort of god of love. The bluish dark figure was *Shiva* – one of the trinity. He looked so real! Perfectly formed eyes and the ink in which the artist had covered himself was realistically natural. There was nothing much for the artist to do except sit in the same pose throughout. And he did it perfectly. He was indeed *Shiva* – who was to tell otherwise!

"*Shiva* sat on the fabled tiger skin on the mount while it snowed around him and one of his legs folded and his other foot rested on a skull above the ground. It was a sight of power. Calm, serene and immersed in meditation he sat unaware of the cold, the surroundings, his own body and most prominently the wails of a desperate and seemingly ravaged woman.

"As for the wails, that was interrupted by a soft sad music that flowed to the audience from the sides of the hall, held the arena of action in stunned attention. The story revealed the demure lass on the stage with torn clothes and teary eyes as the one who experienced the loss of her husband. It was frighteningly sad and poignant. Her smooth skin furrowed away on her forehead and her eyes so wet from the tears she had shed appealing the inconsiderate godhood that sat in front of her but so far away from her prayers. Her blouse was torn and showed fair skin; such a graceful and full bloomed body and her ochre coloured drape which had turned almost a shade of oxblood from the dust, sweat and tears was an unbearable scene. It was rare to see such beauty that radiated purity. Her beautiful lips appealed to the god to bring back her husband he had burned in his anger. I nearly expired at the endearment; the loyalty of the woman and the pain she reflected on her face for her beloved.

"I looked at the god again. He sat there motionless, his third eye so delicately closed as innocent like a child's, while she kissed his foot over the skull.

"The curtains fell.

"It was heart wrenching and soul-churning. And to be carried away by the act, that it almost hurt my inners. Though I knew the rest of the story I wanted to know how it ended. *Parvati* wants to bear a child to save the world and restore balance. But her husband stays in deep meditation when the world is in chaos and requires his attention. So *Kaamdeva* decided to play around *Shiva*, trying to incite seductive thoughts for *Parvati*. But futile effort provokes the love god to shoot one of his mystical arrows that triggers senses for carnal pleasure. He thus successfully breaks the penance of the meditating godhead. Enraged *Shiva* opens his third eye and burns *Kaamdeva*. When *Rathi* hears about the cruel execution of her husband, she faints and later pleads *Shiva* to bring back her husband. Her beauty and purity made it so undeserving for her to live such a fate. I was suddenly sensitive – I observed. I was not the same person that I was in the morning while having the conversation with the people at my boarding. That fat man was correct.

"I am a sculptor. I tried to decipher why I chose to stay when all I was experiencing empathy for the pain depicted by act. I had the choice to get up and walk away but I wanted to stay. It was much more of an outright discovery – the central character was the lady who fought for her husband's life. It was her innocence in her act that made me stay even though I knew the remaining story. Both the actors were brilliantly talented. Otherwise how could a person simply sit portraying a god and just be anything believable other than that! And the lady so fragile and broken managed to take the entire tale on her own. It is like the statue that people worship in sanctum sanctorum even though there are other prominent figures that commanded the same amount of respect. She was the protagonist of the story.

It takes hours and hours of beaten effort on one's craft to portray such an act so flawlessly. Somewhere in my heart I developed a deep respect for the woman – like the one we have for a fellow workman who is a master of his skill.

"The night ended with the scene pending to be continued the next day. Refreshments were served and people interacted with each other. I, too, leaned here and there eavesdropping on the conversations but not mingling fully with any of them. I still had not taken the words of the old man seriously.

"Earlier that day, I had stepped out to explore the city alone and soon found myself wandering the streets aimlessly observing the architecture and beauty of the place. I decided to skip the old man's company; it would be peaceful if I did not have him dictate the route. The streets were well constructed and stretched out into miles – roads merging into intersections at various places. Buildings rose from either side of the roads and each one were crafted with lavish style and taste. I passed in front of many houses that had ponds filled with water lilies. Others had gardens but with beautiful beds of flowers and trees with fruits. Green grass lay like a carpet on which the birds and pets played. Rabbits and squirrels ambled away; some of the houses had peacocks and doves. Almost all the places accommodated visitors giving them space to stay as long as they wanted. That seemed to be the trend in this new place.

"I tried to explore as much as possible and capture what the city had to offer to all those who came. There was not much in my mind to start with so I obviously chose to explore from the point of my vocation. I went from place to place seeing all the sights of architecture; marvellous statues – ranging from gigantic to small in form and delicately carved arches finished to perfection. They all were of pure white stone resembling polished ivory. Unlike the statues I built, these were tastefully decorative with highest form of finishing. It was almost tempting to touch the statues and feel the milky soft radiance of these ivory figures.

"Then I thought to visit the temples in the place. I did not find any – which seemed particularly odd for such a flourishing place. I tried to ask around, but almost all the people I encountered were new to the place like me and they had not the slightest clue about any temples in the region. I tried to ask a few locals who smiled warmly with negation to the knowledge of any temples.

"Among the other oddities of the city that I observed, one that struck me the most was that all the people that lived here were rich. I saw no poor people – none on the streets nor any shabby or modest dwellings. There were hardly any people out on the streets too – another odd thing about this place. The sun was warm and inviting but still hardly anyone stepped out from their houses. The market which I had seen the earlier night bubbling with activity was almost closed. Few remained open that provided food grains, vegetables and milk. The roads held an eerie silence in the middle of the day. Usually such silence fell with the approaching dusk in villages. As much as this place fascinated me about its beauty, the oddities intrigued many questions about the existence of such abnormal, or the fact, unusual way of living.

"In the afternoon, I arrived at the doorstep of beautiful building. Two guards stood in the shade at the entrance. I enquired the whereabouts of a temple as a start to a conversation and then slowly asked them about some public places that served lunch for travellers. They smiled warmly and held the door for me inviting me inside. They said it was their master's pleasure to have a guest for lunch and it would be an honour to them if I obliged. I felt strange at the warm affection and generosity showered on me. I was keen to meet the person of the house who generously held an open door to the on goers.

"I went inside and soon found myself at a hall similar to that of my lodge, filled with people eating food to their heart content. Delicious aromas rose from the far end of the room and my stomach growled with the hunger. A young man approached and led me to the aisle where food was in plenty. He was one of the attendants to the place and offered me a place to sit.

"Soon a big dry leaf thatched together with small thin wood pieces was laid down in front of me. Then a round of attendants with different food items came in serving portions of several delicacies. Chapattis smeared with ample amount of butter, vegetables cooked in spices and condiments, flavoured saffron rice filled with dried grapes, nuts and cashews, sweets and a countless number of items and pickles were laid beautifully on my leaf plate. I was offered water and cold buttermilk in tumblers to drink. After lunch, sweets and betel nuts were passed around. It was a sumptuous meal fit for royals. The host had lavishly entertained the people without any doubt. One of my fellow diners said that in this city food was always served to guests. Surprised by this I enquired whether he too was a guest or an inmate of any kind to the place. He answered with a smirk that he was traveller and was visiting this place on recommendation from one of his friends.

"Indeed this was a strange place. I had visited places in my life where I had to struggle for food and even water but this place offered food without any restraint for free. A smile broke on my face as I wondered as to what would happen if the poor and haggard of the world were to find this place. With the passing of that thought I relished my lunch without any further obstructing idea and enjoyed it thoroughly.

"After lunch, the attendants announced that there was a place adjacent to the hall which people who choose to rest can use. Most of the people moved towards there while a few went strolling inside the building. I, too, chose to go around the place and have a look.

"There were three floors, brightly lit by the sun flooding the space. The place was filled with elegant paintings and statues, all rich in taste and finely crafted. Colourful potteries filled with flowers were placed at many areas along the floor. Curious and anxious onlookers drifted from one piece of work to other exchanging words of admiration for the crafts. It was simply pleasurable for me to walk and admire the paintings. The painter has used a lot of bright colours and the texture seemed so pleasingly surreal. I wished I could paint like this one day. Each and every painting reflected the spark in an artist although the subject was simply flowers or a house on canvas; it still managed to tell something about the artist.

"A small flash of memory passed about my initial days as a sculptor. It was this enthusiasm that haddied in my heart and I was here to rekindle it. I had to let my inhibitions go – like the old man had said about restraining my thinking. The idea lay in feeling of the art rather than the logic in it. That was the only explanation I had to my current predicament. Anything that stimulated my passion was more than welcome. I decided not to hold myself back on calculated thoughts; the principle was to feel and create.

"I spent the remaining time observing all the artifacts in the room. It was the statue of a woman leaning with her back arched. The features of her body was covered by a filament of cloth built in stone, as though her navel and breasts shown through it gave the wavy sheet of stone the feel of a fabric that covered her nude body underneath. Her fingers held the ends of the clothing. Suddenly, I was startled by a person standing beside me who asked with interest and curiosity, 'Do you like it?'

'Indeed. It looks splendid, stable at the same time delicate. The finishing is flawless,' I said. I restrained myself from divulging that I myself was a sculptor. I did not want to give any scope of discussion into the topic with a stranger; I was here to spend my time and enjoy in peace.

'It is one of my creations,' he said casually smiling broadly. I was surprised, nonetheless. He was a young man, younger than me and the statue he had created was flawless. Such workmanship cannot be acquired easily. Either he had worked very hard in his childhood or he was just joking. Nevertheless, I decided to congratulate him before which he promptly interrupted, 'You are *shilpi* too.'

"This young man didn't cease to impress me. His broad grin had disappeared and a smirk had surfaced that he was trying hard to conceal. 'How did you know?' I asked.

'It is very obvious. You spent a lot of time on each statue observing it. Most of the people are concerned about the way it looks but you are interested in how it is built,' he replied. I smiled at myself. Only a sculptor can recognise another fellow worker – no language was required for that.

'You have done an exceedingly flawless job for your…' I suddenly stopped in midst of my congratulation realising my mistake.

'… for my age?' he quipped, chuckling. I was thoroughly embarrassed and was at a loss of words to countermand my retort. After all these years working as a *shilpi* at a hierarchy higher than others I had become judgmental of people and their work.

'Don't be shy. It is all right. I get that a lot and I am used to it. People find it hard to believe that I am a sculptor and much harder to receive their approval when I show them my work. They cannot seem to fathom that I am capable of creating statues with finesse. They feel I have to be an old man to produce brilliance,' said the young fellow. I decided to keep quiet, partially due to the shortage of an appositive opening and partially because of the annoying embarrassment.

'Well I am glad you liked my work,' he said finally giving me an appropriate chance to compliment him for his work, this time with measured words of respect from my part.

"He was humble in his bearing and seemed matured by experience than age. We exchanged pleasantries and after a proper introduction about our former selves, I became a little relaxed to have a company as cheerful as this fellow. This young gentleman was remarkable and excited in me a profound interest and curiosity. I learnt that his father, now long deceased, was a potter and he used carve toys out of wood in his leisure. That was an inspiration for him to learn sculpting and become the man he is today. He was a well renowned artist, in his own respect, like me. Additional to sculpting, he was also a painter and an architect. I too gave him an account of myself as a sculptor and the works I had done. I had finally found a friend.

"We chatted along the hallways and enthusiastically conversed on many things about our professions. He was thorough about the art and the canons it followed but he was more of a casual fellow who allowed passion to dictate the entirety of his work. He explained he used to sway away from the conventional system of measurements just to experiment and see the result. Fortunately, his experiments bore fruit as he created some outstanding figures that people seemed to like and made him a rich man.

'All my works are incomplete. Or so I feel,' he said.

'I do not understand.'

'Well if I was to work on any of the statues you had seen here, it still has a lot of scope to be developed further,' he replied.

"To me all his pieces were refined figures of labour. And the most distinguished part of his work was that, unlike with mine, the finishing of the statues was impeccably smooth – nearly lifelike. In my field I was just supposed to create a figure, but the beauty of the statue did not matter. All that mattered was grace and the context in which the statue was to be designed – like Lord Shiva standing in his eternal dance form of Nataraja or Goddess Kali with her tongue out depicting anger. The statues of gods and goddesses I had created only required the conventional way of chipping and finishing, which ultimately had a coarse texture as opposed to the milky smooth texture of the statues I had just finished viewing. There was nothing more to add to these figures and yet my new acquaintance said he found his work incomplete..

"I did not comment on his view but managed to acknowledge his remark with thoughtful attention. He later explained what he thought could possibly increase the aesthetic value of the sculptures he worked on. Then the topic drifted to painting. I expressed an interest in learning the art. He simply nodded and led me into a room on which hung canvases of huge paintings that he had created. He said he had donated many of his paintings and statues to the place since the host did not accept any money. So he chose to express his gratitude by contributing to the welfare of the building.

"I enquired about the host and learnt that the master of the building was a trade merchant who had travelled the vast ocean to the ends of the world. He was on constant travel and was a lover of art. He built this building to serve the community of artists with the necessary resources from food to anything that we require. I mentally thanked the host and made a note to make a proper donation as and when I could.

"I again expressed my interest to learn painting. He said that I could join him at his place and start whenever I wished. I explained him that I had just been there a day and did not know the places well. He offered to help me out and enquired about my current residence. I gave the details and to my good fortune a few of his acquaintances resided there too. He said that I can accompany them in the evening to his place which apparently held a musical drama in the night. That was where he stayed – not far from my place of accommodation. And as fate would have destined, the drama about which I sneered in the morning as a waste of time, was what I was to spend my evening watching. I simply smiled to myself. I was too hard on myself and the people around; I decided to relax."After a short chat, I took my leave from my friend and headed back to my boarding. When I reached there I found that the old man had left the place homewards. However, he had left a scroll prior to his departure. It read:

Dear friend,

I am happy that you have taken it on yourself to know this new place first hand. By the time you return I will be headed homewards. It is safer to travel alone during the day than at night; hence I could not wait for your permission to leave. However I would like to retire to my work leaving you time and space to find and pursue some new interests that you are likely to find. I have ensured your accommodation here for as long as you like to stay.

Nevertheless, I would like to serve a few reminders about this place. Like I said yesterday – here there are no teachers, only students – so learn as much as you can. Anything and everything here is created from the fire of people's passion; that is the secret of their prosperity. However fire is wild and hard to tame and so is passion when mixed with indulgence. So, whatever you choose from a place so abundant will have a price; hence choose wisely.

And finally, here, there will be no obstruction to thoughts and freedom, so it is obvious that many of the parts that you hold close will eventually get dissolved. You will not be the same person to return. So make the most of the time and let it be the memories of a lifetime that you create here.

I understand your frame of mind and the moods that colour them. The stagnancy that has engulfed you, which seems unflinchingly elusive, is a temporary period. Only those who have passed through can understand that which in itself is difficult to explain. The quest is not to realise the quandary in enthusiasm that is lost but in the knowing the creative force within you. We already have something that is a result of some unknown factor. That existing 'something' is your answer. We are here to discover what causes it.

There is a dark side to creativity; when everything becomes a stimulus it becomes difficult to understand the difference between a creation and indulgence. The quality of genuine inspiration is that it is self creating and has a hairline difference between indulgence and genius. So as much there is a scope of rising high, there exists a scope of decline too. The secret would be to participate and yet be the audience in the participation.

I trust you are a man of genius and simple bearing. This city is filled with new avenues and with a mind like yours, you will surely find something interesting. May grace shine upon you and you find the fire of enthusiasm in your spirit's well to draw upon.

Your old friend

"The old man was indeed elusive in his words. I did not understand why he chose to speak the way he spoke, talk the way he talked or work the way he worked. He tried to be mysterious or he was genuinely mysterious – I did not know but it irritated me very much. He was kind hearted caring lunatic. And he had a way with words. He encouraged me to find my interest but cautioned me mildly of the way I travelled on or what it held in a poetic manner. Though his image has undergone a change from the first time I met him – from a revered learned sculptor to an indulgent self-centered old man who tried hard to project a mysterious air, the care he had for me was not tarnished. And now he is away over the distance and I missed him.

"Later that evening, I arrived at the place with the huge arch at the entrance and found my new acquaintance from the afternoon waiting for me. He had arrived a bit early and was enjoying a stroll along the pond. We met and exchanged jovial banter and moved inside. And for the city the same hustle and bustle regained its frenzy like I had seen the previous night… and then the drama began."

♦ ♦ ♦

"Next day, I rose when the sun had come up and already filled the room with its radiance. I felt well rested. In the room that I occupied, there lay my friend from the previous day, in another bed. The drama had finished late in the night so I stayed at his place that housed the theatre.

"After the routine morning obligations, I and my friend simply stepped out to the hall where a banquet was placed. We helped ourselves and he chatted away on the topic of painting. I was mentally taking note of all the things required for painting. After our breakfast, we strolled in the garden for a while and eventually my friend took me to his chambers. It was a parlour and had an open view of the garden from the balcony. One of his rooms was clean with a bed and household items, but the adjoining room was filled with different types of pastes, colours and canvases. Unfinished, textured paintings lay around and the room was filled with various scents of oil, paste and powders. It ranged from an occasional pungent to sweet whiff s of fumes at various corners of the room.

"He took out a new fresh canvas and fitted it on the walls with some fasteners. The he sprinkled water on the canvas. He let it soak and in the mean time searched for his sets of brushes. He came back with a tray filled with various colourful pastes squeezed at regular spacing and a vessel filled with water. Then mixing ample sky blue and a tinge of green with his feathery brush he touched it to the wet canvas. The water helped the paint to spread like a flame and the original bluish green now became a splatter of turquoise of varying intensity in colour. He did the same movements at two more different places and then took a cloth and soaked the excess water before the paint could reach the entire canvas.

"Then he waited the water to dry. He squat down on his haunches and placed the tray in front of him. Taking ample amount of blue again, he turned to a container and poured viscous oil on to the tray and combined them in the right proportion. He pressed the flat end of a wood to mix the mixture into a batter and at the same time performed a crushing motion. He stopped till the mixture was viscous and gooey. He then added some for oil to make it a dripping oily paste.

"I just waited and watched the motions of the painter without much understanding. He was too busy to be interrupted with questions. And I could not fathom what my friend was trying to create on the canvas. All appeared to be random and undisciplined movements; but my friend had a calm exterior. Only he knew what he was doing.

"He searched for a tube made of wood which taped in diameter from one end to another. He asked me to hold the tube with the wider opening facing towards me. He filled the gooey mass of blue from the opening till the tube filled itself to the brim with the colour. After that, he gently tapped the sides and soon air bubbles surfaced to escape. He then took the canvas down and laid it on the floor and placed the conical tip of the tube on the turquoise spread. Then placing a finger at the wider opening, with gentle but firm motion he dragged the tip on the canvas making a small visible line by abrasion. Then he lifted the tube and repeated the motion again for a couple of times till the line of abrasion showed clearly. Now he placed the tip of the tube again, this time lifting his pressed finger from the opening slowly and dragged it along the scraped line on canvas. To my delight, the paint that was within the tube slowly snaked out on to the canvas. When he reached the end of the trail, the painter pressed his finger on the opening again and the flow of paint stopped. He lifted it and again made the same line – this time a little thicker at one end and tapering to the other end. Although it was a pleasure watching the steps unfolding before me I still couldn't make out the picture. A splatter of turquoise colour with varying intensity and thick paste of deep blue line in its centre was all that appeared to me.

"My friend stood up looking at me with glee and waited for my response. He then laughed childishly on my coyness understanding my failure to decipher the painting. He simply took the canvas and hung it in front of me. As if some veil of magic lifted – lo and behold the picture made perfect sense. My mechanism of vision must have slept keeping my eyes open without registering any information while it was painted in front of me. I felt retarded.

"The painting in front me was simply a tree.

"The blue paste that tapered towards the centre of the canvas was the apex of the trunk while thick end was that of its trunk above ground. And the splatter of turquoise appeared to take the formation of leaves of tree that appeared surreal from a distance with varying texture of colour. Simply beautiful on a white background. 'But why turquoise?' I asked.

"Dejected by my query he asked, 'Why not?' 'But aren't trees green?' I asked. I couldn't contain the curiosity that there existed trees that had deep blue trunks and turquoise leaves with apparently invisible branches.

"He looked more with a gloom and staring at the floor suddenly started laughing. I felt seemingly flushed at this gesture unable to figure the comic in my question. 'I painted a tree and you are concerned with the colour of it.'

"I felt nothing wrong in the obviousness of inquiry. Trees are green – aren't they? I haven't seen a surreal tree like the one before me. 'When I was painting it, did you have any clue that I was painting a tree?' he asked. 'No,' I answered.

'So finally when I paint it and you understand it, you are concerned about its attribute! How quickly you forget the mystery that held you throughout as to what I was painting! My friend, this process is a journey towards discovery - not logic. It is about knowing what we can do rather than what already is.'

"I was confused. What was 'what already is' and what could we do about what already was? Isn't 'what is already', what already is? How could we change to something what can be that what already was? I stood there amused partly in confusion and partly with a conflict of thoughts. My friend was kind enough to explain.

"He said, 'When many things appear simultaneously to our mind we tend to grasp it from the perception we already have. That is how we derive a conclusion about a subject. But our mind is a gate keeper – it only allows one thing at a time so what we experience is in succession. It only sends one particular sensation to process, at a time to understand and hence it deludes the whole picture. And such process made it impossible to distinguish the difference because of the obvious working nature of the mind. Such a mind becomes finite because once he experiences a sensation he is partially satisfied and therefore the rest of the sensations from an experience fail to make a striking mark on one's psyche. The first sensations of any experiences are well received and remembered. That becomes a reference for further experiences of similar nature.

"So if I give you a sweet made of milk, sugar and saffron to taste and you find more sugar in yours while I find the taste of saffron overwhelming in mine then our experiences are different for the same thing. My knowledge will be conformed by the sensation that I experience which will become the part of my nature. So when you see a painting next time, you will investigate it on the same lines as now without understanding the whole picture. Isn't it possible that in the whole wide world that there would be a tree which would appear as 'bluish' and 'turquoise'ish maybe with the changing seasons or maybe with the changing light around?'

"I understood his explanation. It was not an argument about logic but of imagination. If I keep myself limited with expectations of logical outcomes I will not enjoy the scenario. 'And that my friend is what you have to let go – inquiry, reason and rationale. It will give you more possibilities. You will find yourself travelling in an unparalleled universe of experience devoid of logic. That is the beauty of abstractness,' he said.

"Although I did not understand fully the words of my friend then, the days that followed were a revelation and direct experience of its meaning. Unlike my previous vocation that relied on specific rules and distinctive canons on the subject, this new endeavour was not limited to any principles. Imagination was the sole source and anything that provided inspiration was simply entertained. The fate of a creation could not be decided before hand; it was to be allowed to evolve without letting logic dictate the end of a character. This was one of the most prominent aspects; the result was always different from the point we started. It was a journey through evolution. And for that, everything which seemed realistic and logical by its obvious infantine imbecility was to be challenged.

"I learnt my way with colours. It was different from the black stone when broken seemed gray. Colours had a way of lighting up my heart and brimming it with happiness and my days rose from the inexorable shadows of stagnancy. I painted many things – mountains, clouds, cliffs, a storm, landscapes or at times simply a single flower. I painted in the open, at night under a dark night sky filled with stars that studded on the roof of the universe. By giving freedom to the mind, I mastered the aesthetic skills and my days were filled with fruition form the labour which in turn reinforced my determination for newer challenges. The lack of method especially made my work seem more unique…more original. Somehow the thick viscous paint that dissolved with other colours on the canvas made it very contenting; the rise of a mild euphoria at the ending of every session. And the only common thing this pursuit held with respect to my other talents was that it made my solitude enjoyable.

"One day I spoke about my so-called discovery of bliss to my friend. He simply said, 'The mind is always amused to do something that makes it happy. We develop an attachment towards the work we cherish, but when it becomes rudimentary it becomes difficult to divert the mind, which, from its obvious naivety has fallen into the habit of seeking mirth and it shall persist in doing so, till it is given something superior to be amused.'

'So, how does one prevent this process from becoming rudimentary?' I asked.

'Do not develop any expectations from your work. Know that failure is inevitable – we will fail sometime. And the most important – do not plan for a specific outcome.'

'But how can we not plan an outcome? Isn't it the result that we are actually pursuing the reason for setting out on the task in the first place?'

'Imagine a forest fire. What happens when a fire breaks out in a forest?' he asked.

'The trees get burnt. Animals will die. If there are people residing within, they are in harm's way,' I answered wondering what this had to do with my question.

'Well, now observe this scenario. When we are given a situation, we determine its fate based on a logic and common sense. And when everything goes according to our calculations we feel happy because of the sense of control we exert. But in a random chaotic situation like a forest fire where our control is limited we find solace in the most logical outcome based on probability. See, probability makes us incorporate space for unexpected events. This reduces the stress on our minds and relaxes it which indirectly helps our effectiveness. On the contrary, a tightly controlled mind will never find itself flexible to accommodate new ideas. So though we have a goal it is always beneficial to be lenient in our expectations,' he said. Though it made sense, I found hard to relate to it. I just let it go – I would understand it when it came to me.

"Days went by and I progressed in my newly acquired vocation. I did not push myself to master the art; I simply let myself do what I felt in my heart. I realised that mastery of any work is a false impression – more like a fantasy; there always was something that can be added or improved. There would be no end."

♦ ♦ ♦

"One day, taking a stroll as usual, soft music fell on my ears. Delicately spaced sounds turned my attention to a palatial building, from which the tune emanated. My feet automatically followed the sound and soon found myself at the edge of a grove inside the building compound. Someone was pulling on strings and the music that I heard had a happy melancholy in it.

"I moved forward and there at a distance sat the figure of a woman facing the garden, with her back towards me. She sat resting her head and a part of her back on the trunk of a tree while the rest of her body was stretched on the ground. Her hand held a lute, the strings of which she plucked so delicately. The sounds, as if knowing her temper, made a very soft yet audible resonance. Her hair swayed away in the wind and the ends of which waved up and down along with her long cloth that fell from her neck.

"I moved forward. Light green cloth covered her body and her small, bare, and silvery feet showed beneath them –

the soles of which were delicate pink. At intervals in tune with the music she played, her feet tapped each other so lightly that no one in the world would know except for her and the ones who saw it. I felt a force within me – such a pull unknown that extinguished my reason to be there; so I stood there expecting her to notice me.

"But after a while when I realised that she was too immersed in her own world I moved beside her and sat on the ground opposite to her. Her face, the beauty of woman, pleasing and tender, scarlet flushed cheeks and her eyes stayed closed as she played the lute. Her face radiated an intrinsic lustre which I felt deep in my soul; some unknown feeble tremor of a pleasant kind, the explanation to which I was unable to find. I sat there mesmerised by the beauty, unable to take away my eyes from her face. Her soft lips twitched lightly, playfully, as her finger plucked the cords. Her brows and forehead furrowed at the escalation of tune and somehow the tune she played seemed to say something about her. It was painfully sweet – flowing from the covenant of still placid agony that I surprisingly felt familiar with but unable to explain. I felt the tune explored the silent regret of a past that one had undergone. Only a person who is so close to the meaning of sorrow could decorate it in such delicate form and yet endure it. On her forehead lay soft black hair with light curls like the springs of young hyacinth often seen in the garden covered with dew. The radiant deep black tresses of hers melted unnoticeably in the halo of her own aura and the surrounding light seemingly mild, remaining pallor in essence, lifted her rich countenance as the most explained detail in a drawing.

"Her face was bowed, and if her eyes would not have been shut would have gazed away into the blanket of green grass on which we sat. A tear made its way from one eye and slowly moved to the bridge and eventually to the end of her nose. The light around penetrated the drop and made it shine like a gem at the apex.

"I looked at the rest of her body. She was fair and rich as milk and the smoothness from her skin was shiny. She had full breasts and the ends of her blouse around her arms – the hues of soft pale mint green and rich white skin – so distinct and yet so intimately blended. Her neck so straight and slender while her body curled around the lute that ended with her legs stretching out from her clothes which I had seen earlier. I looked at her feet, this time, noticing her toes and the beautifully formed nails on it. This made me wonder how the nails of her hands must be. There wasn't enough of her that I could see and take in at once in that moment. She was effervescent just in her presence. And the notes she plucked spoke of some past blissful memory that had become the anguish of today. Many memories resurfaced as the sound brought the recollections of my past. I had always loved beautiful things, but for the first time I felt that I, too, had a beautiful heart. I felt – I too deserved love; instead of loving which I always did, but to be loved at least once just to be know what it felt like to be taken care of, to be cherished. I never noticed that tears from my eyes had wet my face too. I closed my eyes.

"After a while, the music stopped, suddenly. I opened my eyes. The figure before me stared away into my eyes. Her eyes were perfect – like the petals of the lotus and the pupil was just round enough to stay within those eyelids without touching the sides. She had wiped away her tear, but her eyes stayed soft and almost liquid even long after the drop had dried away. I hastened, as realisation dawned, to wipe mine – but she had already seen it.

'Please do not stop,' I managed to say at last.

'Everything ends. So does this. Prolonging what we feel eventually leads the way to pain. Nothing can be extended forever,' she said.

'I wish to stay,' I said. 'You are welcome. Will you walk with me?' she asked.

"My conscious mind had expired for pleasant exchange of words or any formal introduction. And it did not seem to matter.

"It was not until she rose and stood in front of me till I saw the softness in her being. Her hair, black as the night, was long enough to fall behind her back and reach a little more beyond her hips. Her body curved and her clothes elegantly showed the features with sequins at various places which played along with the light. The light flowed through the fabric revealing the outline of her body from the inside. And beyond the layers of veils her navel shone through them lightly as a lovely depression of vacuum beneath – like a cloud which embraced the summit of a mountain.

"We walked a path that slowly rolled up and then reached a gentle plateau of soft green grass overlooking the ocean. Her body smelt of sandalwood even from the distance. And her hair smelt of jasmine. We never looked at each other but I knew that our mind's eye had a watch on every single, delicate moment we made – even the trinket tied around her arm which rattled to produce the softest of sounds. It was a pleasure to be minute on each and every moment that I spent with her that day.

"We saw the sun moving into the deep water mass of green and the evening spoke of many things that I would have left unseen if I had not been here. Finally I looked at her without swaying my gaze and waited for her to return the gesture. But seemingly aware she stood there watching at the globe slipping into the water as the dusk approached. And I felt sad because she did not turn and look at me. . I could see the light almost penetrate through her body filling it with translucence that remained vague to describe but always create a never ceasing desire to recall in my lonesome time.

"As the last portion of the sinking star had dropped, she turned to me and smiled, 'I have to leave.'

"Please do not. Please stay... my eyes spoke but my lips remained immobile. 'Strangers are not allowed here until they know what they want,' she said.

'And what do I want?' I asked.

'How can I know?' Her callous retort seemed so painfully cruel. I did not want this to end; simply to move on to a plane where this moment would give its way for another where she would not be there. There was a storm in me that I knew nothing of till I met her and my silence concealed it now. I was so close to her gaze but I felt eons away from her affection. I longed and yearned for her but I did not know why. I did not want to touch her, I did not want to talk to her, I did not want to walk with her and I did not want to know that this moment will expire. My mind spanned out to tell her, pray to her that I would be in agony if she left. And now she was about to turn away from a dumb-struck man.

"But I could not let her go. Struggling out of my limpidness, I tried to speak of something but my lips hardy moved. She did not even show a vestige of passion; hardly anything nearing what I felt. She turned her back and walked away. I looked at her feet, so petite and nimble, as it sunk mildly into the grass moving away.

'I want to learn the lute you were playing,' I finally said.

"Half curious with a mischievous hidden mystery she looked at me. Her eyes held the twinkle from some faraway light. 'That is what you really want?'

'Yes. I wish to play the lute, learn it, from you.'

'There are many teachers here who will teach you, but you want to learn it from me! Why?'

'Because I haven't heard them play as you do. And that is why I would not want to learn it from anyone else.' Atleast that part of my answer made sense – atleast to me. I had seen her beauty – so delicate and fragile but there was some mysterious intrinsic quality to her character and that alone was the cause for her to play what she had. It was something that spoke of her and I wanted to know what it was. My request though made in urgency was sensible in meaning, as it dawned later and the relief from knowing that I did not have to come up with any alibis was immensely comforting."

◆ ◆ ◆

"I felt I had been pierced. She lay in my arms, resting against my body as the petals in an unblossomed bud; drops of sweat gliding away from my body, mingling with hers and flowing across her body as her own. We sat near the balcony; I felt her naked back across my chest as the cold wind blow and cooled our body prompting my skin to contract. Soon I felt her body following the same. A satisfaction arose in the depth of my soul to know that we still communicated. I embraced her, bringing my hands on to her breasts and covering them. We could feel the slight shudders from the tremor of our hearts on each other's body. We both had our eyes closed.

"Within the darkness that my eyelids gave as a sanctuary from the real world I felt universes collide, destroy and rise. The nothingness that swallowed and produced the brilliant experiences out in the vastness of space was felt within me. I felt her skin, warm and the layers of flesh underneath still held the reverberations from the apogee of carnal excitement that we achieved moments ago. She lay there waiting for my fingers to explore. I smelt jasmine from her tresses.

"She opened her eyes and turned around to see me. With deep and reverent awe, she was the genius of romance in blessing with the mouth and chin of a goddess; I could feel her gaze even with my eyes closed. She turned and knelt down to sit on her knees and raising her lips slowly to my eyelids kissed them gently. The texture of her lips was much lighter than the skin on my oculus.

"I opened my eyes and looked at her. She was the same person when I met her first. The same light shown through her – a light that itself knew why it shown out. The lovely curly locks behind her ears and the smooth line of her jaw just stayed there as a sheath on it. Her eyes had the depth to dissolve all that I knew and yet I wish to know where its depth lay. I felt drawn and loved and suddenly that changed into a feral rage and I pulled her at to me and kissed her. I felt her that she had a part that belonged to me… so angry and so lively. I wished to possess her and feel her light as my own.

"She did not resist and this only infuriated me further. I knew the sudden change in mood that my anger had brought but she did not react to it. I wish she would have asked me why I was so rough with her all of a sudden. I wish she would have questioned my possessiveness. Her lack of participation, her meek submissiveness for a moment I made me feel worthless.'So you do want it all, don't you?'

"She kept silent. I did not know whether she understood. But I did not stop. I looked at her and my heart melted at her gaze. 'I came to you, spellbound and you did not say a word to me.' She knew I was talking about the evening we met, the tune she played, the lute, the sunset and the walk we had. It had been almost a month after that day we were here, in her chamber at her residence. I went on, 'I stood there gazing at you; you could understand my yearning but still you acted mute. I wanted to hold you then as I hold you now, to let you know the terrible vacuum that I feel when you are not around me. That day you did not show even the slightest of affection or any sentiment and today you lay docile for me here, ready, even to be ravaged.'

"Her gaze did not waver – the same softness shown and her radiance grew even more. She still held my hand and the touch didn't even twitch involuntarily. Nothing moved her – I felt her hand warm but her heart cold. I felt powerless and the innards of my beings just crumbled inwards with a force enough to drive my sanity into nothingness.

"She lowered her unreadable gaze.

"After a long silence, she spoke. 'I saw you first when I opened my eyes, that evening while I played. You sat there with tears in your eyes and that made me feel sad. I wanted to know why you wept; but I did not know you. So staying in my place I tried my best to reach to you…'

'You could have told me that,' I shouted unable to contain my anger after hearing her explain. I felt why it was so obvious to gauge every movement of her passion and why didn't she feel the same need to let her feelings known. I felt alone with her.

'I asked to stay, didn't I?' she asked.

"*So?* my eyes asked the question but I did not say it out.

"Sensing my contempt, she slowly said, 'When you said you wanted to stay, I wanted you to stay too. I felt the hesitation in you, but also your desire to be with me. So I asked you to walk with me. I gave you the opportunity to say your part while I waited for mine in return. I waited for you ask for me, which you eventually did, so I kept my silence. My silence also held the same desire that you held. I am woman and for her, her silence means a lot of things.'

"I was dumbstruck by her remark. Undeniably, she in her own way had had helped me. Remembering the evening, I had felt a little hesitance in her walk and realised that she too wanted to look back – but could not. It struck me right there – she, too, did not know what to say. Here, this moment, she unerringly felt the same thing that I felt.

"I regretted my explosive behaviour. I felt my being cool and look her tenderly. Indeed, she was delicate and as a woman she had done part. I regretted concluding her as callous. I realised another thing. We cannot stay angry on beautiful things – especially those we love and when they are heartless, we find it hard to hurt them. We are afraid of the harm that we may cause because we love them and we are ready to do anything for them even if we are damned for eternity. Somehow we are crippled by beauty.

"I took her face in both my hands and gently leaned forward and kissed her lips. While doing so my fingers gently trailed off to the nape of her neck feeling the protrusion of her spine. Even the hard formed bone seemed so delicate on her. Her breath was irregular and soon found the heaves on her neck against my fingers. My thumb gently touched the small depression below her throat, and gently gliding my hand down felt her erect bosoms, so eager to be felt. She gasped for air as her lips parted from mine feeling my touch. She arched back and I could see her slender neck rise. I too rose on my knees and held her back. She was in ecstasy; she leaned all her weight coaxing me to lay her down.

"I looked at her. She lay there; her fair skin was nearing crimson from the blood coursing within. And her pores had risen from the erotic feelings that I had stimulated. I etched her body into my memory to draw later. Her wholesome breasts stayed round and full and hard while her abdomen rose and fell around the depression of her navel as she struggled convulsing. Vulnerable, with closed eyes, she lay there trusting me. I had the power to love her or to destroy her. I had the choice but she still stayed.

"I bent forward to kiss her navel which for a moment held still as she paused during her breath to feel my lips. I moved down even further driving her limpid making the air in her lungs escape. She held her moans and closed her eyes tightly while her fingers curled around my hair. I rose up and embraced her and took her in the gentlest form. However gentle the impalement was, she still crunched around me and let out a feeble sigh. I was surrounded by the feel of the gleaming rivers and the warm current beneath. The emerald and violet fire burned in the corner of our room casting its luminance on to the gleaming curtains made from rich liquid looking cloth. I wondered if light ever held a shadow in them as the sight of those curtains seemed to change into cataracts of molten gold flowing from the cornices. Is the light the shadow of fire?

"Such spaced and irrelevant thoughts gathered in my mind and I felt the warmth in our bodies reaching a pinnacle, about to explore into the universe. I saw her face lighting like a cosmic torch with brilliant colours of unperceivable brilliance erupting into the core of my being as I heard her ecstatic shrieks in my ear and we both surrendered to the wild flames of passion. There we lay limp, satisfied, spent and content waiting for air to find our lungs and fill it with its momentum.

"After a while when the sweat cooled us again she got up and walked away towards her lute. I lay there still with all the passion of my body spent but my mind longing for more. I saw her ample calves wavering with her flesh underneath as she walked. The wind blew and she felt her naked body stop to take in the breeze. She curled around her lute and, feeling the frets, said, 'The peacock waits for the rain because nothing else can give the mirth that the rain has. The jubilation that it feels to know from the falling drops makes it spread its tail and dance. So is the first note in music inspired by the cry of the peacock. It is called *Shadja*. It is the first note that gives birth to the next six notes which is the key to learning music.' I lay there listening to her. 'Then comes first of her infant sounds. She wishes that her child be strong and so she listens to the sounds in the universe and is mesmerized by the lowing of the bull. Like a strong mother produces a strong child, *Shadja* gives birth to *Rishabha* – inspired from the strong animal.'

"I loved her metaphorical axiom that she used to explain the steps of music. She was my teacher and apart from the pleasure she had taught me a body could derive, she now spoke about the birth of sounds. 'Then she desires that the next child be of gentle nature. So her mind travels in the universe and finally she finds the bleating of a doeling while its feeds from her mother's udder. In that inspiration she gives birth to Gaandhaara – the gentle sound.

'A heron takes her flight and the flap of her wings with the mild wind creates the soothing sound of moderation. A reminder to her to find the moderation between the Strong and the Gentle. So she looks at Rishabha and Gaandhaara and then looks at the heron giving birth to Madhyama – the moderate one.

'Now her heart content and happy she feels the need for something that creates happiness and she hears the cuckoo and then she gives birth to *Panchama* – the fifth note in order.

'After contentment and happiness, she now looks for adventure, speed and agility. She finds the mare running across the green fields – without the worry of tomorrow. The flesh beneath her gleaming skin flowed like water with every stride. A mixture of erotic ecstasy and a frame of classic health, *Shadja* gave birth to Dhaivata.

'Finally she decides the world should know the expanse of itself and inspired by it she finds the elephant and how she nursed her child after her birth. Even the mighty elephant showed humility. So stating that polarities exist in this world in equal portion, reminded of the female nursing mother elephant, Shadja produces Nishaada. That is how all the world knows the sound of music.'

"She gave the account of a paradoxical mother as the sound who brought forth the next six sounds comprising the seven notes of music as we now know it. I was thrilled by the story and more of its surrealism. I was happy to meet her and thanked fortune for the evening that I met her."

Vanaprastham

Asya was spell-struck by the narration so far. She had not the slightest idea that a man could leave his former self and become so despicable. It was hardly believable that the man who remained in front of her so humble in his appearance could have a past as a whore-monger. Veils fell before her eyes by his narration and she felt that story had changed and went on to join a tangent to another persona. It could not be him…at least not the person she saw now. And that is the only reason why after such an explicit descript she still wanted to know how his life went ahead.

Asya felt rage but she decided to keep it down. The *shilpi* narrated:

"The old man, my mentor, did not tell me that the city was a harem – a harem hidden in the lap of mountains facing a sea. Though he did warn me not to judge him since his methods were unconventional, he felt it safe not to provide this information to me. The stagnancy that I had before I came to the city from rudimentary work as a *shilpi* would have not allowed me to take a further step to visit the place if he would have told me about this particular detail.

"The world is a very big place and the things we know that exist in the world are mostly by hearsay. And we are happy to have those rumours stay the way it is as long as it does not affect us. So the conception we have regarding anything, which we do not have real knowledge about or experience with, generally borders innuendo. And that same applies to a harem too.

"The place was a cultural centre of rejects that had been discarded by society. So they built a place away from the world and in the beginning only few knew about it. And since it was a faraway place hidden to the world the righteous did not feel the need to destroy it. Over time it sprung and flourished from contributions from people who had their inclination towards lustful indulgences."

"But how where they misfits?" Asya asked. It seemed odd to her that people who can flourish even after being rejected or thrown away from the society were highly endowed.

The *shilpi* to explain Asya how a brothel formed a part of the society in the simplest manner possible, "In the olden days, the society used to be divided by *Varna* – division of the society for its efficient functioning. Although *varna* system never intended to provide a deliberate distinction in society, its main function was to maintain a very smooth flow of different activities for the development of the human populace. However when the society or the existence of man was challenged by consequences of a sudden event, like natural calamities, wars or new philosophical or spiritual discovery, the society underwent an obvious change in trends and mindset. Past and the existing area of work and thoughts are analysed on the newly found knowledge. This is the natural course of evolution. *Varna*, too, was one such invention. It was simple common sense that working together with the same qualities led to the faster accomplishment of a task at hand. When man found that every persona had a particular trait to him that had an impact on others, they tried to group similar people of same quality under one roof of society. So, the four sects in the society came into existence irrespective of their birth. Earlier every person was allowed to choose the *varna* he or she naturally excelled at. Their goal was to be efficient. The highly learned intellectuals that formed the part of society were called *brahmins*, the protectors of the society became the *khastriyas* and the people skilled in trade became the *vaishyas*. And the crude lot of the society formed the *shudras*.

"But as time passed, the essence of this system was lost in debate over issues of morality. Every system is founded on moral principles and a scheme is derived to work on that foundation. This is how a successful and prosperous society progresses. Every action would be laced with principles that are morally sound, ensuring the welfare of the people. So no action in the society will be prompted by irregular or unrightful thinking. This would be then worthy of calling an ideal society.

"However every working system has a defect and it is only strong as its weakest sections. And it is always from the weakest part the ruptures originate. In this case, society's rejects that formed the *shudras* were the neglected sect. It mostly formed the immoral and corrupt portions of society, or so it was generally believed. But any man's mind can become corrupted.

"A menacing warrior on the battlefield when at time exposed to docile living conditions, for instance, can find it difficult to maintain a calm demeanour all through his life. He can also commit heinous atrocities when prompted but his once reputation of a great warrior would overshadow his misdeeds. It would be appealed to see his actions as a part of his personality rather than a crime. If the same was committed by a *shudra* it would be deemed punishable. But the *khastriya* would not allow himself to be branded as *shudra*. Why would he? Moreover, the 'tribe' he belonged to would consider as an insult to their sect and a threat to their reputation and pride. So eventually, one's particular sect would likely support a corrupt person just because he belonged to their caste. However the elevation in the status of a *shudra* due to his moral conduct may be appreciated, he would go unvalued due to his past. But this never applied to a *khastriya* or *vaishya* or a *brahmin*. They demanded their life to be viewed with respect to their past contributions. *Shudras*, in effect automatically became the minority. The same aspect that was favourable for the majority had an adverse result of the minority. Such a prospect threatened the 'equality' of the people within the society.

"But the society had run on this scheme for hundreds of years. It would have been unwise to overthrow the system in entirety because the smaller portion of the society came to be neglected unintentionally. However, a solution was to be drawn to this problem regardless. A society should be able to differentiate between good and bad, moral and corrupt. That alone would lead to the development of the smooth functioning of the society. So elimination of a complete sect of the society was not possible, neither was it possible to elevate their status yet maintain a distinction in class.

"But when man deliberated and pondered on this, he was obstructed to reach a fair conclusion because the entire system was influenced by the nature of man. He would always be partial to himself. After much deliberation, it was slowly adapted by the society that the ultimate decision can only be made by one entity – The Creator. He was impartial and all pervading so naturally the burden of this decision from such a source would be the rightful place. Hence, a new theory was added to the existing *varna*– it said that the fate of a man's cast was decided by the Omnipotent and therefore born to a particular sect in the human race. This secured the division of society in a prominent manner and the majority profited from it while the minority of *shudras* were reduced to shambles of poverty and ill-treatment. The divide widened the gap between people's hearts and eventually some either left their habitat or were banished. So it wouldn't come as a surprise if these people joined hands together and set up a dwelling together. Such place will not be intruded by the upper classes unless their lives were threatened or their morals challenged."

Though the *shilpi* knew his explanation had some historical inaccuracies, the current general structure of the society was very much parallel to his description. He always found it humorous, while living at the harem, that the upper class always provided all the necessary provisions to the place in terms of money and essentials when they found a place to indulge themselves, but never helped them when they were living within a society. Man always wanted to know the benefit he had; it was always about the advantage one would have in return for the price he pays for. So such a place would be hidden from their personal lives and yet they can fulfil their carnal urges still maintaining their reputation. However this justification would suffice Asya and would be simple for her to understand. Asya seemed content with the explanation too.

The *shilpi* continued:

"It was a very old city. And the harem was indeed started by a group of women who were abused as temple slaves. It slowly flourished into a city".

"How old was this place?" Asya asked.

"It is ancient in its lineage and had centuries to its account. Over time it prospered from a brothel to a sprawling city. As for me, I was reduced to a degenerate slowly. I had always been mesmerised by her except for a single factor about her demeanour that I always held in contempt. She gave all that she could to me but I felt there was a place in her heart that remained untouched by anyone in this world. That singular part that she alone could know, agitated me. All the calmness on her exterior seemed rehearsed and it made no effort to hide that she held something mysterious within her and above all disturbed me the most. It felt unfair lying next to her after giving myself entirely for the spirit lifting adoration, a small part of her remained untouched and unknown by me.

"After a year, the day soon dawned when I discovered the real nature of the place and the true identity of my lover. She was a courtesan – a harlot who shared company with men. And I was one among them with a minor difference. Others knew why they frequented this place but I did not know this place at all."

"How did find out about her real nature?" asked Asya. She was also getting curious.

The *shilpi* moved ahead with his story:

"There was a particular decorum to the place where she lived. There came many visitors but they were not allowed beyond a certain point while in the premises of the building. And every room in the building was a private chamber of a single courtesan. They would never involve or indulge with men belonging to another courtesan; only if men wanted the company of the other was an exception made. Usually men chose their women and stayed with them for long periods of time, and the women would provide pleasure and company in form of sex, liquor or simply by being with them.

"One fine evening, I strolled into their forbidden lair unknown and unwatched. I accidently had tip-toed into the bath area which was commonly used by the courtesans. I was astonished at the women bathing without any restraint of shame nor did they have any discomfort sharing the place naked with each other. I wasn't tempted to watch the scene because as much as this new state of affairs confused me I also wanted to know what was underway.

"I heard their interaction of gossip, mostly about the marks on their body from their lascivious escapades, while bathing each other complimenting their body. In the midst of their tittles, I waited for some familiar sound, if I could hear; just to make sure that this place and the events which unfolded was genuine before me and not hokum. It seemed I may have entered an unknown dimension where naked women had nothing to talk but about sex alone. None seemed familiar but it was real and I did not have the liberty to dismiss it as delusion.

"Suddenly I heard something familiar – the same soft voice that mumbled in my ears when she lay beside me.

'So, how is your man?' asked an unknown voice. Silence. Only the dripping of water and the sound of ripples. 'He is very honest and fragile,' she said.

"I had to make sure it was her. Through the soft translucent curtains, I peered towards them. There were soft coos amongst the female folk and all of them had stopped their activity and moved towards her. Resting themselves at a lower position in water everyone assembled around her to hear her speak. One of the maiden grabbed the sandal paste to apply to her arms. 'We heard he can paint and was a sculptor. But unlike others he is well built and strong. Tell us more about him.'

"She smiled and looked into the milky waters in the bath and said, 'He has rough hands. And I like them.' Everyone laughed. I felt my rough hands to confirm what she had observed.

'But is he like other men? You have had him for so long – over a year; are you going to leave him or not!' giggled one of them. The others tried to hush her. Looking at the events, the maidens had held her in reverence than themselves as one would give to an eminent person. 'I wish to stay with him and he too wishes the same. And somehow he doesn't know who I am.'

"She spoke and all the members froze as of it they had suddenly transformed into statues. They knew what she spoke and were stunned by some apparent revelation that still eluded me. 'Does the Lady know?'

'Yes.'

'You should tell him.'

"She lifted her gaze to the girl who suddenly pursed her lips after the suggestion as if she had spoken something vile. But I wanted to know the answer. 'I am not privileged to choose the life I desire, my sisters. We all have the same condition. Atleast, with him, I have the privilege of his company. It is only a matter of time before that is taken away from me.' Others gazed at her while the youngest of the maiden moved to comfort her.

"After a long pause, she said, 'I am aware that I am being unfair to him but no one would wait for a whore – I would be just a solicitor to him who bore him pleasures.'

"The flabbergasting uprising pressure in my abdomen and the speed of my lifeblood was too much to handle. A furious maelstrom rose from the depth of myself as the veils of her hidden mystery fell. Rancid contempt engulfed me. I stormed out of the building not confronting her, not needing any justification.

"I ran to the quarters of my friend, the painter, and asked him, 'Did you know that this place houses brothels?'

"He laughed hysterically looking away from his painting that he was working on.'Well someone here seems enlightened!'

'Pray tell me the humour in my question,' I said, trying to stay calm.

"Realising my seriousness, my friend quit his work and asked me about the state of my bearing.

'I want to know – did you know this place housed brothels?'

'Why are you speaking in such a surprised tone? Don't you know that this entire city is one? Why would you be treated with kindness and be offered everything for free?' asked my friend astonished. He could not fathom the delirium which I was experiencing.

'I did not know.' Tears sprout forth with no apparent reason, but mostly of guilt, because I did not feel pain but rage. Seething rage coursing through my veins, I smashed the pottery beside me. I felt defeated and violated. My friend, taken aback by this alien nature stood rooted to the ground in fear. He felt that I was experiencing some delusional trauma which may have captured my mind by some disease or spell. I sat down crying – silent tears with sobs in midst. 'I did not know... I... I... I did not...'

"He placed a shoulder on me and asked, 'You did not know what this place was?' He knew me well and well enough to know that I would not play such a jest on him. And he had never seen me in such misery before. 'What happened, my friend?'

"I gave him the account of my meeting with a beautiful woman who played music on her lute and the days I had spent with her learning music and the nights in her arms. I explained the departure from my home prior to the arrival at this place and the advice of the old man. However he did not reveal the true nature of this place. In my mind I resolved to hunt him down and take his life in the most gruesome manner for keeping this from me. 'So why are you upset?' the painter asked.

'I have lived a life of modesty and all the passion I have pursued in my life had been of art. I married young, but god took my beloved away from me. Since then I haven't had the women even for any jovial company.. I never had indulged myself in music or intoxication or anything that my morals didn't agree with. But now, I have desecrated all that I was made of in all its essence. And I could not believe I was so naïve to examine where I have arrived.' Curses fumed within my mind. I felt that I sullied my soul with vile thinking it as love. There would be no river to bathe and wash away all my sins that I had accumulated. I felt the haven of my heart sprayed with colours of lust. I felt the rise of hatred in me. I was, in actual now, two beings – a sinner and a loather for my former self. There remained no force to wipe my soul clean of the guilt that sprung in me. I cursed myself for overlooking the sanctity of my decisions. I fell in love and in return received guilt. Everything felt orchestrated to victimize me.

"Sleep eluded me for days and I collapsed from exhaustion. I never returned to the spiteful place that took my sanity and chastity of soul; I prayed for forgiveness from god and asked him fervently to redeem me. I coaxed and cajoled him with sadness and tears to take my work as a sculptor into account as a service to him and not to deny his grace over me. But I felt that he did not listen to me. I deteriorated in health and the decline cost me my body and I slowly resembled a sack of skin over my skeleton. My reflection reminded me of the old man when I first met him, but a younger imitation. I did not return home because I did not want to face the traitor and liar that I had once regarded as a friend. I was alone again in the world but now I realised the difference – I had lost my will to live. Morbid immobility indicative of a deceased mind made me spend my days at places away from the city – many a times on the cliffs of the mountains which surrounded the city.

"I started consuming liquor to ease myself into sleep. I branded myself as a whore monger and a sinner. I roamed the wilderness during the day and returned the night to the city where alcohol was ample and so were psychedelic inhalants that practically made me feel good about being a reprobate.

"But during all those periods of induced ecstatic flights I still explored why I committed such sin. I did not know what I could do to redeem myself of the guilt – to be spared of the pain that came just from being me and loving. Instead in those hallucinating escapades I heard the same music she played, the thoughts of her limerance and scent of her hair and once again I would be transported to the point where I began my journey on that forsaken place."

"I do not understand," Asya interrupted waking the sculptor from his self absorbed narrative.

"Hallucinogens are powerful agents that make you forget reality and connect you to your subconscious. They practically render you body immobile and transport you to an alternate reality that are mostly your dominant yet hidden thoughts. It is one of the most powerful and surrealistic experiences that one can have."

Asya looked puzzled. The *shilpi* decided to give an account of his own experience to serve an explanation to her.

"When I smoked the hallucinogen for the first time, I felt ecstatic waves of orgasmic delight washing across my body. I felt like a small speck travelling in tunnels of light of varying colours of different intensities. I heard music that relaxed my heart and I heard the humming of beings with bright bodies around me. The speed at which I traveled in those thoughts made me feel real enough to produce supernatural effects, atleast in my mind. I stood in front of a stone and felt myself as a stone and I wished to know my past as the stone. I saw myself lying in the ocean little crumbs of me settling to the bottom, then on me fell carcass of a fish and then again small particles of me falling on it covering it. I lay there for centuries and the ocean with its mighty weight crushed me. I felt the particles coagulate and my being as small particles disappear and my body taking form in bigger pieces. I felt the carcass of the fish press against my body becoming one with me. Later I felt the crushing weight of the water slowly releasing from my breast and soon strong sun shined on my now large body. I finally became a stone and the ocean dried away in the sun. I felt the eons in me and I felt stronger."

The *shilpi* narrated to Asya other experiences of flying in spaces inside his body and visiting alternate universes with beings of light and the time he spent listening to them. Others where he had geometric patterns that mingled with each other in rotations transforming in to one infinite movement that stopped with the passage of his consciousness. He also said that the drugs gave the power to know what lay hidden as thoughts in us but did not give the strength to fortify us in normal periods of time; otherwise these experiences so potent, almost spiritual, would have lifted mankind out of misery a long time ago. The only flaw – it was an influential powerful clout with little understanding.

"After rotting for many months under the influence, while roaming the city grounds at night I returned again to the harem. In one of the windows above sat a lady with a serene smile and a halo around her. I, in my haze, stumbled into the building and soon reached for the stairs. I ran with all my might to that figure.

"This was a lady ripened in age and by the look on her face had matured in experience. But not letting the facade that she put take away the fury of my words, I screamed curses on her. Her serenity remained unmoved and gaze fixed on me. Well built guards ran to capture me before I could reach near her and rendered me immobile with blows on my abdomen. They stopped as the lady signalled them to move and gestured one of the maidens.

"I was helped up by men on to a stool and the maiden served me with some refreshment. When I did not receive the hospitality she calmly placed the pate on the nearby table and disappeared behind the doors. The lady still gazed at me with unnerving quietude. I was suddenly afraid and began to weep. All the effects of intoxication seemed to fade away as my consciousness regained its connection with reality. Still with a haze in my eyes, I looked at her and passed on to the floor.

"I woke up on a bed later and it was in the middle of the night. The room seemed familiar as memory gave away its positive consent that I had been there before. It was the same room in which I had spent the nights with her. I looked around and did not find anyone familiar. Tears welled in my eyes. It might be a while when, suddenly, I felt a warm hand on my shoulder. The warmth was familiar but the touch was alien. I turned around to see the woman I had howled profanities earlier in the evening. She enquired about my well being and then sat beside me. There was sympathy in her eyes.

'Who are you?' I asked.

'This place belongs to me and the people here are my family,' she said.

'So all the women…' my words trailed off.

'Yes, and as you would like to call it as a brothel, this is their residence. Many men frequent here as and when they like and we provide pleasure to them. That is our work in this place.'

'Are you not ashamed?'

'For being a whore?' There was defiance in her eyes, something so bold and colossal that I still remember it. Not a shred of shame or guilt crosses her eyes. I felt so eroded in front of that gaze that I bowed in shame.

'If I would have known that this place was a brothel I would have not come.'

'Yes, I know. And that is exactly why we allowed you to enter that evening when you saw her. You looked like a man so humble in mind, untarnished and chaste. But we have seen the most innocent and pure people change here into the most despicable and vile beings because they always held in their heart the desire to taste the forbidden. Though you looked true in form and radiance shown in you that reflected your soul in your eyes, we did not know what you wanted. We welcomed you like any other guest we have here and felt that you wanted to be served by us. We are whores and after all who are we to judge you?' she added sarcastically.

'Do you enjoy provoking me?' I asked keeping my face in my hands.

'We don't do anything that our lovers don't want, dear. And you certainly wanted what we had to offer – by the looks of it. We do not sell wares here but share our bodies and so if someone walks into our dwelling then we have the right to assume that they are our guest not a naïve intruder.'

'Do you feel happy to paint our lives with your vileness? Does it give you happiness to see a man fall into sin?'

'Sin!' she thundered. 'You think we are content with the life we live and the atrocities that the world inflicts on us including taking away our choice to live the life we want? You, sir, have spoken from your selfish impune self. *Sin*, as you say, is for the people of your kind who take the liberty to assume that we are the consorts born for the destruction of your soul.'

"I did not understand I did not want to get into an argument in such a state of mind. But she did not seem to let it end; I had enraged her beyond her control and she wanted to vent all her fury at me. Suddenly, strong arms grabbed me from both my sides and dragged me out of the room. The guards tried to hold me stable on my feet but I felt weak. The lady signalled them to follow her. We walked on floor with an open balcony overlooking the activities of the harem – singing, dancing and men and women indulging in enjoyment with each other in the open. I looked at every woman in the arena below and all seemed to enjoy the company of men without any regret, shame or dislike. And men too seemed satisfied with their partners. I felt something amiss in the scene.

'Now you see it?' the Lady asked me as if she was waiting for the opportune moment. I felt the grips around me loosen and helping me to stand up. Then they left. I was weak but I wanted to stay so I leaned myself over the railing of the balcony. I looked down again examining the women. All their display of affection was genuine, unlike someone who would serve for the price they pay. They stayed around as their loyalty lay to the men they entertained. It seemed bizarre and impossible for such reflection of fondness and warmth. After all they were human beings and somewhere the fundamental nature of women would show through all the rehearsed practice of their trade. But all of them equally showed surrender to what they felt – they were free from any guilt.

'How is it possible?' I asked.

'If you were to love everyone, there would be no discrimination. There is no need to claim love that is insecure. It would be a sexless state,' she said.

'It is impossible,' I said.

'Impossibility is only a case when there are other options. And we don't have a choice. So under the circumstance of a forced life as a prostitute, it would be wise to learn something that is beneficial to us.' I remembered the contempt I held for the woman I loved, the invisible veil thorough which I could not reach to that guarded corner of her mind that she had held away from me. It was this quality that had made me uncomfortable.

'But I knew she always tried. to hide her true identity from me. I always knew there was some mystery to her and now I know what it is. You forced her to do something that was against her will. Would you justify yourself atleast for that action; that you led her into doing something that she wasn't willing to?'

'Sire, before you find yourself launching into a rage finding reasons to accuse us or maybe particularly me, I would like to remind you that you were resting in her chamber when you were unconscious. Here we allot every person of this house a room so that she can remain with the man that are in mutual consent with each other and they are not allowed to change that space with other woman. If, by some reason, the woman leaves this 'house' of hers, her chamber is left vacant for a year in a hope that she would return; in her memory and nobody is allowed to stay or use it. She left this place the day you stopped coming. A woman knows well what her man thinks. You know, she was the weakest.'

'Weakest! How dare you insult her? This is how you honour her memory?' I spoke in rage

'There is no denying that she is the weakest, because she fell in love with you. But to love ourselves first is the primary lesson that we teach here. Do you think that a person who doesn't love oneself is capable of loving anyone else? She knew that you would not respect her, because you expected her to be a common woman and that terrified her. Yet she chose to love you, remain with you till time allowed. She knew you would break away from her. She is weak because she could not make up her mind while you were here, only to reach a fatal decision after your departure,' the Lady said.

"I was taken aback by her sarcastic retort," said the *shilpi*, looking at Asya. Asya found the Lady's reply witty too.

The *shilpi* continued, "I asked her what she taught the women who sought refuge there. She said, 'We teach them what is necessary. Everything about love and its forms,' said the Lady.

'I wish to know,' I replied.

'We teach the women, who serve the likes of men who frequent here, about principle and morals; that anything principally moral carried to its fullest meaning is extreme. We teach them that all morals are conditional and one cannot exist without another; that both have a common root. And everything has a price to itself that has to be rendered before one could have it,' she said.

'How absurd!' I said, 'You teach this to the women here and damage them. This is untrue, unethical and corrupt.' The Lady of the Harem smiled at me – a smile that I could never forget. That smile had a gesture of defiance and the power of a seasoned individual who had seen life and time's impact on it. It depleted me of the moral strength that I had. I knew there was something that held her stand more resolutely than mine. Nothing could take her power away.

"She said, 'Every woman and girl in this harem spend their nights with a man that she has hardly known and every morning she rises up with the same energy knowing that the following night would be the same as her previous one. Even though the world says that we bring lust to incorrupt people, do you think that a woman will be able to remain the same person every day? After all the impalement to our souls, which itself is a design of society, do you think it is possible for every living being in this world to do that – even with their rudimentary ethical lives! What we do here is an ability nearing to supernatural. Such conduct is not possible without true surrender – and by true surrender I mean acceptance. The person you loved abided to this condition till she met you.'

'Your confidence is born of ignorance, and whores and charlatans in this world are just a product of this ignorance,' I said in my anger.

'Have you met them all – these whores and charlatans you speak of?' the Lady mocked me laughingly.

'You are the destroyer of humanity in the souls of these women you give refuge to and also to those men who come here seeking what you have to offer. Though misled they are, you do the best of your monstrous nature to shove them into the river of plight and guilt for the rest of their lives. You just secure each and every one to a destiny that assures the abolition of their souls,' I blurted.

"I kept my silence after that. All my mind heart and soul reeked of putrid contempt. Though I accused them for their hideous nature and the pride they held, I still felt unrest in my heart. And that unrest originated from the belief they held – that too confidently. There was not a single fragment of doubt in what they had chosen to believe. I have never felt such intense disgust knowing that my words could not even make a scratch to the rationales they believed.

"The Lady sighed and sat opposite to me looking at me for a while. Then she said something that formed the beginning of my reform. And I still remember it till today and it will last to the end of my days. That night was the most important night of my entire life and nothing could ever have an impact as powerful as that. 'Sire, I pray, to listen to me with all the patience you have. What I am about to say is not a justification about myself or the people whom I represent. Neither it is a voice of my ego against which you revolted, nor for the pride we hold. Nothing could tarnish them. This is simply for you, because I see you heartbroken and dejected – guilty.

'You are a sculptor; haven't you noticed that the entire system of your work depends on representing the masculine and the feminine sides of the universe? Why is it impossible to explain creation without the female half? Hasn't it occurred to your observation that all gods have a feminine half to their male counterparts as a consort? And their romance depicted in the scriptures, wouldn't that be erotic? Just because the style of narration chosen by the scribe is politically correct does it mean that the gods would consummate their bond in any other manner than the humans would do? Then why are we ashamed of the actions with respect to the erotic sentiment deemed as unworthy? Why is their lust meaningful and not ours? What motive and purpose does their lust harbour which ours does not?'

"I was not sure where this conversation was leading to but I had nothing to say; I waited till it made sense so that I can make a point of my own. I stayed patient. The Lady sensed this and explained, 'Without understanding the dualities of nature there is no existence for man; his understanding is based on these dualities. The masculine part or Purasha cannot explain itself remaining stagnant and so when it changes into something meaningful it can only explain itself by changing its form – this is creation. Feminine energy or Shakti is creation in its momentum; without it noting is created in this universe.

'But unfortunately, men so naively, in their arrogance of self importance, think that it is the duty of a woman to inspire an erection. Women are meant to be illogical and irrational because they are the part of this creative energy. And creation of new dimension with this energy over an existing one would be seen as destructive by the people attached to the system. Therefore when they try to love something attached to the system, they find it entangled to many elements of the world, thus love becoming a suffering. They fail to understand without destruction there could be no creation. It cannot be dictated only guide – after all it is energy, it will flow like water wherever there is a grove.' The Lady paused. 'Women here come on their own sound understanding and we do not persuade them to be a part of the community we belong. We allow them to stay and give them time to arrive at their own opinion. Most of them are rejected by society for many reasons. It could be their birth into a low–trodden family, exploitations or just poverty. They are aware of the path they are about to tread and they usually do it for the comfort they experience here; but most importantly they stay for security – their lives not threatened here. Imagine an exploited woman in a "decent" society – her kin and the people around will torment her and she has to live a life of cruel punishments and harsh abuse. And she will be reduced to poverty and no matter wherever she tries to run she will soon be caught by her reputation. All her life will be of agony, torment and abuse till her last day. Is there any dignity in such a death?

'In the treatise that Manu, the father of humanity, wrote, he placed importance onthe role of men and placed the order of women beneath them. In all agreement and with due respect to the great scholar who laid the foundation of a new era, he too knew that over the period of time this law would be archaic. But since the masculine populace was the centre of action for the development of society, women were subdued to a passive role. Slavery and abuse of women in the name of service, god and for the decorum of society became prevalent. After their use they were defamed and thrown away to end their days. The progeny of such women became the courtesans in an age and when powerful people invested their interest in this area of amusement and it became organised prostitution.

'But you do not explain the principles that you teach. It is hearsay and blasphemous,' I said.

'Nothing is taught here. This is not a school for the discarded population of the society. We see principles as it is. Every action based on principle is not self sustaining. It is bound to create ripples that would begin to bring a counter-measure to the same idea. When you arrived here did you find any unique traits about this city?' she asked.

'Yes, there are no poor people, food and accommodation is freely provided and the people who visit are free to donate anything but the hosts do not accept money. So any contribution made is seemly from the people here becomes a part of the development of the place. That much I understand. But I do not understand the motive or logic behind it,' I said.

'In affluent societies there exist poor and rich, a divide that is a result of either birth or action. It is an age-old divide and all means known have been tried to remedy it. Have you ever observed that though giving alms is a righteous deed, it also promotes poverty? The beggar receives insufficient alms, enough for a day's meal but inadequate for saving. And when he accumulates enough money for a future, he would have got comfortable with the easier means of begging. The more one receives, the less one seems to have. And it would be ridiculous to think that over the ages, the only people who preached this idea of sharing without expectations were renounciates. And how easy was it for us to defend ourselves with the maxim that one who does not know value of material things will obviously preach about renouncing it.

'Here nothing is abiding, no one feels the need to beg because the meager necessities are fulfilled without being asked for – and the minor difference here is that the person is provided with food and shelter instead of money. When the basic essentials are satisfied the mind does not have to worry about existence, hence he has sufficient amount of time to create a future for him or at least entertain the idea of a future. This indirectly encourages him to move out of poverty. There is no revolution with an empty stomach. Therefore, when the people contribute no one here has to beg for food or accommodation. They only have to ask,' she said.

'But you are encouraging people to enjoy lust and ruin themselves. Isn't that a ripple you create by your actions?' I said.

"She replied, 'None of them come here against their will and we have a duty towards them. Our service is of an unspoken kind which very few people realise. The people are mostly savants – the conjurers of creativity for the urban and flourishing kingdoms, but here they are men; men with vulnerabilities. All that is forbidden out there in the world is enacted here. They visit here to redeem themselves; they come here to act their vulnerabilities without destroying the ego. We let them act their vulnerabilities, inflict on us all the pain they have in their lives and when they leave, that part of them which they dislike changes into something that they can cherish. Here we do not make them feel ashamed for their short comings. And the quality about all vices is the incentive that it provides. So when a man returns, he is without the grip of vices as a forbidden element in his thoughts. He will never feel the cage of seething resentment about any code of conduct and his soul too will be released from the agony of lust. He is a liberated person and that is our goal – to liberate them from the clutches of their own prejudices.

'Lust would be a memory that would have faded away in the midst of his actions here. For that, we have to surrender willingly to their whims. Our gesture releases them from their own conclusions about the act being heinous or unacceptable; making it normal. It is not our intention to help every man who wilfully builds around him a cage from which we should rescue. Our purpose is not deluded by this. The thrill only lasts till it is forbidden. Lust is not cruel; it is misled which finds contentment in acceptance. And a man devoid of a misled emotion will never view women with the same perception. He himself transforms to an elevated position in the recesses of his mind where he has no voluntary control. We help him lose his inhibitions. But he alone cannot do it – the woman who loves him should be open hearted to his ways. Thus their union finds completeness,' the Lady said.

'But these are addictions – how will they possibly take one away from its pursuit?' I asked.

'All the addictions that we acquire are harmful but addiction to body is the least of it, if one chooses to call it an addiction. On account of intoxications, the body becomes a slave to it. But true lust would not harm the body nor impair the mind. It will liberate the soul from the clutches of guilt when one harbours acceptance to one's true nature. Lust happens to be misled because the part that seems coarse about oneself or one's body is reflected in other's persona. So anything not in concurrence with the idea makes the mind feel it beyond reach. The vehement struggle to attain this unreachable object of attraction is lust. That is how the attraction between polarities happens to exist – beauty and ugly, gentle and rough, acceptance and rejection,' the Lady concluded.

'I accept your validation; however man would not pursue lust with an agenda. For him lust is merely an area of exploration and enjoyment, and then this message would slip right through his fingers,' I quoted realising the apparent dilemma.

"The Lady smiled and said, 'Sooner or later, men and women always have an opportunity to realise this. Here the grammar of matrimony is experience – noun and verb; one cannot ignore it. And it is not solely applicable to the masculine gender, but women too have a role in liberating her dearly loved. It happens only with an open heart. The longevity of a consensual relation does not depend upon sacrifice that one is ready to make, but on the contrary depends on the value that they are mutually not ready to sacrifice. Those are the binds that connects the union together.'

"The Lady indeed put the fumes of my ire to rest with her explanations essentially liberating me from the realms of guilt that I would be trapped in. All my actions which I regarded sin also held some meaning to it. And the Lady had helped me draw my sanity together tracing significance to the deeds done in my ignorance.

"All the pieces within my conscience had a glimmer of hope of revival. I had a new beginning. I was opened to a world of possibilities that showed me that opposites can co-exist; but I could not collect myself. I felt all power drained away and my core seemed empty. I did not know where to start. My conscience and body lay scarred by the sufferings of my negligence. I had exhausted my soul of the essential strength to thrive far less begin something. There was nothing to look for and the barrenness of mind, in first of its revelations, came across when desire was completely taken away from within. I realised why desire was so significant to man, how inspiration was the most overlooked element in life. Without nothing to pursue, the memory of your past becomes invading siphoning away the life force into oblivion.

"Dejectedly, I sat in gloom at the harem. I did not want to venture out and let the precincts of the place build a cave around me. Days passed with gloom and the thought of obscurity of a barren future handicapped me. It felt as a requiem.

The Mystique

"I was given consent to stay at the harem out of pity. Everyone except the Lady took sympathy on my state. They knew, somehow, that I was not among the lot that visited them seeking the daily pleasure of dawdling; there was no language required to understand sorrow. Everybody looked at me like a patient recovering from a life threatening disease. But the pities in their eyes bred self-contempt in my heart. I did not have even the ego to make a start. I sat mourning thinking about her, and the nights we shared. I hoped she would return. I missed her company.

"The Lady was the only person that attended me and took the necessary care of my affairs. Despite her age, she had the energy and the unparalleled grace of woman. Her walk was soft and brisk. Her persona radiated command and I was immensely impressed by the will this Lady carried. In my feeble moments, I longed for such a will; a will that she had; to last through the place such as this. It must be the endurance of her experience, I imagined, that gave such strength to this particular woman – the serenity as a result of acceptance at its nucleus – to accept all the ills and elegance of this world yet be unmoved by it.

"One day I asked her, 'How do you remain calm in a place like this? You are always engaged in activities and yet you lead your life with grace! I am intrigued. How do you maintain yourself in such a state? Didn't you ever have the temptation to indulge yourself, atleast once in your life?'

"The Lady smiled warmly at the remark. 'So you think I am one among them and still untouched?' she asked, half humorously and half sarcastically. I did not, now, know the tone of her voice clearly because of my earlier perception of her; I was not sure whether she was being kind or being mockingly cynical. For now I could dismiss it as a rhetorical question. I did not have the will to ponder. She smiled and said, 'Do you know the real history of this place?' I was in no mood to go on for a discussion, and simply shook my head. I just wanted to hear her. She continued, 'Would you believe it if I told you that this place was actually founded by a spiritual aspirant?'

"I was not ready for any more surprises. I was too engrossed in my own dilemma to be interested in some ancient myth. Mildly intrigued, I temporarily pondered but then made my own logical conclusion to this revelation. There are many failed pursuers who want to find god as an excuse rather than looking inside them. So, it may be obvious that after a failed practice to achieve his aim man might succumb to his lower nature. The decline of my life was the sole proof that anything of disastrous nature can happen to oneself. Whatever the case may be I decided to hear her without interrupting.

"The Lady gave me time to collect my thoughts and then proceeded, 'Five centuries ago, this place was a mountain terrain. And the depression where this city remains now, was a huge mountain; the biggest of all, compared to the surrounding. One day an earthquake of terrific magnitude struck this place and the sea roared to foam froth around the mountain. Together, the fury of wind and water broke the bonds of rock as the earth trembled making the entire crust of this projected land mass to sink beneath the ground. Water filled the crater and there lay the mountain buried beneath it.'

"I had to appreciate it; the nature of the narrative as I lay there listening to her, transporting myself into the world that her words painted. It held my interest inspite of the morbid reality I was in; it was a temporary escape.

"She said, 'During this storm, there came a huge ship with one of its mast broken amongst three, uncontrolled, swaying with the wind with no men to steer at its helm. The sails of the ship were torn and the canvas could not hold the spin of the ship which, unlike the numerous maelstroms and hurricanes it had faced, seemed inexperienced at this peculiar spot where the mountains had made a cruel and treacherous plot for wreckage. To witness the fury of nature, strips from man all that are pestilent in his nature and renders him emasculate. The crew, what was left after the majority being hurled into the sea, waited for their approaching inevitable demise. The few on deck looked up at one of its masts and saw a man naked in the wind, standing undaunted by the fury that nature hurled. They recognised him as the mad man who had been along with the crew throughout the journey. He had been in isolation all by himself, without causing any disturbances to anyone enroute, smoking grass and other powders. They only saw him occasionally and dismissed him as a creature of low stature because of his passive and somewhat perceivably queer nature. He would be seen on brief accounts rushing inside the deck without talking to anyone. But now they cursed the gods when they saw this passive man standing high on the mast, miraculously stable and firm grounded. In their last moments, they realised the futility in their courage compared to the man. They were, now, puny and he was mighty.

'The spinning ship wrecked itself against the rocks sending pieces into oblivion along with people. The mast on which the man stood was broken and he was flung, faraway on to the top the mountains. The wreckage did not show any visible signs of surviving life. A few days after the ship wrecked here, the man on the mast went to explore the surrounding ground. He ventured down to the place where the earthquake had altered the shoreline; the sea ended far away from the mountain terrain. Today the harbour is situated there. He surveyed the land and found some resources from the wreckage – some stores of supply drenched in the sea water but enough for him to last months,' she said.

'But where did the ship come from? And who was the naked man that stood fearless from the sea and storm?' I asked.

'Despite what people on the deck saw and assumed; he was not fearless. He was intoxicated at the time of the calamity. And that had rendered him passive to the invading fear of death. He, in a way welcomed it, but was not ready for a suicide. There were other ways to die compared to this but it is not every day that one has the opportunity have a calm exodus in such a threatening dire situation, so he decided to sing his own exequy; waiting for his end. Therefore, he hung on to the mast with ropes and waited for his turn to die. And the herbs he had inhaled gave him enough sense when the rapidity of the occurrences exceeded the expectation of a normal man. He was just a man drunk high on hallucinogens but that provided his body and senses, the extra ability to register the events that changed scene in a blur.'

'Drugs do not ease the senses, they distort them. And what you speak of is inconceivable given such circumstances,' I said sounding rather disappointed. I, myself, had experienced the effects.

'Maybe for you. But the legend says otherwise. And it can be proven. Many spiritual aspirants consume certain herbs that give them clarity about the states they enter, which are unlike the experiences of ecstasy that one gets from inhaling the smoke. The former has a record in memory while the latter doesn't. Inventorially, the former can be recollected consciously after the delirious state. And in such conditions, the senses get tweaked to handle all the unaccounted events at a very swift rate,' the Lady said.

'So this man was an addict?' I asked.

'I do not know how to classify him. What would you call a person who had mastered addiction? Or the stage where he has the power over the hunger that controls others! What would you call a person who consumes the hallucinogens and yet be away from the craving of it! Would you call him an addict?'

'I have never heard of a man with such remarkable control. I have seen people of surrender to the effects. But since this is a story I guess it is acceptable.' I condescended the moment I had a small gap to express sarcasm. To this day I do not know why I chose to speak in that manner when I knew she had done nothing to irritate me.

'Even in the realms of downfall, you still hold your pride of the past. All it took was a little unexpected provocation,' stated the Lady mocking me of my previous loathsome days. I was rendered speechless; the coarse words abraded my conscience. I was once again the man who had surrendered to lust and now I act like a sophist. The words burned me. But the taunt did not end there. She continued, 'So you think that unexplained, miraculous or events bordering the supernatural are all acceptable when they are put together in a myth?' I did not reply. 'You boast confidently about the knowledge you possess. So do you disregard the *Puranas* and *Vedas* and the stories just because you haven't experienced it?' asked the Lady. I maintained my silence. 'That is all right. So you are the learned man, aren't you? Then answer me this – Why was *Krishna* hurt by the arrow of *Barbarik*?' It sounded like a rhetorical question so I did not attempt to think about it. 'Answer me,' she ordered.

"It was a trick question. She would have me somewhere, where I would make a mistake about the story and then point out my folly and again subject me to ridicule. 'Because he had hidden the leaf marked by *Barbarik*'s arrow below his feet,' I said.

"The Lady laughed sarcastically. It was so demeaning that I actually recounted the entire story just to make sure I was correct. I questioned my knowledge, but I believed there was more to this story that I may have overlooked in the urgency to answer the question. 'Be kind enough to narrate the incident to me please,' the Lady said. I had no other means to end this debate but to relive the account from the *Mahabharata*.

"So I narrated to her the story of *Barbarik*, the grandson of *Bhima*. He had meditated for many years to acquire the supreme divine weapons of archery from *Shiva*. Pleased by his austerity, the god appeared to bestow the boon as he desired. This made him a powerful man – the greatest amongst all the archers in the world; even better than *Arjuna*. *Krishna* knew this and the oath that *Barbarik* had undertaken as a responsibility towards his boon. *Barbarik* had undertaken the oath to fight on the side of the weakest party in a war as a gesture to maintain justice and balance.

"But the battle of *Kurukshetra* would be the spoken for the ages to come. Moreover, *Barbarik* being the grandson of *Bhima*, it was his moral duty to fight in the war. But the greatest privilege was the glory that would be sung in all the three worlds about the warriors who would fight in this war which made it more abiding for any *khastriya* to fight. *Krishna* knew that the entire battle would be over in one day if *Barbarik* participated and justice would not prevail. So *Krishna*, in an attempt to dissuade *Barbarik*, met him on the eve of the war. He, first, encouraged *Barbarik's* decision to fight and conveys the blessings fit for a warrior. But then *Krishna* expressed the desire to witness the skills that he had acquired from *Shiva*. Enthusiastically, he displayed his proficiency in archery.

"This peculiar boon; the weapons that he had acquired from *Shiva* consisted of three arrows and a bow. The procedure was to release the first arrow which marked all the objects that *Barbarik* wanted to be destroyed. The second arrow was used to mark all the objects to be saved. And the third arrow was released to destroy all the objects marked by the first arrow. In order to test this, *Krishna* asked *Barbarik* to shoot all the leaves of a tree as a demonstration.

"Thus *Barbarik* sat briefly to meditate before he could execute the display of his talent. In the meantime, *Krishna* silently plucked a leaf and hid it under one of his feet without the knowledge of *Barbarik*. After rising from his mediation and recitals *Barbarik* engages all the three arrows according to the set instructions of its working. The first arrow marks all the leaves including the one under Krishna's feet. The second arrow marks things that are not to be destroyed. And the third arrow destroys all the leaves on the tree. But the leaf hidden under Krishna's feet was also marked. Hence the third arrow that had grown in number equal to the amount of leaves that were marked penetrated *Krishna's* foot under which it lay. Thus Krishna was hurt.

'Hmm...'sighed the Lady after I ended the narrative. I waited for her answer or rather the loophole in this recount. I knew there was none; I was curious about the real intention behind this story from the point of view of this aged sarcastic harlot. But to my astonishment she did not comment. I remembered the old man; he must have got the weird sense of maintaining one's person of mystery from this Lady, I was sure. Everyone here seemed to posses that quality – either borrowed or self invented.

"I broke the silence. I enquired her about the deception, if any, in the story since she was the one who had the query in the first place. 'This story has a loophole. You have missed one factor. Why was Krishna hurt by the arrow of *Barbarik*?' said the Lady.

"She was ridiculing me to the extent of my patience. She was asking the same question again which now seemed more annoying and beyond sarcasm enough to provoke anger. I shut my mouth and decided not to prod further. I did not want a story from *Mahabharata* dissected and neither did I want to know about any spiritual person who laid the foundation to this forsaken place. The interest in listening to a story was gone. The Lady chuckled. 'When a god is involved in a story, people just want to accept anything they hear. It works like a charm and it just removes the ability to enquire, if it means questioning a god.

My dear sir, according to me *Krishna* should not have been hurt by anything. And this is my point.'

'Are you challenging *Ved Vyas* himself? He would be very disappointed if some charlatan was pointing error in his tale. Or maybe *Ganesha* might have lost the pace in scribbling his dictation,' I tried to humour her with my mockery. I was agitated and was being provoked. But the Lady almost lost her demeanour of calm and tranquil and flung into a fit of loud hoarse laugh; manly in tone – astonishingly masculine like the guffaws of a man.

"After settling down from the uprising, she adjusted herself and brought herself down to her prior normal self. I was more amused by the changes that arrived and passed in the facade of this woman. 'In one era of the *Mahabharata,* there was a sage called *Durvasa* who once visited *Krishna* and *Rukmini* to test their patience and loyalty. *Durvasa* was known for his short-temperedness and hence every being treated him with reverence. As a part of the hospitality, *Rukmini* had made the food herself to be served to the sage with utmost devotion, but *Durvasa* ordered that they strip naked and apply the food on their body. Later he asks them for a ride in the chariot driven through their city they ruled in that state. *Krishna* and *Rukmini* follows suit without hesitation, and the sage is happy, and grants them a boon. He utters that the part of the body that had been smeared by food earlier will become impassable and infallible to any attack of any weapons. However to maintain respect the husband and wife duo did not smear the food on the soles of their feet. They had smeared it on the all over the body including the top of their feet. In such a scenario, the arrow from *Barbarik* must not penetrate *Krishna*'s foot from above.'

"I was stunned by this astute detail. I recollected every *Purana* and *Veda* I have read with respect to this detail but was not able to pin point any clear factor to this tale. Is there really a loophole? Can this detail be so callously represented, I wondered. The Lady waited for her well deserved moment of glory. She was not just an old person who was stuck here with some asinine pride. The signs of reasoning stood behind every word of her being, though at the moment I could not decipher it. She had intrigued my interest to a very high level. My ego started to show the first signs of liquidation as I was hit by this sudden throw of detail.

"She said, 'Everyone gets defensive when some dirt is hurled on a god we have believed, no matter we blame him for the misery they have given. But when he or she is asked to follow the path of gods, they simply cannot. Everyone wants to follow a God but no one wants to become a God,' said the Lady.

'Pray tell me, Lady, the true version of this story,' I requested.

'Well I have not been able to extract any true detail to this account by myself. When I showed my query to learned men they accused me of trying to pick a fight with the almighty. Some said the version was wrongly propagated while others said that *Krishna* hadn't applied the food on his feet at all and so forth. None of them had a clear idea but all were struck with the same bewilderment that your face shows now. And wouldn't it be confusing for them since many stories exist for the same god persona over the same account just because the scribe who wrote it believed in that entity more than any other deity. All the stories we hear or the legends that are passed down to us gets lost in translation bit by bit. Though the majority of the content remains the same, the small details are lost because the story revolves around the characters that are influential. And not to mention the effect of the role of a god who takes incarnation in human for the betterment of man. That statement itself is a spear head to pacify any doubts. The man who would speak afterwards is branded as an atheist. That is the unique trait of legends – they ingloriously have the power to silence reason and inquiry just because belief is overwhelmingly important.

This itself proves – 'to believe' is important: not 'what is to be believed' but to believe regardless. And in this quest, true accounts become positive paradoxes because the genuine implorer is stripped of his own thinking under the alleged reasoning of the believers.'

'Then why would these stories exist in the way they are now. Why, would not the truth be revealed! Why are the details left unattended?' I asked, baffled.

'Why would anyone want to hear a tale? Tell me. Is it just to pass time? Or is it because you feel good to listen to a story?' I kept my silence. Not all questions are to be answered.

'We love a tale because we have an opportunity to associate to the possibility of what can be done in a dire situation. The difference between what is and what could have been– the line of action that changed the entire story. It provokes us to think radically for a favourable and beneficial outcome in a situation. The relative tendency of the mind helps us to have the unique quality of association and it somehow provokes man to think. He begins to hope and find a way against despair. And that is where the idea of a story gets incestuous.'

'Incestuous?' I blurted.

'Why? Is that word so demeaning?' asked the Lady. I sealed my lips again. There could be reasoning to this that I was not sure of.

'Something growing out from an origin that degrades its genesis is incestuous. Very few people realise their folly in the pursuit of a story. Man does not know hope until he knows of despair. But somehow the story which propagates the triumph of good over bad or righteous over evil is unable to convey this message of balance. For the audience it is intended to be an inspiration but somehow man confuses it to the way of life – that life is a sphere of unrest and constant state of crisis. They do not get past the veil of commotion and they feel inspired because the story motivates the colossal dormant yet sentient qualities of man when displayed are often termed as sin.'

'He does not have the opportunity to realise that he is misled since no one can overlook a moral at the end of the story. He does not have the chance to be brave and noteworthy every day, but through these tales he realises he can be like one of the great characters. That makes him endure suffering but majority of the people suffers with the silent expectation for their arrival of their role to be significant. And when such a role arrives, if by any chance of events, he will be brave and wise like the characters in the story. But it will be seen too extreme to comprehend in the eyes of others who believe the same lessons but since the actions require surmounting difficulties or changing a situation or simply to fight brings out the feral nature in men. You know, to read about a *Krishna* or a *Rama* looks ideal but being one is threatening in the real sense. Gods are only feared when they walk amongst men; the respect they have is truly questionable. The action of the leaders of our past gives them an antiquity extravagant but in reality it will be opposed by the common man. So the moral of the story lies in the fact that the message will go unreceived nonetheless. God too needs to endure here if he chooses to live amongst humans; otherwise no one will be able to understand the divine. That is why the birth of god is forecasted as a prophecy. It has to live as a message for the people to endure,' said the Lady.

'And what could help him understand this? How will man understand that what needs to be done is to be done?' I asked.

'It is simple. We need to look at principles, ethics and morals as they are; not how they are preached. Every person must analyse what the principles had to offer for him irrespective of the lessons taught. On a very hypothetical note, he can have a start by analysing himself as the only living being on the planet and his adherence to these values then. Will he stick to the standards and morals then? That brings the first lesson – morals exist when a group of people live as a society. It is meant for harmony and does not serve as a dictation to his freedom. To a single man ethics and principles are irrelevant. Prodding further if he was the creator of such principles then what would he create? Will he create it for himself or will he create it for others too? And will he allow his principle, once created, to be changed when the need sets in. If each and every person assumes responsibility to the relevance of these principles to his own individual personal existence then alone harmony can be established. Then alone we can identify what is really necessary. Then there would not be any identification of man's action to sin,' commented the Lady.

"The idea was beautiful. Even whores can find solace and harmoniously co-exist with each and every individual in society. There would be justice along with equality. I saw the system of *Varna* as it were and as it was now and the change in the stream of events that led to its current existence. And that alone was the beginning of things if one was meant to change it. Suddenly I felt myself insignificant compared to the effort that I would have to put to bring even a slight mend in the system. I could not do anything for anyone unless he himself wanted it to happen. The Lady, in her place, was indeed correct. She stood where she had to stand. Otherwise one would be a burden on their own self. And for the first time, the neo society of the land where these harlots resided made sense. It was better than the societies that existed outside this place because there was regard for every person here – even for a person like me. I would not have survived in a society other than this. Here I had an early chance of revival after my downfall. This place responsible for my decline also gave me chance for purgatory. It was up to me to use this opportunity as I would.

"The Lady said, 'What we follow must be truly questioned even if it is god. Otherwise those doubts will be the biggest obstacles to our devotion to oneself. And a person who cannot love oneself is not worthy of loving any god no matter his devotion. It does not complete him. All those taught must be known truly otherwise it is just another fact that can be bent or moulded to suit one's semantics. Do you know, in *Ramayana*, the *Sita* whom *Ravana* abducted was not the actual one born from the earth? She was in fact *Vedavati* in disguise.'

"I did not have the appetite for further thinking so I pleaded to just hear the story since I had never heard about it. The Lady looked outside as the sun had rose high above and soon it would be noon. She began, '*Vedavati*, daughter of *Brahmarishi Kusadhvaja*, the son of *Bṛhaspati*, born with incredible beauty, once sat meditating when *Ravana* passed by her and captivated by her beauty propositions her. She however had spent her entire life chanting the *Vedas*, refuses. Dejected, *Ravana* grabs her by her hair following which enraged *Vedavati* cut off her hair. She says she would enter the fire since she was insulted and ill-treated and perish herself as an offering to the fire. She refused to curse *Ravana* but foretold that she will be born as a cause for his destruction before immolating herself.

'When *Rama*, the incarnation of *Vishnu*, was born and *Sita* was abducted during their exile, *Agni*, the fire god replaces *Sita* with *Vedavati* who had alighted into the fire once. *Agni* entrusts *Sita* to *Swaha*, his consort in the underworld. Thus *Ravana* abducts *Vedavati* instead of *Sita*. But there are variations to this version of the story. In the alternative version, when *Vedavati* commits suicide by jumping into the fire; *Agni* takes her as his consort and *Swaha* is born. It is said that since the prophecy was to be completed, *Swaha* replaces Sita and gets abducted by *Ravana* becoming the cause of his ultimate demise by the hands of *Rama* and fulfilling the prophecy. But this version plays in contradiction with the excerpt from *Venkatachala Mahatmya* of the *Skanda Purana* which coincides with the former version I told.

'My attempt here lies to draw your kind attention, sir, towards the fact that it wasn't *Sita* who was abducted at all as spoken or taught to us. Rather the story has a hidden plot somewhere that only reveals motives and reasons from an all together different epoch. Reliability on stories solely depends on our satisfaction because we try to associate to the events and we have an inherent tendency to want the triumph of good over evil; hence we believe what is propagated or taught without enquiring further.'

"That explanation could not be refuted or argued with. We had our own motives on believing legends; somewhere those formed the medium of ethics that are instilled in men. But the entire truth is not revealed or spread and one day these hidden facts would be the same reason for the loss of trust from these legends that would have turned into belief and devotion. It made me easy to listen to the story of the spiritual aspirant with a more open mind. Legend or not there may be something in it that the Lady expects me to understand. I prepared my ears to attend to her words. 'So what happened to the spiritual aspirant?' I asked coming back to the original tale she had started with. 'Did he survive later?'

'Yes he did. And soon he found four women – slaves from the boat who survived the wreckage. They were banished women of low caste and sold as slaves to merchants and traders. They slaved their way to live and also were the means of amusement for men. But this change of destiny was unexpected when they found stranded in a crater after the storm. They were free but did not know what to do with their freedom. So the five souls regrouped themselves and began to live here. Years later many ships found their way here for a place of rest. In order to earn money these women sold their labour and body. It became a refuge for women who managed to barter a way to the island – usually slaves who wanted a means to escape. This place soon flourished into a town and later into a city as you see today.'

'But why did the place develop into a brothel? Didn't the man, whom you say was a spiritual aspirant come up with a new plan? Or atleast he could have married one of those slave girls and had a family,' I pondered.

"The Lady smiled. 'Yes he could have started a family but unfortunately he didn't.' There was a long pause before she began again. 'He was a eunuch.'

'What!' I exclaimed. The Lady could not resist a chuckle. The story was getting interesting and at the same time surreal. 'Please complete the story,' I pleaded.

'Well the story has been completed. It is the beginning that you should know. I will tell it to you, but first we need to have some food,' saying which the Lady retired from my chamber. I too had my lunch and after some hours the Lady returned. I asked her to resume.

"She began, 'The person who founded this place was indeed a eunuch but before that he was born as a man without any defect at birth. He lived a peaceful life in a village far from here. In his youth he fell in love with a maiden in the village. Hesitantly he approached her and confessed his love to the girl. The girl, however, did not have any interest in him and declined. He asked her over and over again which eventually soured their relation. She did not even tolerate the sight of this man, whose intentions were pure and innocent. He truly loved her but she never understood it. And the day came when she was married away to a wealthy family, and she did not have the slightest regard for how this young man felt.

'Heartbroken and gloomy, this young man sold his possessions and wandered off into the world. He travelled many places till the ache in his heart slowly receded. During one of his travels, he landed himself in a city where he decided to make a new beginning. There, after having a fair start, he found himself attracted to a young lady. They became good friends. She shared everything about her life with him and he too was delighted by the company he had. He too shared his past with her – his love for the girl and the rejection and the grief from it. She consoled him and told that the girl he loved was unlucky because a loyal person like him loved her but she did not have any idea about it. It was truly her loss. He too felt the wounds of his past shed its weight and resume a little life in his cold heart. Her company made it bearable. Eventually, after a long time he felt that someone who liked him could be a nice companion to his life. He was surprised that his once broken heart, now healed, still had the capacity to love someone honestly. So he decided to ask her to marry him. He also thrived well in business and had a stable income.

'Soon the day dawned, and the man laid the proposition in front of the lady. However, she declined him because she considered him only as a friend but importantly she was in love with someone else. After this incident the poor man still hoped that she would miss his company and would atleast return to spend time with him. But he soon found, by accident, her involved with a man whom she loved. Women had a very peculiar nature of breeding company for their own benefit. She did not tell him that she loved some other person but she rejected saying that he was simply her best friend and the thought of them together never occurred to her. She did not have the courtesy to say the real reason for her withdrawal.

'There were days and there were nights when they had spent their time together talking and laughing but never had the woman spoken about her true feelings. He felt miserable on the revelation because he had trusted her. He confronted her for an explanation that was met by silence. He loved her very much and hence he couldn't curse her nor could he make her believe that he loved her more than anything else. He felt misled and broken again over the same wounds. He was devoted to her but since this was what he received he prayed fervently for an answer to his fate. He suffered immensely for being loyal. He became a recluse and simply attended to his inanimate life.

'Time passed by and he flourished into a businessman. He visited many places far and near and came in touch with many people. One such visit took him to a city where his associates lived. He received the hospitality of his friendly associate and was introduced to his family. He and his wife lived there and they were happy to welcome him. In the coming years he had numerous opportunities to stay with them and there were times when his friend was away on business and his wife played the generous host.

'Soon they got to know each other. The man was an honest person and he was simple with his words. Initially, his friend's wife enquired about his family since he seemed to be a man in his prime, it was natural for a person to assume he would be married. She asked him why he was not. Hesitantly he revealed his past and the incident that made him lose interest in worldly life. She said she understood how he felt. It was nothing new to the man; he had already heard this comment from many people about his honesty but since only misery came from such a trait he was not at all inspired by the praise he received.

'Intrigued and pleased by such an honest personality, his friend's wife developed admiration for this man. On further visits, when she was alone, she received him with great care and respect. Soon the bond between them grew strong and one day his friend's wife told him about her life. She was found barren and to her misery could never become a mother and that had made her husband distant from her. Although, he provided for her, he was not interested in her anymore. She indirectly confessed to being attracted to the man. His heart was clear as daylight and he never had any ungrateful thoughts for his friend's wife. He had respect for both his friend and his spouse and never took advantage of their position. However he took the effort to make his friend's wife comfortable even after she expressed her feelings.

'Desire, however, is independent of reason hence indifferent to it. And one of the laws of incessant desire is the law of transcendence. Thoughts have the tendency to manifest itself into reality if they are held for a long time. But it also has a trait of travelling the space when the intentions held are strong. Irrespective of the origin, such thoughts create an impact on other person's life. It can alter one's thinking. And such an incident occurred with the businessman. The friend's wife held this desire to have a man like him as a companion but she was already married, therefore she would desire him but always think this desire to be futile. Soon the love for him turned into reverence.

'The man took this well, as a friend lending his time and patient, understanding ear to the misery of a woman. They had an intimacy only few could achieve; one that inspired the mind for companionship whilst the physical remaining absent without exercising any forceful control. One day it so happened that the man suddenly felt the urge to be close to her since their company became so irrevocably secure. And so he expressed the desire to kiss her. Though flattered, she was extremely baffled between her status as a married woman and her desire. Once, she too had the desire to kiss this humble and honest man. Though she wanted to kiss him, she did not have the courage to move ahead for closure and so in confusion she refused it. It greatly hurt the man but he could do nothing. He loved her and the spark of mature friendship and companionship was actually ignited by his friend's wife.

'She pacified him with excuses. She said that he was a true man and that such thoughts should not be entertained. Moreover she did not have the right to take away the purity of such a person by having a physical relationship with him. But when the man made his desire clear that it was not a physical relation that he wanted but a kiss alone, the woman changed her explanations. It was visible that she had suppressed her initial desire to kiss him but now she tried to get rid of him. One of her most humorous explanations was that the his desire was a result of some external force – some negative entity trying to persuade him to kiss her. It was one of the most pathetic defences that someone could come up with. She initially wanted him but did not know how to approach the situation – now the manifestation was in a manner undesirable to her taste. It was like the wish we long for, but when it is available we don't need or want it anymore. And the very thought of it induces fear. Such an incident too had its end in something destructive.

'Realising the foolishness in his desire, unaware about the sudden change in his thoughts were the result of that woman's desire, he discontinued her company. She remained passive, content with the righteousness of her explanation and averted any further encounters. She was relieved at the riddance.

'The man realised the fickle nature of women. They too want the same and exact things that men wanted and they were concrete about the desires in words and actions. Women however had the nature to shield themselves from these thoughts and console themselves to some make-believe conclusion for the sake of their survival. They can easily lie to themselves and be content with it. It is usually the honest ones who end up as wretched. With this understanding he gave the desire to lead a worldly life and staying within the role of a businessman he devoted most of his time to meditation. He became a renounciate the world would not know.

'But mediation is not a simple and peaceful process. True meditation would plough the mind and it brings forward all the hidden miseries to the surface. Those blinded by the philosophy that meditation can be a cure to the illness of the mind only perceive it as a means to end suffering. On the contrary, mediation breaks oneself down before reaching stability. One who can endure makes it to the other end of the spectrum and has the privilege to look over things as it is.'

'Why did the man consider that meditation was harmful?' I interrupted.

'Have you ever been to a paddy field?' asked the Lady.

'I nodded in positive consent. 'Why does it smell filthy?' she asked.

'Because of the scent of the clay; when it is filled with water.'

'Is that all?' asked the Lady. I remained passive, pondering, but could not offer any answer.

'It stinks because of the seeds. The seeds get broken by the ground as it develops sprouts and the exterior of it rots. Leaves spring forth eventually revealing the entire plant. And at that time it smells of green foliage even when there is water not of rotten mud. To sprout new growth one needs to destroy his older self and the people who do not understand this evolution will always confuse it with destruction. They will never be able to understand the difference between the two because it is the complete obliteration of whatever we once felt was true.

'And so this man who had loved every woman with all his heart eventually burdened his heart with sadness and guilt. Sadness because he offered all that he could and yet no one understood and guilt because he spent his time over and over again on the same mistake. He was not a charmer of words and simplicity was the very thing that attracted women to him but it also took them away when they found him without mystery. Simplicity in a way was mysterious for those who never understood it and once it was deciphered, people would discard it as a used fabric.

'Therefore every time he sat for meditation, his hurt heart used to bring the memories of his past. With great difficulty he made through the threshold of staggering thoughts to the realm of centered wilful concentration. But when he made an inventory of his progress after many years, he realised it far behind his expectations. He reached an impasse from where there seemed no further progress to his penance. So to improve the intensity of this pursuit he renounced all his worldly belongings and retired to the peak of a mountain. He survived on fruits and vegetations and resolved his attempt at meditation with all the austerity.

'Many years went by with the routine. His flesh vanished and he became thin and pale. His hair grew into the typical matted fashion of a saint and his beard grew long to his navel. The finger nails grew long and curved and ugly in sight with dirt and grime in them. His efforts though concrete in practice bore fruit in form of mental strength. He went without food for months. He heard sound of the quantum universe; there was peace, but the idea that this practice should culminate into the realization made him push further. He felt 'something' still remained. That was the only aim which remained to be accomplished – to know god. Somehow the idea hid behind the foggy curtains of thoughts making it evident that behind those veils lay the ultimate truth but no matter what he did to reach close to this objective it seemed a distant cry. Somehow he became lost from the original idea of peace and the initial pursuit he set out for.

'He left the mountain and went in search of people who had undertaken his path. He met many, but all the so-called preachers of truth and realisation never had a single experience of what he had himself achieved. He was looked like an eccentric wanderer who had nothing but god in his mind. He travelled for many places with unsatisfactory results and finally decided to pursue the path himself. He was tired of finding or expecting insight for his practice. He seemed to have landed in a state of spiritual coma waiting for something to happen. He climbed the nearest mountain where he heard was a cave and no human actually ventured out into the creepy place. He thought this to be a perfect recluse to retire.

'As he approached the cave, he saw bright illumination from within, as if thousand of fireflies held a gathering. The light lit the entrance but the source seemed to be inside the cave away from view. It was soothing to look at the smooth luminescence and the glow having a small foggy aura surrounding it. Making a logical calculation that wild animals do not make their homes in places of light, he moved inside to find the source of light. When he entered he saw a sage sitting, smoking some rolled leaf in between his fingers and his body radiated the bright light. The sage's eyes were half closed and watery and the corners of his mouth had saliva tricking down on to his beard.

'The man waited for the sage to awake from whatever trance he was in and in the process fell asleep. When he woke up, he saw the sage sitting in the same place but in a more stable and conscious state. He approached the glowing sage and paid his respects. With all the reverence and courage he could muster he requested the sage to divulge his identity. The sage revealed himself as an aspirant of the almighty and said the cave was his home. Delighted, the man asked the sage permission to stay. He wanted the sage to accept him as his disciple, explaining his years of penance and his apparent dilemma in realising the Ultimate.

'The hermit allowed him to stay but refused to be his teacher. Dejected, the man asked why. The sage told him that he could not be a teacher to anyone; that it was a bond and it binds the pursuer from seeking; if it is learning that he was seeking then he should learn by asking to know, not be taught. The knowledge of the self comes from within and it cannot be taught or tutored.'

'Convinced by the answers, he asked the sage for the necessary amendments that was to be followed. The first step that the sage suggested was to empty the mind of all the old thoughts and principles. And one of it was the Guru-disciple relationship. Although the guru is the representation of the divine bridge between the absolute and the seeker it becomes the limiting barrier to his progress. And the realised soul that helps to elevate suffering on his pupil's end makes the pupil bound to the teacher unknowingly.

'Confused he asked for further explanation from the saint. The sage explained from his own experience that he had met his teacher in the realms of higher dimensions where the souls of realised and greatly developed existed. On that plane he was initiated to the ways of spiritual progress but it made the illusion that he had reached the true point of realisation only to fall by attachment to the experience. And that belief existed because of the expectation from his guru. He mistook it to be the culmination of his penance because he had conditioned his mind to believe that a guru can alone liberate him. And when a soul existing on another leads the way to the path of realisation, that experience itself can cause to hold as major divine experiences.

'On further conversation the saint revealed that one should take the benefit of ignorance at such a place where having a belief can become an obstacle. It is one of the duties of the master or teacher to condition the mind of the student and constantly serve him a reminder that the journey is into uncharted territory and every experience is unique to the seeker's path, hence it will be distinctly different from the teacher. So the only expectation would be to be content with ignorance and prepare the mind for unexpected scenarios rather than burdening oneself with anticipation. Here, to know, not knowing is of utmost benefit.

'The spiritual aspirant then asked the sage about the philosophy of devotion that is propagated to the masses and the shortcoming in it. It was evident that the majority of method followed by the masses was misleading or the practice meant only to reinforce whatever one believed. The truth always eluded man and the very attempt to realise the truth was ironically a path leading away from it.

'The sage explained that spiritual growth has no meaning if it cannot be related to the masses. Atleast some fragments of its meaning should be synthesizable; if the connection between the reality and the all pervading deludes man then such knowledge is of no use. There is no use of a god in front of whom we cannot be vulnerable or weak. And an almighty omnipotent state is without the knowledge of weakness and pain known to men. Such realised souls are no use to a pursuer. Hence the smaller part of the truth about the absolute is implanted in man so that when he pursues, if he chooses to pursue, then he can have continuity to the same idea. It would be disappointing for mankind to know that even though he has a chance to realise the absolute through his body, not everyone can do it nor everyone is entitled to have the experience on this realm.'

'How is that argument possible? Isn't it the reason why we actually seek for a guru?' I interrupted.

'Yes, it is why we seek a guru,' said the Lady. 'But it is not abiding for all the teachers and masters to lead you to the ultimate experience. They are mere guides. In the simplest way to explain, you are shielded from the experience of the absolute because of your karma. If the veil of karma falls giving you the experience then the role of a guru is unnecessary. He alone can be said to be a guru, who takes the karma of a disciple on himself so that his pupil can accelerate in his pursuit; like the rich sharing his wealth with the poor. The effects of such a charity comes out from selflessness but it affects the master too who himself is a realised soul. There is always a risk in undertaking such a task where the karma of others could actually hurl one to the depths of karmic struggle from which he had risen. That is why only the master who has the ability to bear the inevitable can be called the true GURU. All others are mere plaques of guidance along the road of spiritual development for the seeker. Here the protagonist is always the seeker not the teacher.'

'So what is to be expected in the path to self realisation?' I asked.

'It is the same thing that the founder of this place asked the sage in the cave because he knew not how to proceed unless he knew where he was going," said the Lady. "The common or the most usual approach to a spiritual path is the premise that the world and other existing objects including one's body is an obstacle to the truth. This induces undue friction and the approach becomes a struggle. And there is the other idea of good and bad; moral and evil. Most people never achieve the idea of the divine because it is represented by the views of good and bad. They never get past it and always are lost in the battle. They make their perception of divine can only be achieved by overcoming good over bad.

'You see the mind can only be limitless if it realises the possibility of being infinite and that cannot come through doctrines or dogmas alone. But the beginning of any teaching starts by pointing out the deficit of the mind; by painting the picture of a monkey jumping from thought to thought. This is the paradoxical error. It can only be understood by the force of realisation – through means of an experience with no other substitution. And it would be astonishing to know the difference between the two through actual experience.

'But knowing the mind as the vessel that can lead one on the path as well as astray, certain measures are placed in the way to trick the mind for staying on route. And fear is such an invention. The concept of fear is a misled attempt to drive the mind into submission of one's effort. Though fear being powerful initially, the effects derived is faster and stronger but it soon wanes away and the seeker is stuck on a plateau with no upward momentum. This merely creates the factor of fear to boomerang and instill the doubt that the efforts are not correctly applied. This indirectly creates the illusion that our way should be one of consistent, progressive accounts of divine experiences. Else there would be no progress. And the investigation of the error in our approach for practice is often deceivingly considered as a product of karma or sins. Fear becomes the only thing that sets value in everything. The only way to overcome past experiences is by facing the element of fear in it. The sage explained this to the seeker of truth in that cave.

'Unsatisfied by this explanation he asked the sage further for a solution. With a mild disregard to the question, the sage simply rolled a leaf filled it with some powder and grass to cover it and gave it to the man. The he said that it contains herbs and it was good for the health. He lit one end of the lead and asked him to inhale the smoke. Hesitantly he did what he was asked for.

'A strong sense of energy hit him and his brain began to reel similar to that after a loud sneeze. Tears filled his eyes as soon as the smoke made its way to the lungs and the surges of energy came as waves one after another. He fell on his back on the ground and felt his entire body break away like crystalline shards. There his various fragments of the body floated above him and showed him the pictures amongst his memories, the first person he loved and the second and the kiss he asked for. Then his flight increased to the speed of infinite value giving him little chance to absorb the happening around in the unfamiliar realm of consciousness. In that realms he saw the masked goal of his pursuit; the stream of light that he was so relentlessly pursing. There he heard the same exact sounds of the quantum universe as he heard in his meditations. But here he heard them so vividly and his heart remained calm without any breaths. He was still and calm. The experience was divine and unparalleled. The initial bursts of energy have managed to adapt into peaceful rhythm and send enormous relief to his tired soul.

'In that state of induced calmness he made conversation to the images of people that came to his mind. He spoke to them about the guilt and the hatred he had in himself because of them and the way he had suffered. The figures listened to him calmly with their entire attention as if their mere existence was for the purpose to hear him. They absorbed each and every word he said along with the feelings he had experienced and somehow they absorbed all his sadness away and took it with them. Soon all cleared away and he fell into deep slumber.

'When he woke up, he felt his being light and agile. Unlike the heaviness he carried even in his deep hours of meditations, now he felt the burden lifted. He realised the difference between a closed heart and a free one and also through it, the indisputable significance of an experience. To know, gave understanding but to feel was supremely incomparable. On enquiry about the herbs the sage explained that they were hallucinogens. He debated on the ill effects of drugs on the body but the sage took the opportunity to explain the alteration of the regular contents of the mind by it. All the fears have been shuffled and taken away by breaking the norm that drugs are harmful. Drugs were harmful only on the condition of abuse.

'There was no arguing the experience it had. Undoubtedly, he had been relieved of the fears and burden of his mind. He broke the fear of fear itself. Now he clearly understood that once fear is experienced, it had no power over us. Fear exists only for the people who are not ready to experience; it is because they seek to understand the unknown before experiencing it. What propagated as harmful or undesirable is not necessarily as they were projected.

'In the days to come he progressed faster and crossed many dimensions of divine barriers and found himself rooted in his meditations. He experienced the astral worlds and gained insight about it by his occasional trips via psychedelics. He used caution to use them only when required and the sage greatly helped him by educating the quantity and quality of the herbs to be used and techniques to maintain the state of induced ecstasy without being addicted to it. But still he felt incomplete and even the sage could not help to find an answer. Somewhere he knew that there was one more threshold to cross beyond which lay his liberation. In the silent hours of contemplation, he traced his source and finally arrived at the discovery that it was his decision to quit the worldly life which was the emotional barrier that stopped him from realising his true goal.'

'How could the decision to renounce the world be wrong?' I asked.

'Sir,' said the Lady, 'His renunciation was due to the unrest in his previous life that he had left incomplete. The decision was not in favour of the natural course of events but was a cause of rejection from the world. In other words, the desire to pursue the absolute was indeed true to its core but his emotional issues remained untouched and were pending all these years. You see there is no complete fulfilment of life if those karmas that changed you remain unfulfilled. They will not allow the manifestation of your true self no matter however long you choose to sit silently in contemplation. Thus they will manifest simply because there is no other way but manifestation. This is ample reason for you to take another birth just to fulfil those actions you desired. Desires are immutably eternal, you are not. Therefore the ultimate choice remains with us.

'Realising this, the seeker left the cave and resumed the life of a common man. Miraculously, his body did not show any signs of aging and looked like that of a man in his prime. It was a result of his penance that he could control his body without decay. Armed with this he began a life where he confronted everything that he had held a prejudice for. He realized that being a householder would just be a routine and would take a long time to understand his missing link. The only thing that can radically accelerate his understanding would be through whatever was termed as sin. He explored all the areas of sin whenever necessary without being afraid. There were only so much wrong one could do to investigate where he is the weakest.

'So he worked hard and earned the comfort of a rich man then indulged in liquor, psychedelics and other luxurious and self absorbing activities. But they did not even scratch his resolute surface. He found himself deeply centered with his own self indifferent to the ebb and flow. The only fragment of unhappiness that remained in him was his inability to realise his goal, but he did not overwhelm himself with grief. He took care to follow the path he was set out for and eventually the day arrived when he encountered his weakest part of the soul.

'The unique thing about the mind in transformation is that when it encounters even one positive quality that endears, it automatically entwines itself to other positives thus making the process of change enjoyable and effortless. That is why some people progress faster than others. The same is true for negative qualities; one must just find the triggering factor to accumulate all the other negative qualities. And every man has one unique trait that can lead him to his downfall and an equally opposite force that can lead him to the pinnacle of his life.

'The man had never indulged in lust. And that is where he encountered the quakes which lay in his heart. Intimacy was the unresolved subject in question because he had never experienced the trust of a woman. He was always disturbed by the feminine gender's trait of retracing their emotion and being comfortable with it. The day he indulged in the art of carnal excitement and pleasure, he was again in an unknown region. He felt fear in the highest form – because it was the only fear left to overcome. He was clueless. His heart only knew to love and loyalty was an automatic trait he had. It was the goodness within himself that wouldn't allow salvation and that was overwhelmingly self destructive.

'But there was no retreat from this path he had tread on. And therefore he kept indulging and analysing the occurrences in his heart. Some days he grieved, but for a brief moment he seemed to have found the clarity. Then he would fall back into his dilemma. His internal life was split between two interests that could not seem to relate to each other. He tried to calm his nerves by retreating to his psychedelic state but there too he experienced grief unlike the earlier experiences he had. There he realised what his ego was – that after all these years of penance and self control, he had just replaced his prior self with new ways of treatment; that belief from his experiences still remained the core centre and therefore had an expectation to be saved from this predicament based on that belief. He had overcome this trait with respect to every other aspect but he just didn't trust people. He blamed his heart for being so innocent and loyal. Guilt-ridden, he just provoked bitterness from himself and from the world. He felt lost from his purpose again – his initial quest for truth. He had taken the risk and failed.

'Soon his existence was reduced to shambles and he thrived as a whore monger and indulged in sexual conquests just to forget his ever exploding thoughts. He fled from himself. He found his entire life useless as compared to a common man who lived happily with his brutish and lowly nature while he suffered travelling through sin just to understand what the truth was. Who was to understand that he had suffered silently without complaining and had taken a great deal of courage on his part to stay strong? He realised that he had opened the gates of an uncontrollable flood that seemed never to give him even momentary peace,' the Lady said.

'How did he overcome the state?' I asked.

'He did not because he could not,' said the Lady. 'Until one day in haze of his intoxication he castrated himself wishing to be an impotent. He was unable to control the sway of his life so he decided to end it by inflicting the inevitable. He wanted to know what would happen if there was no accessory. Where would this energy flow? He was drunk and in his delirium he cut his nether regions as a challenge to the force within him that did not seem to stop flowing. He mistakenly assumed that lust had conquered his heart and there was no escape from it.

'But soon he was proven wrong. After this brutal self infliction, he was taken care of by one of the harlots whom he used to frequent. She had realised his situation long ago but was hesitant to speak to him. She loved him and she knew that he was pure – that his true nature was very different from what he displayed. His wounds healed but he never trusted the woman that took care for him thinking the act was out of pity. But she did not quit and continued to serve him.

'One day, infuriated and agitated, he hurled curses and asked her why she was caring for him this way. The harlot expressed her heart, but he could not trust her. He gave her all the reasons why he was ineligible and said that she, too, was a whore; whatever she had done in her life was what she had practiced and trained to do; there was no depth to her affection. She explained that a woman's heart recognizes a man she loves and all it takes was willingness to love and be loved. In her own words she enlightened him about the true nature of his inner being.

'He found that she had felt his presence superior to any man she had known in her life. That was the reason why other women felt it uncomfortable to be with him – because they were not able to decipher him. They felt a vibe of unfamiliarity with him because of the purity he carried. People are always content to share their company with like minded folks; however, he was different and hence the other prostitutes felt it hard to be with him because they were constantly irritated by his being. His purity made them aware that they had surrendered to sin while he was being untouched even in those impure waters. They chose to distance him because they could not afford to lose their sanity. And that alone was the reason why she chose to serve him while others abandoned him.

'Moved by her devotion, he thanked the woman for her indisputable love and accepted her affection and trust. And lo and behold, the final hindrance cast itself off like the clouds of a dry summer day. With a bolt of change he realised his true nature. He was everything, a reflection of the universe and he saw the universe in him. He existed as many but still was one. There was no more suffering, no more joy. It was the state of bliss indifferent to any ups and downs he had experienced. He felt the fury and tranquil in the same manner; effortlessly undeterred and undaunted both as a part of his own.

'And that is the story of the person who found this place after years of his self realisation. And it became an obvious choice for him when the survivors from the wreckage were women exploited by the society and had got used to the ways of the harem. He did not alter their decisions; after all who was he to do so? But this place functions on the outlines he suggested,' the Lady concluded.

"I looked out of the window and saw dusk approaching. The story explored sin as a step on the path to self development. It made sense from the point of view of a debate – to place an idea in the mind via a story. But it seemed very surreal at the same time.. I sat there ruminating on the story. After all, my suffering too was on the same lines. But at the same time I wondered whether this story was devised just to send a subtle message for me to understand the nature of my current predicament – to make me understand that there was a chance. I tried to ignore it but the echoes of that story made it impossible to divert my attention. Somewhere, inside, I too wanted to get away from my reality," the *shilpi* said, ponderingly.

Asya too felt the story to be unrealistic, similar to a fable or a legend told to children before they drifted off to sleep. Usually those stories have the element of a message in it meant to grab the attention of the mind. With the curiosity of a child Asya asked, "Then what happened?"

"Late in the night the Lady returned with food but I was not interested in it. She asked me if I was uncomfortable but I kept my silence. I wasn't able to put in words the effect the story had had on me. The Lady calmly said, 'You feel it hard to trust what I have told you.' I had mocked her once but this time I was not ready to argue. I was going to let it pass.

"Then the unbelievable happened. The Lady slowly took away her robes and undid her clothing. I was staring out from the window looking at the stars. Without sound she stood naked behind me, waiting for me to turn and gaze at her. After a while, I moved around to see the body of a mature, fully grown woman, but with a minor difference. The nether extremities bore scars of an alien kind; something grotesque inflicted without mercy.

"Suddenly a voice said, 'Now do you believe me?' The voice was masculine unlike the elegant feminine voice I had heard till that day. Sounding rough in texture I was taken aback and almost frightened. Ceaseless thoughts crossed my minds of various natures ranging from the being standing in front of me as a monster or a witch or some wicked delirium playing in my mind.

"It took me years to understand that the Lady was indeed the spiritual aspirant whose story she had narrated. She was the man who pursued the area of sin and astoundingly lived for over five centuries. She was the eunuch."

"How is that even possible?" asked Asya disbelievingly. She felt fooled. She questioned this man again, now, with another set of doubts in her mind. He now seemed to be a lunatic. She was suddenly afraid.

The *shilpi* looked calm and unmoved. He waited for Asya to assimilate the development – to settle all fluttering of sudden emotions.

"It would be unlikely to say here that nothing is impossible once you live to know it. I would have to believe that the eunuch was indeed the spiritual aspirant now because my life is the living proof of it. I, too, disbelieved it but it took me years to understand the truth behind it."

"What truth?" asked a bewildered Asya.

"Do you know when the last war fought in this nation was?"

"About a century ago," Asya replied wondering what held now to be revealed from this particular change of topic.

"And yet you believed that a *brahmin* became a *khastriya* to fight a war to avenge his beloved before becoming a *shilpi*; to be precise – a century old war. That you were able to believe?"

Asya felt the ground beneath her slip. She felt part of an illusion; far away from reality. She thought of running away. The excitement was too much to contain. Maybe coming here was the wrong decision.

Asya

Asya looked outside to see the children playing. They ambled away chasing butterflies and dragonflies in their beautiful garden. She heard them scurrying away at the sight of their mother, returning from the river after bathing. They did not want to be seen with muddy hands and feet. It left a chuckle on Asya's face that she could not manage to hide, seeing the children vanish and hide in midst of the bushes and trees. The woman carried the pot around her hip, crossed the garden without noticing the children and approached the house.

"Mother," the woman said entering, keeping the pot down. "You must be cold. I will make you hot tea." Asya watched the slender woman pace quickly into the kitchen. Her daughter has got her hips, and her hair, and her nose. Asya smiled.

Her daughter warmed the vessels and poured some water into it. When it began bubbling, she put tea leaves, grated ginger and some jaggery. The room filled with the aroma of the beverage. The smell was enough to arouse the knots of hunger in Asya.

As the woman handed over the tumbler of tea to her, Asya said, "Make some sweet porridge today." The young lady smiled and nodded in acknowledgement; she knew her mother loved porridge – the lumpy rice and jaggery mixture kind.

It was the onset of winter. The trace of sunlight in the room was increasing with the morning sun. Both of them sipped on their tea. Asya looked out through the door on to their beautiful garden again as the green grass became brighter with the yellow hues of the sun. She slowly got up and went to the veranda and smelt the air. The mist had the whiff of mud in it. Asya looked down on the grass, wet with dew.

The children rushed beside their grandmother and tugged playfully. Asya joined them, taking the smallest of the three children in her hand. The other two started clinging to her begging to be held. So she sat down, there, on the ground. One begged her to sing a song. Another asked her to say a story – not just any story but the story they have heard countless number of times. The story their grandmother invented – about the *One-Eyed Monster*.

In this version of story the One-Eyed Monster was a colossal demon who lived in a lake that fell in love with a damsel when she arrived at his lake. In his previous life, he was cursed to this fate by a beautiful nymph at the same lake, when approached seeking her affection. She asked him to sing a song about the love he had in his heart for her. The lover asked her for one day to prepare it. While bidding farewell she laid the condition that his song should make her happy, otherwise she would not consider him. He agreed and left. He did not sleep the entire night thinking about the words he could put in his song to give life to his emotions.

Next day early at the lake, he called for the nymph. She came out and looked at the weary persuader. Her friends hid under the blanket of water away from the man's vision, to listen to his song.

He began to sing. He sang about the unknown world of the water nymph as a fantasy of his imagination. He sang about the depth of their world and the beauty of various life forms it held. He spoke about the beauty as synonymous to the spotless beauty of the nymph that stood before him so delicately, giving her patient ear to listen to his song. He spoke about the rage that the oceans hold and to show the world how water could behave, god created lakes but she was the one who worked to maintain its sweetness and so did the travellers throng towards her. He sang about her eyes as the clear mass of water in which two black pearls dwelled as her pupils.

Then he spoke of the sun, the moon and the stars. He spoke about the love that bees and flowers have for each other; how each relies on the other. He sang of the wind that carries itself the beauty of every place it visits and brings something new with it to places unknown. He sang of the people who lived in the world; a mother who is happy about her child; a father who is happy to come to his family. He sang how the rain marries the sunlight and their ceremony is attended by the universe under the rainbow. He then asked her to marry him because he was a seeker of her tranquillity.

The friends of the water nymph rose to the surface mesmerized by the song. They cooed at their fellow mate and her luck. But the water nymph was not at all amused at the song. When he sang, all she could see was the difference of the two worlds that they lived in. She felt sad instead of feeling happy. She did not see the man's love, but the grief and sorrow she would find in loving him. Her sadness turned into rage, and to the astonishment of her friends and the gods, she cursed him into an ugly demon with a single eye. The man instantly transformed into the ugly form, but his heart remained the same. Her friends shrieked with horror at his sight. They pitied him and asked the nymph why she committed such heinous crime.

Before she turned to leave, he said to the nymph that he still loved her and he was ready to wait for her return. He begged her to tell him the reason for his state that she put him in. Suddenly, overwhelmed with guilt, she cried, but she did not say anything. She left the lake, much to his dismay, and so did her friends. The demon decided to stay at the lake anticipating her return.

Centuries passed by. The water nymph, now, haunted by her gruesome act, could not find her interest in any affairs of the world. She simply failed to understand her grief; unable to concentrate, she became recluse. She hid away from the world. Her powers diminished and guilt eroded her will. Finally she reached the lakes where she cursed the man. She found that the lake had become a marsh where no vegetation grew. People had abandoned the place and it poured out rotten odour. Unable to control her grief, she cried and a tear, dropped to the ground.

Suddenly the demon rose from the marshy ground and moved towards her. He said he had hoped that she would return to him one day. She asked him how he could hope when there was nothing for him to believe. He explained to her that she had left without explaining her cause for his predicament. He spoke about his quandary everyday to the gods, the plants and to the lake. He spoke about his sadness to the grass that grew and the mud beneath the lake. Hearing him cry and seeing him sad all the vegetation around him turned sad. They too waited for her return to know the reason of her curse. They waited for years and eventually died, but the earth retained the memory of his sadness. That is why all the vegetation refused to grow in this place till they knew the reason. And when her tear fell on the ground, the earth told the demon of her return.

She told him about the sadness that she would have felt if she were to have loved him. She told him that she was not aware that one has to endure with love, and that idea suddenly frightened her. She was happy to meet him and but his idea of love made her sad. She was infuriated by it and therefore she cursed him. The demon smiled and consoled her. Moved by his behaviour she felt the love of the man for the first time. But she did not know how to undo the curse. She sat sobbing realising her folly. No matter how dark she had painted him he was still the same.

The demon pacified the lamenting nymph. She pleaded for forgiveness. He told her that he did not hold any ill will against her and he only loved her. She revealed that she did not know how to undo the curse. She said she loves him. He consoled her and told her that that was enough. That was his initial desire.

But she felt she had committed a crime in her distress; she had to remedy and repair it.

She promised the demon that she would find a way to undo the curse and he would be free. Touched, he pledged to wait for her and retreated back to the marsh. The nymph undergoes severe penance and finally nearing her death she had the fortune to have god appear in front of her. She pleaded for forgiveness from the god and asked for a way. The god revealed to her that her powers had been extinguished from the guilt she had carried within her, so she found herself helpless to undo the curse. The only thing that she could do was sing back the words of his love song to him, and the curse would be undone – that was the only way. And now only her life breath remained – all her remaining energy had been spent in the rigorous penance. She was about to die.

She pleaded the god to atleast undo the curse for her and asks to shower happiness on her love. The god expresses the futility in that wish – the demon had wanted her always and his happiness was always entwined with hers. So after her death, though he may be lifted from the curse, he will still be unhappy. Her love was the only hope he had carried. Hearing this, the dame collapsed heartbroken.

Feeling pity, the god finally gave her a solution. She would be born again, if she chose to, as a human being and then she would have the opportunity to undo the curse. She had to sing the same song to the demon and the curse would be relieved. She agreed and the god disappeared. The nymph breathed her last and died.

After a century she is born in a village near the lake. She grows up unaware of the demon that waited for his love. When she had matured into a fine woman and seasoned to the age of marriage, she has a dream about a song from the lips of a man who sung about the ocean, lake and water, about beautiful world and the creatures that lay beneath the water mass. She heard the call of love in his voice for a girl who had eyes with pupils like black pearls. Then she heard him sing about the world he lived in. She remembers the dream after waking up. The world he lived in sounded similar to the world she lived, but, the world below fascinated her more.

One day she goes to the lake to bathe. Humming the poem while she stood still feeling the cold water of the lake, she stared at the reflection and surprisingly found her eyes similar to the description in the verse she had heard in her dream. The demon that lay rest beneath slowly surfaced and waited for her departure. While she was about to leave the banks of the lake, he calls out to her. She felt the same voice that she heard in her dream. All the foliage and the wind grew still. It was the voice, and only her. Rest of the universe halted. Still lying in the shadows, the demon called her again. She turned and enquired in a high tone to reveal the person behind the mysterious voice.

He refused, saying that he is ugly and he did not mean to frighten her. But with curiosity at its peak, she cajoles to divulge himself. He gives many excuses but the damsel was determined to find the anonymous. Finally he agrees to reveal himself on a condition – she was to sing the song that she was humming earlier. She agrees to sing it to a real person and not an invisible entity.

Challenged by this, the demon slowly rises to the surface and stands above the lake. Though frightened, the girl maintains her composure and keeps her promise. She sings with closed eyes and when she finishes, she finds a handsome young man in place of the ugly demon. Taken by his poise, she asks him about his identity. He narrates the story of his past and the purpose of his wait. He thanks her for keeping her promise. Unable to understand the developments, the girl finds herself on unfamiliar grounds again. But unlike the previous time, she wonders the truth behind the story and remembers the dream she had. Of all the dreams she had had, this particular dream was a memory that resurfaced for a purpose. This time she takes the effort to understand.

The young man touches her and the floodgates of memories from her previous birth open in her mind. She relives them again and looks at the man who had waited ages for her. She surrenders to him weeping finding closure in him.

He says, "It is because of your love I endured. It is because you made me what I am; for this reason you and I are one."

The children stopped Asya knowing the end, and the narration began amongst them – the eldest continued the story of the marriage of the nymph and the monster. They always felt the victory of love and the sentiment it gave them. Asya too joined them in their jovial completion and sighed. They scrambled away back to their play.

Asya sat there thinking about the story she had invented. She had recited this to her daughter and now her grandchildren. Her daughter loved it. When Asya narrated this story for the first time, her husband too had enjoyed it. Both father and daughter had sat beside her to listen to it. They were curious to know where she had learned this story from. She later told them that she invented for the sake of good passage of time. The soldier congratulated Asya for her imagination but most of all praised her for the message of love in it. Everybody felt the need for love be victorious; to be righteous and to be all conquering.

But no one seemed to know about endurance; everyone overlooked its part in the course of loving. But Asya knew what it took to resign oneself to maintain forbearance. Persistence was a weak word to give representation to the vague idea of endurance. And to endure meant to look the truth in the eye like scaling a mountain whose peak lay hidden in the clouds – into unknown territory. It was a unique way to meet the shreds of our souls; love, indeed, was an opportunity for this.

And Asya knew the importance of the message in her story; it was not only an essential to make the story satisfyingly content but also a responsibility. Anyone coming in touch with love initially paves the way for a fantastical land; a journey into the realm full of promises, because it gives life a moment to think about things that we were unable to comprehend or imagine. With love, our hearts takes flights with the wings of emotion and that makes life more interesting, conceivable, more possible. We begin to find completeness when the parts of ourselves we ignored begins to be taken care by someone else. We begin to realise the value that others find in us. We begin to love ourselves for the part that we have become because we can love. And those feelings cannot be tamed. We love the colours that the other's soul paints us with for this love must be understood; persevered – love has the ultimate responsibility.

But how are we to realise the wisdom in those feelings? Feelings are meant only to be experienced. The effort to understand those feelings only set in at the moment of loss. And Asya too had the similar fate of revelation.

Her rendezvous with the *shilpi* marked an important phase in her life. Naïve and young, then, she too was similar to the sculptor's reflection of his youth. She did not understand the nature of polarities; that they could co-exist, that they indeed co-exist and that is the only order of things. But to realise this she had to wait till the return of her husband from war.

The war ended a few months after she met the *shilpi*. She never returned to the sculptor again simply because she doubted him. But all the insight she had gained from him somehow resonated in her subconscious appeasing it to rest. The immediate effect in Asya after meeting the sculptor was that she found the groove to make a stand; to undertake a decision and adhere to it. And one of the first decisions she took was to give away her grief and concentrate on the possibility of her husband's return. But it was undeniable that this sudden change in her psyche's demeanour was certainly accredited to the *shilpi*.

Her husband returned when the war ended. The nation reunited and so did the couple. Prosperity reigned and content with the life they had, her husband decided to withdraw and resign from the life of a soldier. On his return he spoke of a peculiar feeling he had had throughout the war; the thought of Asya with him incessantly. He spoke how he felt her company even at a distant land, while he fought and while he rested. He was shy at first to say this, afraid of being ridiculed, but no one knew that it was truly believable except Asya. It was the fruit of her penance in grief that she was now blessed with this revelation. She had felt the words of the *shilpi* come true.

She soon became blessed with motherhood and nurtured a girl child. The parents were happy. Asya was happy but contentment eluded her. Normalcy almost had a concussive quality to it and lacked to motivate her. That was the beginning of ruminant life.

It was later, in the prime of her life that she noticed the subtle change of life and the attention it required. While she had cried the night with devastating thoughts in her head, that was the most intense period of her life. Nothing had kept her impetus on the precipice when she had the fear of plunging into an abyss. Fear was a stimulus that set the value in the things she held meaningful. And slowly all the words learnt from meeting the *shilpi* was beginning to show.

Love proved the security of her matrimonial companionship but failed to provide the contentment in it. Numerous reasons existed to be happy but her heart sat in a lull. She was the most powerful being when her love was threatened, but now she felt lacking; misplaced. She failed to understand the changes and she stayed deluded.

Late in her life, she realised her folly. Her child had grown and married a good man. It was, again, the same old fashion of living – Asya and her husband lived together on the hill. She remembered the days of youth and the fervour in the epoch. She did not know in her young age that the notion of love would evolve over time and mature. The feeling of loss gives the meaning to pursue and endure. Hope only existed in despair and like the *shilpi* said, it was indeed a distraction. Despair imparts the drive to do the impossible. We conjure our imagination with the most demanding exemplars of endurance in misery and states of despondency. Love creates a purpose, so understandable and implicit in nature that we find worth existing. Everything becomes value based and bearing.

Asya, now, is more than one hundred years old. But she still retains the agility of a woman in her prime. And age too had been extraordinarily kind to her. Her face and her body resembled a little elder in form to her own daughter. If people would look at them, they can easily confuse the mother and daughter to be sisters. As for her husband, he aged well with time and passed away many years ago. Astonishingly, Asya never aged in body after meeting the *shilpi*. And her life was the living testimony to the words of the *shilpi* she had doubted once.

She remembers the day of her departure from the hillock every day. She had disbelieved the sculptor when he revealed that he had lived for more than a hundred years. Along with that she had discarded the story of the eunuch whom the *shilpi* met in the harem. It was odd; beyond her conception for a person to live almost five centuries without even a slight deterioration in body. But as she now lives the implausible herself, she realises the truth in the lives of the people that she had doubted. And those are the ones that anyone can easily disbelieve. There is nothing enticing in a rudimentary life.

She recollects the frightening excitement of that day when the truth about the *shilpi* was told. She had asked the *shilpi* about such a possibility of existence and she remembers his exact words till this day.

He had said:

"Transcendence – that is the key. I doubted the eunuch, like you do now, but years later when my body stopped decaying I realised the possibility of the life that she had endured as a man. My doubt somehow managed to cling on to the astonishing detail of the eunuch every day. It was irrefutably strong and made its significance evident, powerfully by each passing day. Moreover the truth has the right to be felt because it endures through time. It was indeed a gesture from the Lady of the Harem to make me believe in my after years that what I have heard or learnt was the truth. I doubted the Lady's story based on her years she had lived and now live in the same fashion disbelieved by you. But that is the least of the concerns with regard to this world. It is easier to believe that a demon was good in the *Puranas* that he could have devotion for gods irrespective of his birth but in reality it is really questionable. The real question is – Will you believe a truth if it comes from an unlikely unexpected or prejudicially a 'wrong' source – like a eunuch?

"My life is a testament of truth but I retain it in my heart and mind as a burden unable to share it. I have to watch my loved ones fall prey to the beliefs they harbour because I could not devise an easier method to make them understand the truth. I cannot give enough proof that truth is the greatest of all desire one can have. And all I have is life now – the years that I have accumulated; the rest I loved had passed away making me just as inanimate as the statue I carve out of this stone. I would have quit this life, but Ultimate Truth has the ability to be silent and in turn impart that silence to us as its testimony. That state makes me human – one of the privileges that truth allows me."

It was highly unbelievable for her to know that the *shilpi* had lived for more than a hundred and eighty years.

And most of his journey though filled with adventure did not meet the generic expectations to trust him. The end proved uncanny to the extent of suspicion in the nature of the man she had met in that period. She never returned to him to ask about him further. And now she harboured a regret of not exploring further. She doubted him. And that is the difference between reality and a story. We will believe a quick story but disbelieve life. The only way to believe is to live it; to journey to the end and perceive for ourselves. Asya too had to endure life.

Asya had tried to impart this knowledge to others. She brought up her child based on the freedom that love would provide. She made it understand, that our expectation is always feeble and incomplete. We do not want someone to understand us, we just long for someone to be there. Though love provided a fulfilling idea, it too had a hollow part. It made us dependent on our object of fancy and this eventually leaves us imprisoned than liberated because of the unspoken expectation we harbour from love; that it will always be fulfilling. After all we have made ourselves believe that love alone can heal us and it cannot be substituted. Truth indeed was enduring but it has to be experienced to gain familiarity.

◆ ◆ ◆

Asya looks forward to the future without expectation. She feels the contentment in herself devoid of the feeling or necessity to endure. There is nothing she has left to fight for, nothing to envisage, nothing to quell nor there's anything afforded to chance. Her beloved husband is gone, but she never grieved for her loss. It felt that she had already grieved for him in another era. Time had already taken that in account – she remembered the time he had been at war and how she cried at the imaginable loss of her husband, but today she felt closer to him.

And she had the chance to relive an entire life time again. After all she too had the gift of transcendence maybe from the *shilpi*; the gift of longevity. She has the opportunity to choose and create happiness every day.

She had fallen in love again but she, now, loves the most neglected person – Her own Self.

Thoughtful, yet content Asya rises and slowly walks back to her home.

A new day begins. Again.

Epilogue

The 3000 year old sculpture sat behind the glass box in the museum. It was preserved carefully in a cool ventilated room at constant temperature. A plaque was placed describing the approximate year in which the statue was made. It also described the carbon dating procedure used to determine the age of the statue assuring its authenticity. It weighed almost a ton of stone.

People passed by the worn out statue glancing at it briefly. The face of the statue was partially broken and disfigured. Tiny circular erosions marked the body of the statue resembling as warts invading. The stone was grey and showed decay.

In spite of this, the rest of the body was erect and every feature stood remarkably composite.

The waist was slender and demonstrated sensuality. The broken fragmented lip on the statue still had a strong outline. The small but prominent breast line showed with elegance. The lute stood on an angular line with hands holding it. The statue ended with small proportional feet protruding from its stone fabric.

Archaeological reports reflected the statue excavated from almost 900 meters below ground along with many fossils, coins and pottery. The discoverers boasted their find with pride and wrote articles and published theories about the civilization of that time concurring with the statue. Scriptures and long forgotten dusty books on canons and iconometry were shuffled to the surface for references. An ancient piece of history makes an impact on today's world.

The efforts and work of someone who existed centuries ago survived and reached out in time to meet the new world again. Though the world seeing the sculpture does not know the story behind it, you do.

www.ingramcontent.com/pod-product-compliance
Lightning Source LLC
Chambersburg PA
CBHW022111040426
42450CB00006B/662